CW00518785

The Internet and Politics

Can the Internet really make a difference in building, preserving or challenging democracy? This new volume explores the Internet's impact on civil society and the challenges posed by such a new and uncharted pathway of communication.

This edited collection uses a set of compelling case studies to examine ideas about the Internet's role in building civil society around the globe. It offers thorough grounding in the way the Internet builds social capital, engages citizens, motivates voters and encourages protest activity. This timely volume includes studies of the role of the Internet in:

- Drawing young people into politics in the US, including the 2004 election.
- Widening the appeal and increasing the organization of the UK's pro-hunt protestors, 'The Countryside Alliance'.
- Aiding freedom of speech and protest in Ukraine, including in the 2004 presidential election.
- Palestinian and Northern Irish terrorism.

This book will be of interest to students and scholars of international politics, the Internet and civil society.

Sarah Oates is a Senior Lecturer in Politics at the University of Glasgow, UK.

Diana Owen is Associate Professor of Political Science at Georgetown University, USA.

Rachel K. Gibson is a Senior Research Fellow in the Research School of Social Sciences, The Australian National University, Australia.

Democratization Studies
(Formerly Democratization Studies, Frank Cass)
Series Editors: Peter Burnell and Peter Calvert

Democratization Studies combines theoretical and comparative studies with detailed analyses of issues central to democratic progress and its performance, all over the world.

The books in this series aim to encourage debate on the many aspects of democratization that are of interest to policy-makers, administrators and journalists, aid and development personnel, as well as to all those involved in education.

Democratization and the Media
Edited by Vicky Randall

The Resilience of Democracy
Persistent practice, durable idea
Edited by Peter Burnell and Peter Calvert

The Internet, Democracy and Democratization
Edited by Peter Ferdinand

Party Development and Democratic Change in Post-communist Europe
Edited by Paul Lewis

Democracy Assistance
International co-operation for democratization
Edited by Peter Burnell

Opposition and Democracy in South Africa
Edited by Roger Southall

The European Union and Democracy Promotion
The case of North Africa
Edited by Richard Gillespie and Richard Youngs

Democratization and the Judiciary
Edited by Siri Gloppen, Roberto Gargarella and Elin Skaar

Civil Society in Democratization
Edited by Peter Burnell and Peter Calvert

The Internet and Politics
Citizens, voters and activists
Edited by Sarah Oates, Diana Owen and Rachel K. Gibson

The Internet and Politics

Citizens, voters and activists

**Edited by Sarah Oates, Diana Owen
and Rachel K. Gibson**

Routledge
Taylor & Francis Group

LONDON AND NEW YORK

First published 2006
by Routledge
2 Park Square, Milton Park, Abingdon, Oxon OX14 4RN

Simultaneously published in the USA and Canada
by Routledge
270 Madison Ave, New York, NY 10016

Routledge is an imprint of the Taylor & Francis Group

Transferred to Digital Printing 2006

Typeset in Times by RefineCatch Ltd, Bungay, Suffolk

British Library Cataloguing in Publication Data
A catalogue record for this book is available from the British Library

Library of Congress Cataloging in Publication Data
    The Internet and politics : citizens, voters, and activists / edited by
Sarah Oates, Diana Owen, and Rachel Gibson.
        p. cm.
    "Based on papers written for a 2003 European Consortium of
Political Research workshop."
    Includes bibliographical references.
    1. Political participation—Technological innovations—
Congresses.   2. Information technology—Political aspects—
Congresses.   3. Internet—Political aspects—Congresses.   I. Oates,
Sarah.   II. Owen, Diana Marie.   III. Gibson, Rachel Kay.
    JF799.I62 2005
    323'.042'02854678—dc22
    2005006117

ISBN10: 0-415-34784-X
ISBN13: 9-78-0-415-34784-6
ISBN10: 0-415-43587-0 (paperback)
ISBN13: 9-78-0-415-43587-1(paperback)

Printed and bound by CPI Antony Rowe, Eastbourne

Contents

Figures

Tables

Contributors

Heinz Brandenburg joined the Political Science department at the University of Aberdeen to lecture in political communication and rational choice theory in January 2005. Previously, he was a Lecturer in Political Science at the Norwegian University of Science and Technology, Trondheim. His core field of interest is political communication, where he has published on the role of strategy and media relations in elections as well as military campaigns. He is currently working on a comparative study on agenda building.

Maura Conway is a Ph.D. candidate in the Department of Political Science at Trinity College Dublin, Ireland, and a teaching fellow in the School of International Relations at the University of St Andrews. Her research interests are in the area of terrorism and the Internet. She has published in *First Monday, Current History*, the *Journal of Information Warfare* and elsewhere.

Rachel K. Gibson is a Senior Research Fellow in the ACSPRI Centre for Social Research at the Australian National University. She has published widely on the subject of new media and politics, with a particular focus on parties and web campaigning. Her most recent publications include an edited volume on electronic democracy (*Political Parties and the Internet: Net gain?*, Routledge, 2003), co-edited with Stephen Ward and Paul Nixon. She is currently working on a co-authored book entitled *Difficult Democracy* that examines how the Internet has affected political organisations and participation in the United Kingdom.

Natalya Krasnoboka is a Ph.D. student and assistant at the Faculty of Political and Social Sciences, University of Antwerp, Belgium. Her research focuses on the political and civil role of traditional media and the Internet in Eastern European societies in transition.

Jakob Linaa Jensen is Assistant Professor at the Institute of Information and Media Studies, University of Aarhus, Denmark. He has published several articles and a book on the Internet as a medium for democratic dialogue. His research interests include social life online, digital democracy and internet-mediated tourist experiences.

Wainer Lusoli is a Research Fellow at the European Studies Research Institute, University of Salford. He is currently working on the research project on representation in the Internet age, a part of the British e-Society Programme funded by the Economic and Social Research Council. He has published on politics and new media in the *European Journal of Communication*, *Parliamentary Affairs*, *Representation*, *The Information Polity* and other journals.

Luke March is Lecturer in Soviet and Post-Soviet Politics at the University of Edinburgh. He has published on left-wing and nationalist movements, and the role of new communications technologies in democratisation. His most recent publications include *The Communist Party in Post-Soviet Russia* (Manchester University Press, 2002). He is currently working both on democratisation in Moldova and the development of the radical left in Europe.

Sarah Oates is Lecturer in Politics at the University of Glasgow. She has published widely on the mass media, elections and public opinion in the former Soviet Union. Currently, she is principal of a project in the New Security Challenges Programme of the Economic and Social Research Council to compare media coverage and voter response to security issues and terrorist threats in Russian, American and British election campaigns.

Diana Owen is Associate Professor of Political Science at Georgetown University. She is the author of *Media Messages in Presidential Elections* and *New Media in American Politics* (with Richard Davis). She is the co-founder of Georgetown's Graduate Program in Communication, Culture, and Technology.

Paul Reilly is a Ph.D. candidate in the Politics Department at the University of Glasgow. He is working on issues surrounding the use of the Internet by terrorist groups.

Diana Schmidt is a Ph.D. candidate at the Institute of Governance, Public Policy and Social Research, Queen's University Belfast. She has researched and published on local civil society formation around global issues in the Russian context. Her current research focuses on civic networking against corruption in Russia.

Holli A. Semetko is Vice Provost for International Affairs, Director of The Claus M. Halle Institute for Global Learning, and Professor of Political Science at Emory University in Atlanta, Georgia. She is also Professor of Audience and Public Opinion Research at the Amsterdam School of Communications Research at the University of Amsterdam. Her most recent articles appear in *The Journal of Politics*, *British Journal of Political Science* and *Political Communication*. Her most recent book, *Political Campaigning in Referendums: Framing the Referendum Issue* (Routledge,

2004), co-authored with Claes de Vreese, focuses on the impact of the media in referendum campaigns.

Stephen Ward is a research fellow at the Oxford Internet Institute. His research interests are in the area of e-democracy, particularly political participation and campaigning online. Since 1997, he has tracked the development of online campaign efforts by political parties. Currently, he is working on the British e-Society Programme funded by the British Economic and Social Research Council to compare British and Australian use of the Internet in parliaments. His recent publications in these areas include: *Political Parties and the Internet: Net Gain?* (Routledge, 2003), co-edited with Rachel Gibson and Paul Nixon, and *Electronic Democracy* (Routledge, 2003), co-edited with Rachel Gibson and Andrea Roemele.

Scott Wright is currently an Economic and Social Research Council-funded Postdoctoral Research Fellow at the University of East Anglia. His research focuses on government-run discussion forums, with a particular interest in the role of website design in relation to theories of technology and the public sphere.

1 The Internet, civil society and democracy

A comparative perspective

Sarah Oates and Rachel K. Gibson

Changes in the media landscape present new challenges for scholars interested in the relationship between the mass media and civil society. The explosion of the Internet that started in advanced industrial democracies and has spread through much of the globe provides new and unexplored pathways for communication. The inclusion of the Internet in the media mix raises new questions and challenges for citizens, journalists, politicians and governments alike. The central idea to this volume is the exploration of the nature of the Internet's impact on civil society. In particular, this book addresses the following central questions in the discipline of Internet studies: Is the Internet qualitatively different from the more traditional forms of the media? Has it demonstrated real potential to improve civil society through a wider provision of information, through an enhancement of communication between government and citizen or via better state transparency? Alternatively, does the Internet actually present a threat to the coherence of civil society, as people are encouraged to abandon shared media experiences and pursue narrower interests?

This book presents a series of new research writings on the Internet, not only to address these issues, but also to give scholars the tools to answer these questions in their own research. The study of the Internet has defied traditional scholarship in two primary ways. First, the Internet has changed so rapidly and so fast that it is enormously difficult to keep up with its content and direction, much less try to predict how it may affect political behaviour and civil society. At the same time, it is often difficult to know where to fit the Internet into a discussion of politics and society. Is it a dependent variable, an element that is shaped and formed by the forces of society? Or does it function as an independent variable on existing political institutions, changing the nature of the relationship among citizens and parties, the mass media, public opinion, leaders and other political institutions? There are many opinions about the Internet and its role in politics, but relatively little research that can be replicated and discussed across country boundaries. This book represents a new generation of research on the Internet that places it within the tradition of empirical and philosophical research into politics and society. It is particularly important to consider whether research on the Internet, civil society and politics addresses a well-defined hypothesis, one that can be tested in a range of countries and political systems. All of the chapters in this book ask a central question, ranging from the efficacy of the E-democracy program in a single state in the United States to examining how Russian political parties have used the Internet to attract supporters.

One of the primary problems in looking at the Internet is one that is paralleled in the study of the mass media in general. The Internet is a sphere that can involve virtually all levels of the political world simultaneously, from the officials who are broadcasting their policies via websites, to the mass media that are interpreting these messages on separate websites, to the citizens sitting at their computers and absorbing Internet content. Just as with the traditional mass media, it is important to consider which level of analysis is under examination. For example, the study of the political messages broadcast by a party is distinct from a study of how the Internet users are accessing, interpreting or believing those messages. In addition, it is impossible to understand the meaning or impact of a party website in a vacuum. How does the website relate to the party communication strategy overall? Is the information on the website unique or different from party information in the traditional forms of the mass media? Is it targeted at a different audience? Does it attract a different audience? Perhaps most important of all, does it mobilise that particular audience in a new and different way from the traditional methods of political mobilisation?

This volume offers three important perspectives on the study of the Internet and politics. The chapters, based on papers written for a European Consortium of Political Research workshop on the changing media and civil society, explicitly address the role of the Internet within civil society. In addition, the book offers a range of important case studies in various regime types to help to build a cross-national understanding of how the Internet transforms familiar political institutions and interactions within the nation-state. Finally, each chapter works at building a concrete understanding of the methods needed to approach the study of the Internet, from the formulation of hypotheses to research design to data analysis. This book should provide an advance in the way that scholars can conceptualise and carry out their studies of the Internet in comparative perspective. The chapter authors for this volume have updated all of the work since the conference for this volume.

The chapters in this book span a number of countries and include different elements of the role of the Internet in politics. Yet, the chapters share the central notion of a definition of a central hypothesis about this role and a research approach that should be relevant to other case studies. This book is concerned with four central themes in the study of the Internet:

1   a definition of the role of the Internet in the promotion of civil society in advanced industrial democracies;
2   an analysis of whether the Internet serves as a particular catalyst for 'outsider' groups, defined in this study as terrorists;

3   gauging whether the Internet serves as a beacon of democracy or a tool
    for oppression in non-free states;
4   focusing on central research questions and methodologies in the field of
    Internet studies.

While these are all broad themes, this volume is intended to offer a range of
chapter-length comparative studies in order to give readers a well-rounded
introduction into the state of Internet studies that crosses country boundaries
and regime types. Turning to the first theme in the book, it is important to
consider the role of the Internet within the general discussion about the
media, civil society and political engagement in advanced industrial democracies. While the mass media have faced much criticism for their alleged
undermining of civic society (Putnam, 2000), Pippa Norris *et al.* in *A Virtuous
Circle* (2000) suggest that the mass media actually serve a useful function in
keeping citizens engaged and informed about elections in democracies. The
question of where the Internet fits on this spectrum of opinion is still open for
debate.

Certainly, the initial work on e-democracy and political participation was
exuberant in its hopes for a betterment of society. Along with Howard
Rheingold (1995), writers such as Toffler and Toffler (1995), Negroponte
(1995), Rash (1997) and Dyson (1998) saw the new digital technologies as key
to the renewal of direct democracy and citizen empowerment. The inherent
structural logic of new media, it was thought, would inexorably lead to the
opening up of a decentralized interactive public space in which people, or
'netizens', would form new social bonds and create new fora for political
decision making. Others adopted a less utopian perspective, seeing the potential of the new ICTs to lie in their ability to improve and 'pare down' current
governance apparatus rather than replace it entirely (Mulgan and Adonis,
1994; Heilemann, 1996; Poster, 1997; Shenk, 1997; Morris, 2000). There were
still others, however, who saw the Internet and its associated applications as
inherently dangerous to democracy, reducing the possibility for collective
action (Wu and Weaver, 1996; Street, 1992; Lipow and Seyd, 1996) and erod-
ing social capital and community ties (Etzioni and Etzioni, 1999; Galston,
2003). Others also perceived its problematic potential to reduce both the
quality of political debate and discourse (Streck, 1999; Sunstein, 2001) and
the accountability of the government (Wilhelm, 2000; Lessig, 1999; Adkeniz,
2000; Liberty, 1999; Elmer, 1997).

While provocative and insightful, such arguments constituted a 'blue skies'
approach to the question of Internet effects. Shortly afterward, empirical
social scientists stepped into the debate to conduct more data-driven analyses
of the issue. As the results rolled in, accusations of 'hype' came thick and fast,
particularly in relation to the more positive mobilisation-related claims. Key
to these counter-claims was the consistent finding that only a minority of
the population in most Western countries enjoyed access to the Internet, and
that this was an affluent minority at best. The Internet, it was concluded, was

neither the agent of the glorious revolution nor apocalypse now, but a reinforcer of the status quo (Bimber, 1998a; Hill and Hughes, 1998; Davis and Owen, 1998; Margolis and Resnick, 2000; Norris, 2001; Schuefele and Nisbet, 2002).

Even more dispiriting for the e-democrat hopes was the additional finding that, despite Internet users being among the better-resourced section of the population, levels of interest in online politics were surprisingly low. Less than one-quarter of the population apparently engaged in even the most basic level of political activity, such as looking for information about the US election in 1996. This compared highly unfavourably with the 61 per cent that reported tuning into a news bulletin during the previous day or the 50 per cent who said they had read a newspaper (Pew, 1996). Pippa Norris summed up the position well in her statement that 'the rise of the virtual political system seems most likely to facilitate further knowledge, interest, and activism of those who are already most predisposed toward civic engagement, reinforcing patterns of political participation' (2001: 228).

Even more worrying than the inequality of interest in the web have been the objective measures showing the relative inequality in access to ICTs. If the web is, in fact, a tool that can empower citizens, it is particularly worrying to reflect that access is overwhelmingly the privilege of the wealthiest citizens in the most advanced democracies (Norris, 2001). Even within countries, there are significant barriers to the poorest citizens having the same quality and ease of access to the web, creating divisions of potential web empowerment not only across countries, but within them as well.

In the realm of social capital, a concept central to this book, the stories of gloom intensified. In a challenge to the eulogies of Rheingold and Grossman about the community-building properties of the new media, critics charged that social 'balkanisation' and isolation were more likely results. Dire warnings about the potential for greater disconnection and alienation among citizens emerged as scholars pointed to the de-humanising effects of sitting at a computer all day (Boggs, 1997; Hightower, 1998). A number of empirical studies of these questions started to emerge that appeared to bear these negative hypotheses out. Work by Nie and Erbring (2000) reported that the levels of sociability of individuals actually dropped and their feelings of alienation and disconnection to society increased with higher use of the Internet. Cummings *et al.* (2002) discovered that computer-mediated communication and particularly email were inferior means of building close social relationships when compared with physical interaction or even the telephone.

Other studies offered more ambivalent conclusions. For instance, Putnam (2000) used data from a DDB Needham Lifestyle survey to maintain that, after demographic controls were applied, Internet users and non-users did not differ significantly in their levels of civic engagement. In his analysis of data from the Pew Research Center and the US National Election Survey in 1996, Uslaner (2001) also argued for a largely 'nil' effect of Internet use on social capital, although he came to the conclusion through a more circular logic. While the heaviest users of the Internet did have wider social circles, those engaging in online chat were more mistrustful of others. Overall, Uslaner concluded 'there is little evidence that the Internet will create new communities to make up for the decline in civic engagement that has occurred over the past four decades in the United States'. Using data from the 1998 National Geographic Web Survey, Wellman *et al.* (2001) present a similarly mixed set of findings. While a positive association does exist between online and offline participation, online interaction largely supplements face-to-face and telephone communication and higher levels of Internet use actually are associated with decreased commitment to online community. Weber *et al.* (2003) also report a positive link between the Internet and civic participation but alongside an exacerbation of the socio-economic bias associated with this activity in the pre-Internet era.

Some brief respite from the bleak picture of negative or nil effects was offered by events such as the Arizona Democrats online primary in 2000, in which record levels of participation were recorded (Gibson, 2001), as well as in reports of the take-up of e-government services in the United States and the United Kingdom (Coleman, 2001).[1] Closer examination, however, succeeded in dashing any revived hopes. In-depth analysis of online voting in the Arizona primary revealed the practice had actually worsened race and educational barriers to participation (Solop, 2001; Alvarez and Nagler, 2000). Similarly, the closer examination by Tolbert *et al.* (2003) of attitudes toward e-government initiatives revealed compelling evidence for those who argue that online politics will mirror, or exacerbate existing disparities in the composition of the electorate based on socio-economic status.

Thus, the evidence presented to this point had effectively dashed the early exuberance of the e-democrats. As one scholar describes it, a consensus has basically emerged that the Internet will only 'reinforce the existing patterns of political inequality' (Krueger, 2002). Yet, there are findings that offer some hope that the Internet can contribute to civil society in new and useful ways. Ferdinand (2000) finds significant evidence the Internet has widened democracy, particularly in the case of linking citizens in oppressive regimes both to each other and to the international sphere, yet concludes that time will be needed to determine whether citizens, parties and other groups are able to benefit from the civic potential offered by the technology. A number of authors attest in particular to the youth appeal of the technology. Tolbert *et al.* (2003) did find reinforcement of patterns of political inequality, but also noted that younger respondents are more supportive of digital democracy, a finding that is significant since it suggests the medium's potential for 'expanding the electorate to include a group that has been traditionally under-represented' (2003: 27). Shah *et al.* (2001) found that it is important to specify the nature of Internet activities under study, as this is key to unravelling the ambivalence of both positive and negative effects or the so-called 'Internet paradox'. Information gathering was positively linked with the production of social capital, while recreational uses emerged as negatively related to people's store of community spirit. In a further study, after accounting for the reciprocal effects between Internet use and social engagement, Shah *et al.* (2002) reported further positive results, finding time spent online was associated with higher levels of civic engagement. Finally, in a third and highly significant twist, Krueger (2002) made the argument that the models suggesting that political engagement and the Internet were inversely related left out crucial independent variables – such as time online, Internet skills and familiarity of individuals with ICTs – in explaining online participation. While traditional resources were clearly important in gaining access to the Internet, other Internet-specific factors also should be considered when looking at activity online. His empirical research supported the point with socio-economic resources moving to the background in determining online engagement once the new online skills were included in the analysis.

Thus, while it may be true that the new medium perpetuates and reinforces existing levels of engagement, it also appears that it can promote connection and participation among some less traditional players. Picking up on this theme of a revised or more qualified understanding of the normalisation thesis, the next four chapters of the book make important contributions to the debate. In particular, the chapter by Diana Owen examining the Internet, youth and civic engagement in the United States takes on the normalisation argument, dispelling the idea that it is the same old faces using Internet technology to engage in politics more fervently.

Survey evidence presented in Chapter 2 by Owen suggests that this image of the young, politically disengaged Internet user is not accurate. Young people have been using the Internet both to monitor conventional political processes, such as election campaigns, and to facilitate overt political activity. What researchers may be missing is proper empirical mechanisms for assessing the scope and intensity of this engagement. As Internet access has become nearly universal among young Americans, their facility with the technology has increased along with their trust in the veracity of the content on the Internet. Young people have become producers of much political content, even as it remains largely outside the purview of mainstream media organisations and political elites. Further, they have started to use Internet information in their political decision making, a trend that should continue to develop over time. While the Internet's influence on political information dissemination has occurred in plain sight, its effect on political engagement has been more covert. It may be the case that the Internet has nurtured a kind of 'stealth' political activism among young people who have become galvanised by a series of extraordinary world events in the wake of the terrorist attacks on 9/11. Owen's research suggests that the claim that the 'online' world does not translate into 'offline' action can no longer be supported. Her analysis shows that, once the socio-economic background of the adolescents is accounted for, Internet use and skills move to the fore in predicting involvement in information gathering. Indeed, experience with the Internet, measured in terms of the amount of time spent online, is the greatest determinant of their tendency to seek news and information about current events, express opinions and create web pages. She argues that many of these activities, while not expressly political, can legitimately be seen as precursors to the development of citizenship skills behaviour in terms of signalling an engagement in the world. The chapter includes information from the youth online engagement in the 2004 US presidential election.

Jakob Linaa Jensen continues the theme of empirical studies of mobilisation via the Internet in Chapter 3 by examining the Minnesota E-democracy project. Linaa Jensen is concerned with whether this type of Internet initiative can strengthen civil society. What he finds in his analysis of the E-democracy project is that the Internet is not really introducing new people to political participation; rather it is strengthening the resources of those who were already politically involved. Linaa Jensen's research suggests that participants in the Minnesota E-democracy programme typically have more political resources than the population in general. In particular, the E-democracy participants are far better educated than the general population. The E-democracy participants are not turning to the web for their first taste of politics. Rather, the Internet tends to complement their relatively high involvement in more traditional forms of political participation. At the same time, it does not seem that online participation replaces more traditional forms of participation. Among other resources that determine whether citizens become involved in political activities online, it would appear that Internet use promotes additional online activism rather than the Internet empowering those who had long been uninvolved in the political process. The vast majority of the E-democracy participants are 'super users' who access the Internet both at home and at work or school. In this chapter, a study of online participants does not confirm a democratic promise that the Internet would mobilise new groups of people. Rather the Internet 'gladiators' now have yet another medium for political involvement and influence. Online participation, however, seems to have the positive effect of strengthening political interest and involvement (an echo of Owen's findings in Chapter 2).

In Chapter 4, Wainer Lusoli and Stephen Ward consider the role of the Internet in the apparent upsurge of protest activity over the past decade by examining the experience of the Countryside Alliance in the United Kingdom. Can the Internet revive traditional representative organisations, such as organisations, parties and trade unions, that appear to be in decline in many liberal democracies? A number of accounts have highlighted the importance of the Internet and other new media in the mobilisation of specific mass protests as well as in the general activity of campaigning organisations. Can these new communication technologies provide a catalyst for political participation and a more active citizenry and, if so, what types of political organisations are likely to benefit? While there has been a growing amount of evidence examining the online strategies of political organisations from a top-down perspective, there has been little evidence emerging from the grass roots about the role of the Internet. This chapter examines this empirical gap through a survey of members of a countryside-lobbying organisation in Britain.

The Countryside Alliance has come to prominence over the past several years for its opposition to a British government ban on hunting with dogs. It has received fairly wide coverage in the traditional mass media, particularly for its large 'Liberty and Livelihood' protest march in London in September 2002, a march that drew hundreds of thousands of participants. While the alliance has a reputation for representing an ageing, conservative, rural, middle-class membership – apparently unpromising ground for Internet campaigning – the organisation has devoted considerable resources to using the Internet for mobilisation purposes. Lusoli and Ward use both a postal survey and an online poll to examine the profile of members online, their use of the Internet as well as the attitudes of members toward the Internet and participation. In particular, the study was concerned with whether the Internet widened participation in this cause through one of two methods. First, did the Internet facilitate inclusion of a greater number and diversity of citizens into the participatory process? In addition, did it deepen or extend the range and efficacy of participatory activity? Results from the study tend to parallel the findings of Linaa Jensen with the E-democracy project. Lusoli and Ward found that, while the presence of the Internet (particularly email) can amplify political involvement, it is the underlying cause or organisation that remains central to the activism.

If identifiable sectors of society and interest groups are using the Internet, how is the government tackling the potential of the new medium in advanced industrial democracies? In Chapter 5, Scott Wright examines how the British government is attempting to use a variety of institutional techniques on the Internet to encourage and shape political participation. The development of policies that are intended to encourage participation is only one side of the coin. The flip side is how will these policies be received? Will people actually take advantage of these new opportunities? These arguments fit within a broader debate about the balance between social capital and institutional design in the overall contribution to political participation. This chapter uses an analysis of two local government Internet discussion boards in Cumbria and Suffolk. Each of these discussion boards had different aims and was structured in different ways in order to achieve its goals. The chapter will argue that there are a number of factors shaping how, if at all, people partici-pate on discussion boards and that some scholars are right to suggest that the relationship between institutional design and social capital is a two-way one. However, it will be argued that some scholars have not fully accounted for how much institutional issues – in this case website design – can affect the nature of discussion on a micro level, i.e. the interface between government and citizen.

The next section of the book turns away from groups operating mostly in mainstream politics and considers the role of the Internet in the aggregation of the more isolated, outsider communities. Can the Internet, as a new medium, reach those who typically sit at the margins of civil society? What initiatives are taking place among groups generally lacking decision-making power in society (i.e. the homeless, the working poor, the elderly) or lack of political rights (such as refugees) to aggregate interests in a more effective and efficient way via the Internet? While the literature on such topics is perhaps less extensive and empirically conclusive at this stage than that examining the impact of the Internet on the more formalised institutions of civil society and behaviours, it nevertheless points to some fascinating possibilities.

One particular form of insurgency that has attracted much attention for its effective use of the new media is the Zapatista movement in the Chiapas region of Mexico. The National Zapatista Liberation (ELZN), a resistance movement formed in 1994 by Indian peasants to combat what they saw as their continuing economic and cultural oppression by the Mexican govern-ment and particularly the new free trade agreement with the United States, exploited the new ICTs extensively to transmit their message to the outside world. Circumventing the state media, and with the help of sympathetic friends in the US (particularly academics based at the University of Texas[2]), the ELZN successfully publicised their struggle to the wider world on the web and email networks. This stimulated greater traditional media coverage as well as a meeting of more than 3,000 global activists in Lacandon forest to formulate a new worldwide network of resistance to neo-liberal forces (Cleaver, 1995; Ronfeldt *et al.*, 1998; Jeffries, 2001).

A second and highly noteworthy instance of the articulation and multipli-cation of non-mainstream voices via Internet-based methods has been the series of anti-globalisation demonstrations that have occurred across the world since the infamous 'battle of Seattle' in late 1999. As delegates met at the World Trade Organisation Ministerial Conference that year, approxi-mately 50,000 protestors representing a wide range of minority interests and economically disadvantaged groups coordinated one of the most powerful demonstrations seen in the United States for many decades. This brought the city of Seattle to a state of civil emergency and night curfew. A crucial aspect of the protestors' success was the advance coordination of blockades and tactics via the Internet. During the meeting itself, protestors also used mobile phones and various independent media sites on the web to coordinate the logistics of the demonstrations and provide visual footage of events, unavail-able from conventional news coverage[3] (Denning, 2001; Capling and Nossal, 2001; Shepard and Hayduk, 2002; Burbach, 2001). Subsequent protests at meetings of world trade bodies in places such as Melbourne and Genoa saw similar tactics being deployed, although with diminished effect as the author-ities became more effective in their efforts to counter the actions of the activists.

In addition to the growth of social movement activism online, non-mainstream e-activism has also emerged in recent years in a more individual-istic form – that of 'hacktivism'. This is an Internet-specific type of protest, consisting mainly of the defacement or shutting down of well-known 'enemy' websites. While the expressly political nature of this activity has been questioned, with practitioners being seen as motivated by the desire to take high-profile scalps such as government agencies or well-known international companies to gain peer recognition, there clearly have been instances in which these attacks have constituted genuine attempts to redress power imbalances. The motivating idea here is that the correct target for anti-capitalist protest had switched to information networks and away from the streets (Sterling, 1992). Among the most well known of these are the 'sit-ins' coordinated by the Electronic Disturbance Theatre in 1998, in which the Frankfurt Stock Exchange, the Pentagon and the Mexican President's home page were disabled after falling victim to attack. However, despite creating some media headlines and annoyance for the organisations involved, the practical effects of such actions have come under question (Meikle, 2002). The Critical Art Ensemble, an amorphous group of cyberactivists and champions of electronic civil disobedience in the 1990s (Critical Art Ensemble, 1994, 1995), since have notably shifted position on this issue, arguing that the tactic had become moribund and should not serve as replacement for real world protest (Critical Art Ensemble, 2001).

Given the priority many countries have now attached to universal public access to the Internet, one can argue this is a sign that they do not see their own power bases as agents of the state to be under serious threat from such types of attack. At the same time, as the US Defense Department learnt through its development of ARPANET (a forerunner to the Internet), it is impossible to foresee the complete spectrum of future use of the Internet. Certainly, the multi-way communication that is now possible as well as the sophisticated encryption that can be practised does make governments mindful to track and control civilian communication. Chapters 6 and 7 pick up this debate, considering in particular the Internet's ability to amplify the power of terrorists.

In a chapter on 'cybercortical' warfare, Maura Conway examines the case of Hizbollah.org, the website that broadcasts the interests of a key Palestinian group. She argues that terrorists are not limiting themselves to the traditional means of communication and increasingly employ the new media to pursue their goals. The terrorists of today, like those of yesteryear, are keen to exploit the traditional mass media as well as recognise the value of more direct communication channels. By 2002, 19 of the 34 organisations on the US list of Designated Foreign Terrorist Organizations had established an online presence. Conway argues that Hizbollah represents a particularly interesting case among those groups. Despite its appearance on the terrorist list, Hizbollah is a political party with a wide base of support in Lebanon. It also differs from the other groups in that its campaign of 'cybercortical' warfare has met with a high level of success. This chapter discusses how groups such as Hizbollah can use the Internet as a tool for mobilisation and organisation – and how this can challenge the notion of the Internet's role in civil society.

In contrast, Paul Reilly finds the Internet to be quite a limited tool for terrorists. Reilly examines the general threat of 'cyber-terrorism' in Chapter 7 by looking at how terrorist groups in Northern Ireland use the Internet. He argues that the threat of cyber-terrorism is vastly exaggerated by nation-states as a means of justifying Internet restrictions. Terrorists are not free to act with impunity on the Internet. Legislation such as the UK Regulation of Investigatory Powers Act in 2000 has limited the ability of the terrorist to utilise the Internet as an offensive weapon. Meanwhile, nation-states manipulate public distrust of the Internet to implement policies that restrict Internet freedoms. This is because nation-states do not want arguments counter to their conception of civil society to be readily available on the Internet. With the exception of religiously motivated groups in the Middle East, terrorist groups are likely to use the Internet as a supplementary tool of covert communication. Meanwhile, 'big spectaculars' in the physical world such as bombings and murder will continue to provide effective publicity for terrorists. Psychological warfare, a necessary component of terrorism, is effectively conducted through manipulation of the television news and the front pages of newspapers. The Internet cannot replicate the shared experience of the mass media, as it is a private viewing box rather than a public medium. Reilly argues that the longevity of organisations such as the Provisional Irish Republican Army reflects the efficacy of manipulation of the conventional mass media. If this strategy is to remain effective, Northern Irish terrorist organisations are likely to view the cost of achieving a cyber-terror capability as a price not worth paying.

The third section of the book examines the role the Internet is playing in non-democratic states. Three chapters with new evidence from Russia and Ukraine gauge how much the new medium can balance a lack of civil society in former Soviet states. As is clear from the experience of the Zapatistas in Mexico, it is possible for the Internet to provide a channel for free speech. However, there are many who see the technology as boding ill for free society, raising the prospect of it being subverted to the needs of the state in relatively closed media systems. Building on the notion of the panopticon, first identified by Bentham in the nineteenth century and developed more recently by Foucault (1975), dystopian theorists have argued in the most extreme instance that the Internet age may usher in a new era of repression of citizen rights and Orwellian-style constant surveillance (Robins and Webster, 1988; Zuboff, 1988). While they raise an unsettling prospect, to date such visions do not appear to have come close to realisation. Indeed, the approach taken by most authoritarian states to the Internet confirms to a degree the arguments of those emphasising the medium's inherent democratising properties. Adopting a defensive posture, non-democratic regimes have sought to limit rather than promulgate the Internet's spread across society. The Chinese state in particular went to great lengths to control network development in the country as well as blocking the content and images available. However, for the most part, non-democratic governments have had to settle for a more post-hoc approach to Internet access and control. For example, Internet use not authorised by the state has been defined as a criminal offence in North Korea, Myanmar and Iraq in the days of Saddam Hussein (Chivakula, 2001).

Despite full panoptic control and subversion of the Internet not appearing as a realistic option even for the more authoritarian societies of the world at this point, this does not necessarily mean that the medium becomes an automatic defender of the rights and freedoms of civil society. More subtle shifts toward greater elite control of society through the new technologies cannot be entirely ruled out. For example, Mander (2001) has warned of the dangerous centralisation of power that will occur as the cultural homogenisation and bureaucratisation of society introduced by new ICTs takes hold. Barney (2000) also identifies the dehumanising and mechanistic aspects of the technology as a concern for the diversity and ultimate health of democracy. Adopting an approach more driven by human agency, some scholars have argued the new media will erode present opportunities for skilful and manipulative politicians to advance their own agendas under the cloak of democratic legitimacy (Lipow and Seyd, 1996). The individualised nature of communication, it is argued, promotes the fragmentation and disaggregation of interests, reducing the possibility for holding leaders accountable. Taking the argument one stage further, there are those who fear an overall meltdown of the collective voice and descent of political debate into ignorance and impulsiveness as the new ICTs are increasingly applied to decision making (Shenk, 1997; Bimber, 1998b). One might argue that these trends are most likely as an outcome for those societies without firm democratic traditions anchoring their aggregative bodies, such as parties and parliaments. The chapters in this third section of the book allow us to gain some insight into this question by placing the spotlight on the effects of new media within the former Soviet sphere.

In Chapter 8, Luke March explores the longer-term prospects for the Internet to aid the development of political parties in Russia. While confirming a lag in the adoption of the Internet by parties compared with developed democracies, the data presented in this chapter do not present a uniformly bleak picture. The Internet at least offers new party systems the possibility of greater organisational integrity, efficiency and visibility in relatively open electoral fields. In theory, this should help educate an inexperienced electorate as well as compensate for the deficiencies or biases of the mass media. At the same time, the Internet should provide the linkage between civil society and the state that is so tenuous in many newer democracies. There is indeed evidence of limited movements in this direction, particularly from the younger, more liberal politicians who have dabbled in virtual party building. Russian parties may use their websites primarily for information broadcasting, yet in the context of non-free media they may become alternative information portals for an information-starved electorate. In this way, they can contribute to the pluralisation of the media in general.

Yet, March goes on to stress that the case of Russia shows that the political use of the Internet is very much defined by existing constraints in the political communication system rather than any mystical 'democratic' quality intrinsic to the technology itself. New democracies, particularly post-Soviet ones, are neither a political *tabula rasa* nor a level playing field from the outset. As such, structural, institutional and cultural factors play at the least a contextual or at most a conditioning role in terms of the Internet. In the case of Russia, this means far lower rates of Internet access on the part of the public – as well as parties that must contend with the fact that they have had no guaranteed national governing role. Thus, political parties, the public and the Internet all have much more limited potential within the system. While in principle the Internet offers political parties unparalleled exposure and unmediated communication, in practice their message is transmitted between electronic media and an electorate socialised in a less information-friendly milieu, perhaps more risk averse, and understandably sceptical of rapid change.

Outside of the electoral arena, Diana Schmidt focuses in Chapter 9 on whether the Internet is important for Russian non-governmental organisations (NGOs). She finds that non-governmental organisations can play an increasing role in informing and educating citizens in diverse, new kinds of collective engagement on a community level in Russia. Within local communities, however, this engagement is typically achieved without using the Internet, as the citizens concerned very rarely have access to this medium. Yet, the Internet can help non-government organisations by facilitating information gathering, the public expression of ideas as well as the creation of new communication links with other organizations in Russia and abroad. The new medium thus opens up two important functions of a civic public sphere, i.e. information and discussion. However, a lack of funding, technological problems and a dearth of expertise limit access for non-governmental organisations (and others) to this sphere. Whether Internet technologies might eventually also become operational for the third function of a civic public sphere – impact on democratic decision making – has to be assessed with regard to the complex and unstable institutional context in Russia.

The third chapter in this section tests the notion of whether the Internet can challenge the hegemony of the traditional mass media in a non-democratic state. In Chapter 10, Natalya Krasnoboka and Holli A. Semetko compare the news coverage of political protest in the first phase of the on-going political crisis in Ukraine for three months in 2000. They examine this coverage in three of the most popular and politically neutral news outlets: one national daily newspaper, one national commercial television channel and one online-only news website. The chapter finds that the newspaper content was quite distinctive from the other two media sources in its coverage of the protest, reacting as if it were still publishing in Soviet times. Qualitative analysis of the political reporting on the Internet and television news reveals that, while broadcast news was more open and inclusive in its reporting than the newspaper coverage, it was still more constrained and less inclusive than the

Internet content. The Internet coverage gave meaningful background on the protest coverage, which was not a feature of the television news reporting or the newspaper articles. The Internet site also provided more details on the size and location of the protests in comparison with the two traditional media, which appeared to be reflecting the interests of their owners. The chapter also draws conclusions about the role of the Internet in the development of contentious politics in a post-Soviet society, conclusions which are particularly relevant given the populist challenge to the hegemonic power of one group of power elites in the 2004 Ukrainian presidential elections.

In the final chapter of the book, Heinz Brandenburg places the Internet within the important, on-going debate drawn from the ideas of Jürgen Habermas and civil society. Brandenburg argues that the dialogue about revitalising democracy through online citizen deliberation suffers from a number of deficiencies, inconsistencies and false assumptions. First, it is entirely unwarranted that deliberation and the existence of a functioning public sphere is almost uncritically accepted as a necessary and sufficient condition for the existence of 'true' democracy. Second, the public sphere (or spheres) generated by the online world tends to be asymmetrical with regard to access, use, group polarisation, individual filtering and patterns of online engagement. Thus, the technology of the Internet may be regarded as a useful tool for organisational and social purposes and it may even have strong subversive potential. However, the Internet itself cannot alter the nature of the established Eurocentric and non-participatory model of representative democracy. Finally, the lesson that 'public sphere engineers' in the United Kingdom and elsewhere have learnt from their analysis of the insufficiency of Internet technology to create an online commons is also problematic. At the root of the problem is citizenship. While the Internet can remove the boundary between civil society and state, it cannot generate a feeling of citizenship. That means that, in order to effectively engineer an online public sphere, one also has to effectively engineer an online public.

Conclusions

One of the most pervasive problems in studying the Internet remains the lack of clarity about the structure of the research question as well as a failure to specify the level of the analysis. It is possible to consider the mass media both as a dependent variable, i.e. an element that is affected by certain independent variables, and as an independent variable itself. There is often confusion about this, as we understand the media as something that is influenced at the same time as it is influential in other spheres. To avoid this confusion, it is important to address immediately in research questions the expected role of the media, especially the Internet. Is the researcher seeking to clarify how the Internet is formed or how the Internet itself is influencing other political institutions within a society? Throughout this book, the Internet is studied generally as an independent variable, as scholars discuss its impact on civil society, youth involvement in politics, political parties, community action, local governance, non-governmental organisations, the success of terrorist groups and the freedom of speech. This means that the Internet is placed in perspective alongside other factors that can influence civil society, parties, community action, terrorism and democracy in general.

The other key point is to consider the level of analysis, as the Internet simultaneously produces information as well as spawns information consumers. Thus, it is important to consider whether the study is about those that provide information on the Internet and the legal/cultural environment in which they work; the content itself; or the Internet audience. Each level of the Internet calls for separate attention in order to generate meaningful hypotheses and research questions, particularly ones that can travel across country borders. In this book, the chapters by Conway and Reilly look specifically at how terrorist groups attempt to use the Internet to further their aims as well as the constraints that they face both logistically and legally in those attempts. The chapters by Owen, Wright, Schmidt and Lusoli and Ward are concerned with how well attempts to mobilise groups, ranging from youthful voters to activists to the common citizen, are carried out on the Internet. Thus, their studies discuss the range of the spectrum, from production through content to audience. March's chapter on Russian political parties includes a detailed content analysis of party websites, modelled on Gibson and Ward (2000). Krasnoboka and Semetko offer one of the few direct comparisons between content on a web-only information source and traditional mass media.

Overall, these chapters are united in arguing that our study of Internet use and its effects needs to be systematic and grounded in empirical evidence. Casual observations about the Internet or even philosophising about the new technologies, while it may set up the dialectic necessary for a body of literature to evolve and develop, also can deflect a lot of energy toward heated and ultimately empty debate. It is hoped that the case studies, analysis and hypotheses found in this book will provide a significant and useful basis for further evolution of the growing corpus of knowledge on Internet effects, particularly as they apply to the realm of civil society.

Notes

1   For US data, see Elena Larsen and Lee Rainie, *The Rise of the E-Citizen: How People Use Government Agencies*, a report from the Pew Internet and American Life Project, 3 April 2002. Another useful report from the Pew Center is *How Americans Get in Touch with Government* by John Horrigan, which was published on 24 May 2004. For access to Pew reports, visit their website at http://www.pewinternet.org.

2   See Acción Zapatista de Austin, 'Zapatismo in Cyberspace', at http://studentorgs.utexas.edu/nave/cyber.html.

3   See *Indymedia Seattle*, http://seattle.indymedia.org.

References

Adkeniz, Y. (2000) 'Policing the Internet: Concerns for Cyber-Rights', in Gibson, R. and Ward, S. (eds), *Reinvigorating Democracy?: British Politics and the Internet*, Aldershot: Ashgate.

Alvarez, R.M. and Nagler, J. (2000) 'The Likely Consequences of Internet Voting for Political Representation', Paper presented at the Internet Voting and Democracy Symposium, Loyola Law School, Los Angeles, CA.

Barney, D. (2000) *Prometheus Wired: The Hope for Democracy in the Age of Network Technology*, Sydney: University of New South Wales Press.

Bimber, B. (1998a) 'Toward an Empirical Map of Political Participation on the Internet', Paper presented at the annual meeting of the American Political Science Association, Boston, MA.

Bimber, B. (1998b) 'The Internet and Political Transformation: Populism, Community, and Accelerated Pluralism', *Polity* 31 (1): 133–160.

Boggs, C. (1997) 'The Great Retreat: Decline of the Public Sphere in Late Twentieth Century America', *Theory and Society* 26: 741–780.

Burbach, R. (ed.) (2001) *Globalization and Postmodern Politics: From Zapatistas to High-Tech Robber Barons*, London: Pluto Press.

Capling, A. and Nossal, K.R. (2001) 'Death of Distance or Tyranny of Distance?: The Internet, Deterritorialization and the Anti-Globalization Movement', *Pacific Review* 14 (3): 443–465.

Chivakula, K. (2001) 'Global Internet Regulation a Reality?', *Vector* 77 (24), 12 April. Online. Available http://thevector.njit.edu/.

Cleaver, H. (1995) *The Zapatistas and the Electronic Fabric of Struggle*. Online. Available http://www.eco.utexas.edu./faculty/Cleaver/zaps.html.

Coleman, S. (2001) *Democracy Online: What Do We Want from MPs' Web Sites?*, London: Hansard Society. Online. Available http://www.hansardsociety.org.uk/MPWEB.pdf.

Critical Art Ensemble (1994) *The Electronic Disturbance*, New York: Autonomedia.

Critical Art Ensemble (1995) *Electronic Civil Disobedience and Other Unpopular Ideas*, New York: Autonomedia.

Critical Art Ensemble (2001) *Digital Resistance: Explorations in Tactical Media*, New York: Autonomedia.

Cummings, J., Butler, B. and Kraut, R. (2002) 'The Quality of Online Social Relationships', *Communications of the ACM* [Association for Computing Machinery] 45 (7): 103–108.

Davis, R. and Owen, D. (1998) *New Media and American Politics*, New York: Oxford University Press.

Denning, D. (2001) 'Cyberwarriors: Activists and Terrorists Turn to Cyberspace', *Harvard International Review* (23) 2: 70–75.

Dyson, E. (1998) *Release 2.1: A Design for Living in the Digital Age*, London: Penguin.

Elmer, G. (1997) 'Spaces of Surveillance: Indexicality and Solicitation on the Internet', *Critical Studies in Mass Communication* 14 (2): 182–191.

Etzioni, A. and Etzioni, O. (1999) 'Face-to-Face and Computer-mediated Communities, A Comparative Analysis', Paper presented at Virtual Communities: Eighth Annual Conference on Computers, Freedom and Privacy, University of Texas, Austin.

Ferdinand, P. (ed.) (2000) *The Internet, Democracy and Democratization*, London: Frank Cass Publishers Ltd.

Foucault, M. (1975) *Discipline and Punish: The Birth of the Prison*, London: Allen Lane.

Galston, W. (2003) 'The Impact of the Internet on Civic Life: An Early Assessment', in Kamarck, E.C. and Nye, J.S. (eds), *Governance.com: Democracy in the Information Age*, Washington DC: Brookings Institution Press.

Gibson, R.K. (2001) 'Elections Online: Assessing Internet Voting in Light of the Arizona Democratic Primary', *Political Science Quarterly* 116 (4): 561–583.

Gibson, R.K. and Ward, S. (2000) 'A Proposed Methodology for Studying the Function and Effectiveness of Party and Candidate Websites', *Social Science Computer Review* 18 (3): 301–319.

Heilemann, J. (1996) 'Old Politics RIP', *Wired* 4 (11). Online. Available www.wired.com/wired/archive?4.11/netizen.html.

Hightower, J. (1998) 'Virtual Communities as Communities: Net Surfers Don't Ride Alone', in Smith, A.A. and Kollock, P. (eds), *Communities in Cyberspace*, London: Routledge.

Hill, K. and Hughes, J. (1998) *Cyberpolitics: Citizen Activism in the Age of the Internet*, Oxford: Rowman & Littlefield.

Jeffries, F. (2001) 'Zapatismo and Intergalactic Age', in Burbach, R. (ed.), *Globalization and Postmodern Politics: From Zapatistas to High-Tech Robber Barons*, 129–144, London: Pluto Press.

Krueger, B. (2002) 'Assessing the Potential of Internet Political Participation in the United States: A Resource Approach', *American Politics Research* 30 (5): 476–498.

Lessig, L. (1999) *Code and Other Laws of Cyberspace*, New York: Basic Books.

Liberty (ed.) (1999) *Liberating Cyberspace: Civil Liberties, Human Rights and the Internet*, London: Pluto Press and Liberty.

Lipow, A. and Seyd, P. (1996) 'The Politics of Anti-Partyism', *Parliamentary Affairs* 49 (2): 273–84.

Mander, J. (2001) 'Technologies of Globalization', in Goldsmith, E. and Mander, J. (eds), *The Case against the Global Economy and for a Turn towards Localization*, London: Earthscan.

Margolis, M. and Resnick, D. (2000) *Politics as Usual: The Cyberspace 'Revolution'*, London: Sage.

Meikle, G. (2002) *Future Active: Media Activism and the Internet*, New York: Pluto Press.

Morris, D. (2000) *Vote.com*, Los Angeles, CA: Renaissance.

Mulgan, G. and Adonis, A. (1994) 'Back to Greece: The Scope for Direct Democracy', *Demos Quarterly* 3: 2–9.

Negroponte, N. (1995) *Being Digital*, London: Coronet.

Nie, N.H. and Erbring, L. (2000) 'Internet and Society: A Preliminary Report', Stanford, CA: Stanford Institute for the Quantitative Study of Society.

Norris, P. (2001) *Digital Divide*, Cambridge: Cambridge University Press.

Norris, P., Bennett, W.L. and Entman, R.M. (eds) (2000) *A Virtuous Circle: Political Communications in Postindustrial Societies*, Cambridge: Cambridge University Press.

Pew Research Center for the People and the Press (1996) *One in Ten Voters Online for Campaign '96*, Washington, DC: Pew Research Center for the People and the Press. Online. Available http://people-press.org/reports/display.php3?ReportID=117.

Poster, M. (1997) 'Cyberdemocracy: The Internet and the Public Sphere', in Holmes, D. (ed.), *Virtual Politics: Identity and Community in Cyberspace*, London: Sage.

Putnam, R. (2000) *Bowling Alone*, New York: Simon & Schuster.

Rash, W. (1997) *Politics on the Nets: Wiring the Political Process*, New York: W.H. Freeman.

Rheingold, H. (1995) *The Virtual Community: Finding Connection in a Computerised World*, London: Minerva.

Robins, K. and Webster, F. (1988) 'Cybernetic Capitalism: Information, Technology and Everyday Life', in Mosco, V. and Wasko, J. (eds), *The Political Economy of Information*, Madison, WI: University of Wisconsin Press.

Ronfeldt, D., Arquilla, J., Fuller, G.E. and Fuller, M. (1998) *The Zapatista Social Netwar in Mexcio*, Santa Monica, CA: Rand Corporation.

Schuefele, D.A. and Nisbet, M.C. (2002) 'Being a Citizen Online: New Opportunities and Dead Ends', *Harvard Journal of Press/Politics* 7 (3): 55–75.

Shah, D.V., Kwak, N. and Holbert, R.L. (2001) ' "Connecting" and "Disconnecting" with Civic Life: Patterns of Internet Use and the Production of Social Capital', *Political Communication* 18: 141–162.

Shah, D., Schmierbach, M., Hawkins, J., Espino, R. and Donavan, J. (2002) 'Non-Recursive Models of Internet Use and Community Engagement: Questioning Whether Time Spent Online Erodes Social Capital', *Journalism and Mass Communication Quarterly* 79 (4): 964–987.

Shenk, D. (1997) *Data Smog*, San Francisco, CA: Abacus.

Shepard, B. and Hayduk, R. (2002) 'Urban Protest and Community Building in the Age of Globalization', in Shephard, B. and Hayduk, R. (eds), *From ACT UP to the WTO: Urban Protest and Community Building in the Age of Globalization*, London: Verso.

Solop, F. (2001) 'Digital Democracy Comes of Age: Internet Voting and the 2000 Arizona Democratic Primary Election', *PSOnline* 34 (2), June.

Sterling, B. (1992) *The Hacker Crackdown*, New York: Bantam Books.

Streck, J. (1999) 'Pulling the Plug on Electronic Town Meetings: Participatory Democracy and the Reality of Usenet', in Toulouse, C. and Luke, T. (eds), *The Politics of Cyberspace*, 18–47, London: Routledge.

Street, J. (1992) *Politics and Technology*, New York: Guildford Press.

Sunstein, C. (2001) *Republic.com*, Princeton, NJ: Princeton University Press.

Toffler, A. and Toffler, H. (1995) *Creating a New Civilization: The Politics of the Third Wave*, Atlanta, GA: Turner Publications.

Tolbert, C., Mossberger, K. and McNeal, R. (2003) 'Beyond the Digital Divide: Exploring Attitudes about Information Technology, Political Participation and Electronic Government', Paper presented at the annual meeting of the American Political Science Association, Boston, MA.

Uslaner, E. (2001) 'Trust, Civic Engagement and the Internet', Paper presented at the European Consortium of Political Research, Grenoble, France.

Weber, L., Loumake, A. and Bergman, J. (2003) 'Who Participates and Why?': An Analysis of Citizens on the Internet and the Mass Public', *Social Science Computer Review* 21 (1): 26–42.

Wellman, B., Quan Haase, A., Witte, J. and Hampton, K. (2001) 'Does the Internet increase, decrease, or supplement social capital?', *American Behavioral Scientist* 45 (3): 436–455.

Wilhelm, A.G. (2000) *Democracy in the Digital Age: Challenges to Political Life in Cyberspace*, New York: Routledge.

Wu, W. and Weaver, D. (1996) 'On-line Democracy or On-line Demagoguery?: Public Opinion "Polls" on the Internet', *Harvard International Journal of Press/Politics* 2 (4): 71–86.

Zuboff, S. (1988) *In the Age of the Smart Machine: The Future of Work and Power*, New York: Basic Books.

2 The Internet and youth civic engagement in the United States

Diana Owen

New forms of mass communication traditionally have had great appeal for younger people. Not only are the younger generation less likely to have established long-standing habits of media use, but they also are more willing to experiment with new technologies and formats. Younger citizens may claim new communications technologies as their own, developing particular expertise and novel applications. They view new technologies as a means of gaining advantage in the educational arena, in the workforce and in the political realm. Despite the conclusions of much research that young citizens fail to engage in traditional forms of participation, there are indications that the Internet may be facilitating, if not invigorating, youth civic engagement.

There has been much speculation about the Internet's potential to facilitate the engagement of younger citizens in politics, especially given the conventional wisdom regarding this group's civic orientations. This group of Americans under the age of 35, frequently labelled 'Generations X and Y', have been derided for their lack of political interest and activity for the last two decades. They have a different orientation toward politics than older cohorts (Keeter *et al.*, 2002). They know relatively little about politics and government (Delli Carpini and Keeter, 1996); distrust politicians and other citizens; and exhibit depressed levels of patriotism and pride of country (Delli Carpini, 2000). Younger citizens are disaffected from formal political institutions, processes and actors. They are especially disenchanted with the two major political parties in the United States. Members of the younger generation are more likely to be political independents, favour candidates running without party labels and support third-party candidates than older citizens (Owen, 1997a; Dennis and Owen, 1997). In addition, youth are less likely to register to vote and turn out to vote in elections than older people. A small minority have worked on a campaign, contacted a public official or attended a political meeting. Even fewer have taken part in governmental affairs, including at the local level. Generation X is substantially under-represented among the ranks of formal government office-holders. While there is a perception that young people may be more heavily vested in community-based volunteer activities, the evidence is mixed (Verba *et al.*, 1995).

It is becoming increasingly clear, however, that young people in the United

States have been far from idle in the political sphere. This is particularly true if one looks to Internet use among citizens. Evidence suggests that young people are more likely than older citizens to use web-based platforms to carry out research and gain political information, including during election campaigns (Pew Research Center, 2003). Youth audiences gravitate to websites designed to attract their attention, including political sites (Rainie, 2002). In addition, young people are well inclined to communicate and express their views via online platforms. Perhaps more importantly, younger citizens have been engaging in political activities below the radar screens of observers and scholars who focus on conventional behaviours indexed to traditional institutions (Davis *et al.*, 2002). Young people are following the broader American trend toward single-issue politics, as they strive to find a way to connect more meaningfully to an increasingly complex political world (Schudson, 1998). They have been forming issue-based organizations online as a means of expressing their concerns. The Internet has become a conduit for significant youth political activation, as disparate groups organise protest movements online in conjunction with other new media formats, such as talk radio and low-power FM radio.

In order to place the analysis of the Internet and youth civic engagement in context, this chapter begins with a discussion of the new media's evolution in American politics. The Internet is but a single factor, albeit an important one, in a dynamic transformation of the media system. The online world acts as a hub for the coordination, integration and restructuring of political discourse and action.

The new media come of age

For almost 20 years, the American media landscape has been undergoing a significant transformation galvanized by the advent of 'new media'. Existing media platforms, such as print tabloids, broadcast call-in programmes, television news magazines and music television, have accommodated political content to an unprecedented degree. Simultaneously, technological innovations, especially computer networks and the more recent introduction of personal digital appliances, have enabled the development of new communication forms. In fact, the US media system is in the midst of a dramatic transformation that has momentous implications for younger generations of citizens. The traditional media have been joined by 'new media' actors who have been steadily encroaching upon their turf. This transition has resulted in changes in the form of both the manner of distribution and the content of political news and information. Perhaps even more significantly, it has contributed to a shift in the nature of political engagement and activation. Communications media, especially online sources, are creating unprecedented linkages among citizens – and these connections are precursors to political participation. This is a particularly significant factor for a younger generation that appreciates and enjoys use of the Internet and other new media to a greater degree than older citizens.

The new media's emergence in the United States was facilitated by a regulatory environment that downplayed the public service imperative for communications organizations. It coincided as well with the first Gulf War and a number of high-profile legal cases. These proved a boon for talk formats, and prompted innovation and expansion into other realms of news and politics. New media became firmly established during the 1992 presidential election, as candidates sought to bypass the constraints of traditional media by appealing to voters via alternative channels (Davis and Owen, 1998). Although its use was still relatively rudimentary, the Internet first became a factor in election campaigns in 1996 (Davis, 1999; Andersen and Cornfield, 2002). By the 2004 presidential contest, the Internet had become an integral part of candidates' electoral presence and a rich source of campaign information, especially for young voters (Pew Internet, 2004b).

A free-for-all atmosphere characterised the early years of the new media era. New media were – and still are – highly diverse. They were unreliable and sporadic in providing serious forums for political discourse and activity. Some new media, such as electronic town meetings, offered citizens novel options for meaningfully accessing politics. Other forms, such as talk radio, openly spurned established journalistic norms and practices in favour of entertainment values and increasingly sensational content as they unabashedly pursued profits (Owen, 1997b; Barker, 2002).

These divergent profiles of new media sparked differing interpretations of their democratic potential. Optimistic observers credited new media with stimulating a new democratic populism. They claimed this could be done by the new media's mechanisms for activating average citizens by facilitating a more inclusive public discourse. These sanguine expectations were offset by realistic evaluations that recognised that the democratic potential of the new media was frequently undercut. New media only superficially served underrepresented constituencies, and most often provided additional outlets for expression to those who already were politically well entrenched and well connected (Owen, 1996; Davis and Owen, 1998). Outward appearances to the contrary, new media gatekeepers actually limited access to the airwaves, as they sought formulas that maximised their profit-making capacity. 'Digital divide' issues relating to access and the development of appropriate skills to use innovative technologies were especially pronounced in the political applications of new media. Although more than half the US population had access to the Internet, only 8.5 per cent of the public had any connections to politics online in 1997. A knowledge gap based on education, income and occupation was related to disparities in the inclination to take advantage of the political opportunities offered by the Internet (Katz, 1997).

Today, the free-for-all that has characterised the new media environment has begun to sort itself out. New media are no longer novel or marginal in the American political process. They have evolved in a manner that favours greater citizen input and control over the communications process. Committed audiences have been established. While initially new media were used by citizens to supplement their mainstream media habits, a growing number of people now are turning exclusively to new media for news and information. Innovation promotes greater public accessibility to media outlets that accommodate a broader spectrum of voices – including youth.

Perhaps the most significant developments surround the platforms associated with newer communications technologies, especially the Internet. Online platforms in the United States erect few barriers to entry, and they represent the most open options for disseminating political content. As individuals have developed greater facility with the Internet, they have discovered new ways of exploiting its political possibilities. Younger generations of citizens are leading the way in terms of use and innovation.

The Internet as a political medium

Access to the Internet and its use are astoundingly high for Americans, making it a viable tool for mass engagement rather than an enclave for political junkies, specialists and outsiders. The diffusion of Internet technology in American society has been rapid (Norris, 2001). A healthy majority of Americans have access to the Internet and go online. *The UCLA Internet Report – Year 3* reported that 71 per cent of the population were online in 2003, a figure that differed little from the previous year (Cole *et al.*, 2003). Pew Internet and American Life data suggest that approximately 128 million adults, or 63 per cent of the US population, were online in 2004, with 68 million daily users. The 'digital divide' is closing, as Internet facilities are made increasingly available in schools, libraries and other public spaces (Pew Internet and American Life Project, 2004a). Americans spend an average of over 11 hours online per week (Cole *et al.*, 2003).

An extraordinarily high percentage of young people use the Internet. As a result of Clinton–Gore era initiatives to have Internet access in all secondary schools and libraries (including the $2.25 billion E-Rate programme that subsidised equipment and training), 98 per cent of school-aged children had Internet access by 2001 (Fabos, 2002). Census Bureau statistics indicate that over 70 per cent of children between the ages of 3 and 8 as well as 90 per cent of those between ages 9 and 17 were online in 2001. UCLA data show that 97 per cent of people 18 and under were using the Internet in late 2002. Pew Internet and American Life Project data reveal that, in 2004, 78 per cent of 18- to 29-year-olds and 74 per cent of 30- to 49-year-olds went online. The percentage of those online decreases as age increases and only 25 per cent of people over the age of 65 were online in 2004. Further, young people spend a significant amount of time using the Internet. Teens between the ages of 12 and 17 spent an average of approximately one hour per day online, while one-third of older adolescents (15–17) used the Internet for more than six hours a week (Kaiser Family Foundation, 2002).

Over time, new media formats, especially online news and information sites, have gained greater public legitimacy. People have more faith in the accuracy of web content. Young people are especially comfortable with online news: over 80 per cent of those under age 30 consider it to be extremely credible. In fact, the younger generation considers online news sources to be *more* reliable than national television news, local television news, national radio news or local newspapers. These findings can be explained in part by the fact that online news producers come largely from the ranks of younger citizens (Radio and Television Director's Foundation, 2001). In addition, young people who regularly engage with the Internet have become familiar with the standards of fact checking and sourcing that have evolved in the online world.

The number of people relying on the Internet for political news has reached a stable mass of approximately 40 per cent of the US population (Pew Internet, 2004a). While many Internet users also consult print newspapers and television news, there is a growing trend toward sole reliance on online news sources. *The UCLA Internet Report* indicates that television viewing among online news audiences has been steadily declining since 2001. Experienced users, many of whom are younger people, increasingly cut into their television viewing time to go online (Cole *et al.*, 2003).

Because of its seemingly limitless capacity, the Internet accommodates virtually anyone with an inclination to take part in the production of news and information. Thus, the Internet has contributed to the rise of amateur journalists. Young people are well represented among the ranks of both amateur and professional content providers. They have highly developed technical skills, accept new media channels as legitimate, and perceive online journalism as a mechanism for bypassing roadblocks to entry into mainstream media establishments. Propelled by their distrust of mainstream news organizations, amateur reporters will delve deeply into issues that are either glossed over or ignored entirely by the mainstream media (Downie and Kaiser, 2003). Online news organizations have tended to hire people for their technical abilities, rather than their training in journalism (Finberg *et al.*, 2002). As a result, a young cohort occupies many online newsrooms. Online news producers spend much of their time reprocessing content from the print and broadcast news products of their affiliates, but they are increasingly given the opportunity to make their own contributions. As news bureaus have cut their budgets for newsgathering and production, they have substituted information, commentary and speciality segments (such as online photo galleries and chats) that are largely the work of younger online newsroom workers.

Adolescent Internet use

As the data on Internet access and use indicate, adolescents are well represented online. There is, in fact, evidence of a generational shift in media orientations as the lifestyles of adolescents increasingly centre around online technology. Some scholars have gone so far as to label the generation of Americans born after 1976 the 'DotNets' (Bennett and Xenos, 2004).

Experience with the medium, and the heightened levels of proficiency and comfort in using the Internet this affords, may prompt younger generations to develop a lively political life online as they age. Schools, non-profit organizations and corporations have implemented a host of programmes designed to socialise young people to online politics. One example during the 2004 presidential election was Freedom's Answer, a web-based campaign to engage high school students in get-out-the-vote drives that involved over 1 million students (www.freedomsanswer.org).

Relatively few data account for the political uses of online sources by young people. This study employs data from an October 2000 survey of Internet activities by parents and their children conducted by the Pew Internet and American Life Project. These data are limited in the degree to which they specifically address political uses of the Internet. However, they can be used in two key ways. First, it is possible to use the data to develop a profile of the types of online activities in which adolescents engage. In addition, the data make it possible to theorise about the related skill sets adolescents have mastered that may facilitate their future online political activities.

The questionnaire asks the adolescents in the sample to indicate whether they have ever engaged in a range of online activities. These activities were classified into five categories based on their characteristics and degree of relevance to politics. Activities related to getting and disseminating information are the most directly pertinent to politics. These activities include seeking news and information about current events; going to websites and bulletin boards to publish opinions; and creating web pages. While the ambiguity of these indicators leaves their political relevance open to interpretation, these activities may prepare adolescents to engage in online political activities later in life. Communication activities – such as sending and receiving email, engaging in instant messaging and participating in online chats – also constitute pre-political activities. Another category includes information-seeking activities that are non-political. This includes using online sources to find out about television shows, movies, music, hobbies, products, clubs, groups, teams, health and issues that are difficult to discuss in person. Non-political online activities include using the Internet to play games, listen to music, download music as well as buy, trade or sell things. These activities involve using some of the more advanced features of the Internet that are increasingly relevant to politics, such as multimedia functions and the use of online payment systems. A final category, labelled 'time burning', addresses the degree to which adolescents go online for no specific reason.

Adolescents aged 12 to 17 were compared to older age groups in an effort to determine the extent to which younger citizens are more or less active in particular domains of online engagement. Unfortunately, the parent sample was not asked the battery of Internet activity questions presented to the adolescents, so the children cannot be compared directly with their parents. The best resort was to use the Pew Internet and American Life Project's Longitudinal Tracking Survey released in March 2001, approximately five months after the parent–child study. This database contained most, but not all, of the questions asked of the adolescents. The analysis includes one additional measure of getting information: visiting local, state and national government websites (for the adult sample).

Table 2.1 indicates that younger people generally are more prolific in their use of the Internet than older respondents. Those under the age of 25 are the most likely to use the Internet to obtain and disseminate information about current affairs. This finding tracks with their decreased inclination to use traditional sources of news, such as newspapers and network news broadcasts (Pew Research Center, 2002). Adolescents are more likely to engage in online communications activities than older people. More than 90 per cent of 12- to 17-year-olds use email, almost 75 per cent send instant messages and 55 per cent participate in online chat rooms. Young people will seek information about entertainment and sports more often than information about products and health issues. Not surprisingly, the reverse holds for older individuals. Finally, respondents under the age of 21 were substantially more inclined to go online purely for entertainment (see Table 2.1).

As one would expect, older adolescents (15–17 years old) generally are more likely to engage in activities that are most relevant for political engagement, information dissemination/seeking and communicating than younger children (12–14 years old). There were a few exceptions to this pattern. As Table 2.2 suggests, notable gender differences are apparent, as the overall trend shows that 12- to 14-year-old females are more inclined to seek information, disseminate information and communicate than their male counterparts. Yet, gender differences almost disappear among older adolescents. The one exception to this trend is that males are more likely than females to create web pages.

In order to gain a greater understanding of the factors influencing the tendencies of adolescents to engage in online news and information activities, this analysis uses a series of binary logistic regression analyses. The models included age, gender, the frequency with which the adolescent goes online, the age at which he or she first went online, family income, education of parents, and race.[1] The model is limited by the scope and measurement of available indicators.[2] As Table 2.3 shows, the experience of adolescents with the Internet, measured in terms of the amount of time spent online, is the greatest determinant of their tendency to seek news and information about current events, express opinions and create web pages. Consistent with the bivariate analysis, the regression model shows that older adolescents are more inclined to seek news and information online than younger people, although this relationship does not hold up for expressing opinions and creating web pages. Gender differences remain evident when additional controls are introduced, as females are somewhat more likely to seek information and males are more inclined to create web pages. Young people in households that include a more educated parent seek information with greater frequency.

These findings support the proposition that adolescents are developing

Table 2.1 Activities done online

	Percentage who have ever done the activity (by age group)									
	12–17	18–20	21–24	25–29	30–39	40–49	50–59	60–69	70+
Getting/disseminating news/information:									
Get news/information	68	63	67	47	44	45	45	50	33
Write opinions	38	—	—	—	—	—	—	—	—
Create web page	24	—	—	—	—	—	—	—	—
Government website	—	43	53	47	40	51	61	47	46
Communicating:									
Email	92	80	89	83	82	78	80	91	62
Instant message	74	58	24	35	33	30	26	26	15
Chat	55	—	—	—	—	—	—	—	—
Get information about:									
TV shows, movies, music	83	89	84	68	57	44	44	41	39
Hobby	69	100	100	79	76	78	69	52	54
New products/purchases	66	80	73	70	71	79	66	50	39
Sports scores	47	51	49	31	39	27	28	28	8
Clubs, groups, teams	39	—	—	—	—	—	—	—	—
Health	26	31	65	45	59	51	52	47	31
Things hard to talk about	18	—	—	—	—	—	—	—	—

continued

Table 2.1 continued

	Percentage who have ever done the activity (by age group)							
	12–17	*18–20*	*21–24*	*25–29*	*30–39*	*40–49*	*50–59*	*60–69*	*70+*

	12–17	*18–20*	*21–24*	*25–29*	*30–39*	*40–49*	*50–59*	*60–69*	*70+*
Non-political activities:									
Play games	66	76	62	24	32	28	32	31	33
Listen to music	59	79	57	24	31	22	18	16	25
Download music	53	—	—	—	—	—	—	—	—
Buy things	31	55	60	57	47	46	39	41	54
Trade or sell things	31	—	—	—	—	—	—	—	—
Time burning:									
No reason	84	87	56	65	56	49	54	34	77
Number of respondents	753	56	37	71	164	138	61	32	12

Data source for 12 to 17-year-olds: Pew Internet and American Life Project (2000).
Data source for 18 and older: Pew Internet and American Life Project (2001).

Table 2.2 Activities done online by adolescents' age and gender

| | Percentage who have ever done the activity | | | | | |
| | Male | | | Female | | |
	12–14 %	15–17 %	sign. chi-square	12–14 %	15–17 %	sign. chi-square
Getting/disseminating news/information:						
Get news/information	60	72	0.01	67	74	0.09
Write opinions	33	42	0.05	40	37	ns
Create web page	23	34	0.01	19	18	ns
Communicating:						
Email	84	94	0.00	93	96	ns
Instant message	60	80	0.00	72	83	0.00
Chat	49	59	0.05	49	62	0.00
N	167	212		174	200	

Data source: Pew Internet and American Life Project (2000).

Table 2.3 OLS regression analysis of Internet participation in the 2000 presidential election campaign

	beta	stat. sign.
Age	−0.07	0.05
Gender	−0.05	0.05
Education	0.02	ns
White	−0.04	ns
Black	0.02	ns
Ideology	−0.06	0.03
Go online	0.19	0.00
Get info not available elsewhere	0.05	0.06
Online info convenient	0.02	ns
Web sources reflect interests	0.07	0.01
Not enough news from other sources	0.11	0.00
N	1404	
R^2	0.06	0.00

Data source: Pew Research Center (2000).

skills that will serve them well in the online political world, should they choose to take part. The greater their experience with the medium, the more likely adolescents are to engage in activities related to creating and disseminating information. This generation's proficiency with the Internet will likely continue to develop as they reach political maturity.

Online election activity

The new millennium witnessed a continuation of the long-term trend of low levels of youth participation in election campaigns. Between 1972 (when 18-year-olds first gained the right to vote) and 2000, turnout declined among voters under the age of 25 by 15 percentage points.[3] Thirty-seven per cent of young people participated in the 2000 presidential election, compared with 61 per cent of the adult population (Levine and Lopez, 2002).[4] Turnout in midterm elections is substantially lower, as 16 per cent of young people participated in the 2002 contest (Association of American Colleges and Universities, 2002). Young voters were substantially more active in the 2004 election (CIRCLE, 2004a). The turnout rate among young voters increased by 5.8 per cent in 2004, as 10.5 million voters ages 18–24 went to the polls, representing 1.8 million more voters than in 2000. Forty-two per cent of voters under age 30 were first-time voters (CIRCLE, 2004b).

Young people typically claim that they are not inspired by candidates who avoid addressing their concerns. This was the case during the 2002 midterm election in which voters aged 30 and under were significantly more interested in education issues than older voters. Older voters instead focused on the economy, a topic that received more attention from candidates and the press (DePledge and Bustos, 2002). Young people were more attentive to the 2004 presidential election, driven by concerns about jobs, the economy, terrorism and national security. Seventy-four per cent of 18- to 29-year-olds believed that this election would be the most important of their lifetime (CIRCLE, 2004a).

Stimulating youth participation in the electoral process is a daunting task, despite the increase in turnout in 2004. The disenchantment of youth with political parties leaves them lacking strong linkage mechanisms to connect them to the electoral process (Dennis and Owen, 1997). The Internet has been touted as a promising avenue for fostering young adult campaign involvement, and perhaps filling the traditional role of parties, because of the medium's more general appeal to the under-35 age group. The most prominent use of the web in the electoral context is as a political information source and expression forum. Young voters were more oriented toward online sources to gain campaign news and information during the 2000 presidential contest than older voters (Pew Research Center, 2000), a trend that remained in evidence during the 2002 midterm election (Pew Research Center, 2003) and 2004 presidential race (Pew Research Center, 2004).

Previews of the Internet's potential for informing and engaging the public during the 1996 and 1998 elections led to great anticipation that the 2000 presidential campaign would establish the Internet as a powerful force in elections. There was a tremendous amount of high-quality election resources available online, representing the efforts of many constituencies, including campaigns, parties, news organisations, civic groups, individual citizens and even school children. Websites provided a wealth of information, including technical details about registration and voting; the full text of candidates' position on issues; and campaign strategies. They also furnished resources for how to get involved offline. Reacting to criticisms voiced by young people about political websites in past elections, designers sought to maintain interest and involvement by making the sites conform to the expectations of web-savvy visitors. Sites were visually striking, easy to use and interactive, including features such as discussion boards, chat rooms and online polls. Unfiltered interactive discussions with candidates, political leaders and journalists were hosted online. Some sites incorporated sophisticated innovations, such as streaming audio and video of original content, some of which was produced by and for young citizens (Owen, 2001).

The 2004 presidential election may have been the long-awaited 'Internet campaign'. Candidate, party and political organisation websites included unprecedented features that caught the attention of voters and, in some cases, made Internet users part of the campaign. The 'air wars' took to the Internet, as campaigns launched ads and rebuttals via the web. Voters were invited to create and air their own campaign ads on sites, such as moveon.org, which sponsored a contest for the best voter-produced spot and funded $15 million in television airplay for the winner (Jamieson, 2004). Campaign web logs or 'blogs' allowed candidates, their spouses and friends as well as journalists and ordinary people to convey their thoughts about the campaign. In addition, they could field comments from a wide range of people. Political websites took on the role traditionally played by parties of facilitating voter engagement in campaigns. They organised volunteers, promoted events and raised large amounts of money for candidates.

The vitality of the online presidential campaign in 2004 is reflected in the increased use of the Internet by voters. In 2000, campaign websites associated with candidates, parties or civic organizations did not generate a tremendous amount of voter traffic among any age group, although young people were slightly more inclined to visit candidate sites than older voters. Approximately 14 per cent of the public visited candidate websites in 2000, including 19 per cent of 18- to 24-year-olds, while 10 per cent visited a party website. In contrast, 32 per cent of adults had consulted a candidate's website in 2004, as visits to party websites fell to 2 per cent (Harris Interactive, 2004). Websites designed specifically for young people, including civic engagement sites that encourage self-expression and volunteerism, are among the most popular with this audience (Center for Media Education, 2001). Such youth-specific sites were prominent during the 2000 and 2004 presidential election campaigns, and included MTV's site (rockthevote.org) and the National Association of Secretaries of State site (stateofthevote.org). Political parody websites, such as jibjab.com, theonion.com and whitehousewest.com, which poked fun at the candidates, were especially popular among 18- to 24-year-old voters. The web addresses of these sites were distributed widely by email, resulting in visits by more than 60 per cent of young voters (Owen and Davis, 2004).

There are age-related differences in the types of online campaign activities in which people take part. Looking for more information about the positions of the candidates on issues is by far the most popular election use of the Internet, and 75 per cent of young voters go online for this purpose. Young people are more likely than older voters to go online to find out logistical information about voting and to engage in chats. Citizens over the age of 50 are the most likely to register their opinions by participating in an electronic poll, to get online information about a candidate's voting record and contribute money online (Pew Research Center, 2003).

A study focusing on the campaign Internet use of 18- to 29-year-old voters in the 2004 presidential contest[5] reveals that the online campaign greatly facilitated the political engagement of those expressing at least some interest in the campaign. While most young people continued to use the Internet primarily to seek information about the campaign, a significant number used the online environment to express their opinions and to become active in the election. Twenty-eight per cent went online at least once a day to get information about the campaign. Seventy-two per cent visited a candidate's website and 23 per cent subscribed to a campaign's email alerts. Twenty-two per cent used the Internet to express their views about the presidential candidates by participating in an online discussion group, while 14 per cent read or contributed to a candidate's blog. Of the 21 per cent who volunteered for a presidential candidate, 7 per cent used the Internet to solicit donations, recruit volunteers or organise an event for George W. Bush or John Kerry. Thirty per cent rated candidates' websites as 'excellent' for providing opportunities for getting involved with the campaign. Nine per cent became involved offline because of email solicitations for volunteers from candidates.

In an effort to determine what factors might predict Internet-based participation in an election campaign, an ordinary least squares regression analysis was performed using data from the 2000 Pew Research Center election study. An additive index of online participation was created that incorporated seven types of online election activities. These activities are defined as: participating in online discussions; registering opinions; getting information about voting records; finding out where and when to vote; emailing support or opposition to a candidate; contributing money; and looking for issue information. The model included age as a primary variable of interest. Controls were entered for gender, education, race and ideology. The amount of time spent online getting campaign information and four measures of motivations for using the Internet – getting information not available elsewhere, convenience, web sources reflecting personal interest and not enough news provided by other sources – also were included. As Table 2.3 indicates, age is a statistically significant predictor of Internet participation in the multivariate model, with younger people being the most active online. Gender is the only demographic control to achieve statistical significance, as men engage in more online campaign activities than women. Conservatives participate more online during elections than liberals. All of the motivational measures were statistically significant with the exception of convenience.

Pew Research Center data revealed that the Internet was a factor in voter decision making for a substantial number of people in the 2000 presidential contest. Forty-four per cent of the survey respondents reported that information they received online made them want to vote for or against a particular candidate. This finding is especially striking for younger voters, as 54 per cent of 18- to 24-year olds were influenced by online information compared to 29 per cent of voters over the age of 60. In order to identify factors that might predict whether or not the Internet had an impact on voter decision making, we estimated a model using binary logistic regression analysis. The same predictors that were used in the multivariate analysis of Internet participation were included in the model. The measure of online election participation was added as well. The findings in Table 2.4 confirm that age is a statistically significant determinant of Internet influence on vote choice as described in the bivariate analysis. Women are more likely than men to rely on online information for decision making. Ideology approaches statistical significance, with liberals being more likely than conservatives to base their vote on information accessed online. The only motivational factor that achieves significance is the desire to use the Internet to provide information that is not available in traditional news media. Finally, those who score high on the index of online election participation are the most inclined to be influenced by the Internet when casting a ballot for a candidate.

These findings provide substantial support for the proposition that young people are using the Internet to engage in the electoral process to a greater extent than older cohorts. The number of young voters using online sources

Table 2.4 Binary logistic regression analysis of Internet influence on vote choice in the 2000 presidential election campaign

	b	*SE*	*stat. sign.*
Age	−0.02	0.00	0.00
Gender	0.38	0.15	0.01
Education	0.05	0.06	ns
White	−0.15	0.29	ns
Black	0.12	0.38	ns
Ideology	0.12	0.08	0.11
Go online	0.06	0.06	ns
Get info not available elsewhere	0.33	0.34	ns
Online info convenient	0.11	0.21	ns
Web sources reflect interests	−0.03	0.46	ns
Not enough news from other sources	0.51	0.24	0.03
Internet election participation	0.41	0.06	0.00
Constant	−1.42	0.56	0.02
N	809		
Nagelkerke R^2	0.13	0.00	
% of cases correctly classified	64%		

Data source: Pew Research Center (2000).

for information seeking, communicating and networking grows markedly with the passing of each presidential contest (Davis *et al.*, 2002). The online election environment brought young people into the campaign in both the virtual world and the 'real' world as their online experiences led them to offline activity. Of special note is the finding that a majority of young people in the survey reported using Internet information to guide their vote choice. Traditionally, studies have indicated that the media's influence on vote choice is limited as partisan and group ties structure voting decisions (Berelson *et al.*, 1954). While these data are hardly definitive, and the relationship warrants far more thorough investigation, this finding suggests that the Internet is capable of replacing the linkage mechanisms of party and face-to-face agents in the campaign process for future generations of citizens.

Political protest

Initial enthusiasm about the new media's potential to stimulate citizen activism was tempered by observations that, while they provided seemingly endless opportunities for expression, the new media did little to help people transform this discourse into meaningful political action. Critics argue that both new and traditional media, for that matter, leave people with the impression that they are participating when they are not really taking part. Some analysts claim that the new media merely distract people from genuine political engagement (Hart, 1994; Putnam, 2001).

Despite this criticism, the ability to use new media to facilitate political action is perhaps the biggest development in their evolution, and younger generations are at the forefront of this movement. The new media's activating influence has been underestimated because of the tendency for political observers and most survey researchers to focus on established institutional structures and related behaviours. Those who lament the limited role of the Internet during the 2000 presidential campaign failed to observe the scope of online community-building it stimulated by bringing together millions of people who shared similar concerns, but were separated from one another by time and space (Davis *et al.*, 2002). The uniqueness of Internet communities large and small is vested in their ability to unite individuals from diverse backgrounds by transcending established societal hierarchies. Internet communities formed around the 2000 presidential campaign, a good number of which were created in conjunction with youth-oriented websites, continued to exist after the election. Some of their members have moved beyond the realm of virtual connectivity to real-world action. Young people were activated during the 2004 presidential election through sites such as meetup.org, which facilitates meetings between people with like interests. This can include anything from politics to a fondness for particular breeds of dogs and cats, showing that the division between politics and social interests can be just a click away.

New communications technologies and media formats are revolutionizing the ways in which political movements take shape (Norris, 2001). In the past, movements were orchestrated from organisational hierarchies that took significant time to form. New-style social movements emerge from decentralised networks of previously uncoordinated groups that may be associated with a vast array of individualised concerns. Although they lack a single, identifiable leader, their high level of connectivity through communications networks allows them to quickly adapt to changing political conditions (Rheingold, 2002). Thus, online organisational connections that are established prior to events that spark activation can allow protest movements to come together quickly and efficiently. The time, place and focus of demonstrations can be changed with relative ease. Protestors at World Trade Organization meetings in Seattle, Washington, DC, Quebec City and other locations used the Internet to coordinate logistics, including how to deal with law enforcement. 'Books not Bombs', an anti-war protest involving 230 campuses nationwide sponsored by the National Youth and Student Peace Coalition, was organised using the Internet and regional talk radio. Referring to protests against the possible war with Iraq, demonstrations that attracted more than 800,000 people in the United States and 1.5 million in Europe, Todd Gitlin observed, 'It took four and a half years to multiply the size of the Vietnam protests twenty fold. . . . This time the same thing has happened in six months' (Lee, 2003: 25). The first 'virtual march' on Washington, organised by moveon.org with the organisation of the 'Win Without War' coalition, involved 32 groups and several hundred thousand people who flooded Capitol Hill offices with calls, faxes and emails (Tierney, 2003).

As younger people have a facility not only with Internet technology, but also with personal digital appliances, they are positioned to be leaders in this transformed environment for political activism. Field movements can be orchestrated via mobile phones and portable computers. In addition, mobilisation can be instigated readily across national boundaries, resulting in simultaneous actions around the world.

Conclusions

The conclusions of numerous investigations express disappointment that young people are not participating and, further, that they are not using Internet technology to participate in politics more actively. This study begs to differ with that assessment. Compelling evidence demonstrates that young people have been using the Internet both to monitor conventional political processes, such as election campaigns, and to engage actively in politics. Perhaps what has been missing is proper empirical mechanisms for assessing the scope and intensity of this engagement.

As Internet access has become nearly universal among young Americans, their facility with the technology has increased along with their trust in the veracity of the content it conveys. Young people have become producers of much political content, which has now come to influence mainstream media organization reports. That bloggers broke the story of a racially charged statement at the 100th birthday party of Senator Strom Thurmond, a scandal that forced the resignation of Senator Trent Lott from his leadership position, illustrates this point. Further, young people use Internet information in their political decision making. As the 2004 presidential campaign demonstrates, these trends likely will continue to develop. The claim that the online world does not translate into offline action can no longer be supported.

Notes

Author's note: I would like to thank Valerie K. Hardy for her exceptional research assistance. This chapter is dedicated to her memory – a very small way to remember a truly magnificent soul.

1   The coding scheme is as follows: age (in years), gender (1 = male, 2 = female), online frequency (1 = less often, 4 = every day), age first online (in years), family income (1 = less than $10,000, 8 = $100,000 or more), parent's education (1 = none/grades 1–8, 7 = post-graduate training/professional school after college), race (0 = white, 1 = non-white).
2   The study did not include any indicators of either the parents' or the children's political orientations, which would have been useful given the focus of this research. Further, parent's education reflects the highest degree attained by the parent who was interviewed and does not take into account the educational level of other adults in the household. The sample included a small percentage of non-white respondents, which necessitated creating a binary measure in which all these respondents were collapsed into a single category.
3   1992 was an exception to this trend, as there was a surge in turnout among voters under the age of 25 to approximately 51 per cent. This increase in turnout was partially attributed to young voters' connection to the political process via new media, especially sources such as MTV and other entertainment-oriented venues. Candidates Bill Clinton and Ross Perot appealed directly to young people through new media channels.
4   Measures of turnout differ vastly based on the methodology employed. During the 2000 election, turnout estimates ranged from 66 per cent to 51 per cent, depending upon who was included in the calculation of the eligible voter population. The statistics reported here are based on data from the Census Current Population Survey, which were considered by the researchers to be the most reflective of actual trends (Levine and Lopez, 2002).
5   The Georgetown University/Brigham Young University 2004 Presidential Election Internet Study is a three-wave panel experiment conducted in October and November of 2004. The study consists of online surveys that used over-sampling 18- to 29-year-olds and respondents in battleground states. For further information, contact the author at owend@georgetown.edu.

References

Andersen, D. and Cornfield, M. (2002) *The Civic Web: Online Politics and Democratic Values*, Lanham, MD: Rowman & Littlefield.
Association of American Colleges and Universities (2002) 'Young Voters Feel Their Vote Won't Count', www.aacu.org/aacu_news, November.
Barker, D.C. (2002) *Rushed to Judgment: Talk Radio, Persuasion, and American Political Behavior*, New York: Columbia University Press.

Bennett, W.L. and Xenos, M. (2004) 'Young Voters and the Web of Politics', Working Paper 24, August, College Park, MD: CIRCLE.

Berelson, B., Lazarsfeld, P. and McPhee, W. (1954) *Voting*, Chicago, IL: University of Chicago Press.

Center for Information and Research on Civic Learning and Engagement (CIRCLE) (2004a) 'Young Voters Favor Kerry but Find Bush More Likeable', College Park, MD: School of Public Policy, 21 September.

Center for Information and Research on Civic Learning and Engagement (CIRCLE) (2004b) 'The 2004 Presidential Election and Young Voters', College Park, MD: School of Public Policy, 28 October.

Center for Media Education (2001) 'TeenSites: A Field Guide to the New Digital Landscape', Washington, DC: Center for Media Education.

Cole, J.I., Suman, M., Schramm, P., Lunn, R., Aquino, J.-S. *et al.* (2003) *The UCLA Internet Report – Surveying the Digital Future, Year 3*, Los Angeles, CA: UCLA Center for Communication Policy.

Davis, R. (1999) *The Web of Politics: The Internet's Impact on the American Political System*, New York: Oxford University Press.

Davis, R. and Owen, D. (1998) *New Media and American Politics*, New York: Oxford University Press.

Davis, S., Elin, L. and Reeher, G. (2002) *Click on Democracy: The Internet's Power to Change Political Apathy into Civic Action*, Boulder, CO: Westview.

Delli Carpini, M.X. (2000) 'Gen.com: Youth, Civic Engagement, and the New Information Environment', *Political Communication* 17: 341–349.

Delli Carpini, M.X. and Keeter, S. (1996) *What Americans Know about Politics and Why It Matters*, New Haven, CT: Yale University Press.

Dennis, J. and Owen, D. (1997) 'The Partisanship Puzzle: Identification and Attitudes of Generation X', in Craig, S.C. and Bennett, S.E. (eds), *After the Boom: The Politics of Generation X*, Totowa, NJ: Rowman & Littlefield.

DePledge, D. and Bustos, S. (2002) 'Poll: Young People See Voting as a Choice, not a Duty', *Decision 2002: Gannett News Service Special Report*, 31 October.

Downie, Jr, L. and Kaiser, R. (2003) *The News about the News*, New York: Vintage.

Fabos, B. (2002) 'Searching for Educational Content in the For-Profit Internet', Michigan State University manuscript.

Finberg, Howard *et al.* (2002) 'Report: Online News Widely Accepted as Credible', Poynteronline, 1 February. Online. Available http://poynteronline.org/content/content_view.asp?id=3509 (accessed 27 June 2005).

Harris Interactive (2004) 'Visits to Candidate Web Sites Are Up', www.emarketer.com/Article.aspx?1003086, 12 October.

Hart, R.P. (1994) *Seducing America: How Television Charms the American Voter*, New York: Oxford University Press.

Jamieson, Kathleen Hall (2004) 'How the 2004 Election Changed Political Communication', PBS, 9 November.

Kaiser Family Foundation (2002) 'Teens Online', Fall, Menlo Park, CA: Kaiser Family Foundation.

Katz, J. (1997) 'Birth of a Digital Nation', *Wired*, April: 48–57.

Keeter, S. *et al.* (2002) 'The Civic and Political Health of the Nation: A Generational Portrait', College Park, MD: Center for Information and Research on Civic Learning and Engagement, 19 September.

Lee, J. (2003) 'How the Protesters Mobilized', *New York Times*, 23 February online.

Levine, P. and Lopez, M.H. (2002) 'Youth Voter Turnout Has Declined, by Any Measure', College Park, MD: Center for Information and Research on Civic Learning and Engagement, September.

Norris, Pippa (2001) *Digital Divide: Civic Engagement, Information Poverty, and the Internet Worldwide*, New York: Cambridge University Press.

Owen, D. (1996) 'Who's Talking? Who's Listening? The New Politics of Radio Talk Shows', in Craig, S.C. (ed.), *Broken Contract: Changing Relationships between Americans and their Government*, Boulder, CO: Westview.

Owen, D. (1997a) 'Mixed Signals: Generation X's Attitudes toward the Political System', in Craig, S.C. and Bennett, S.E. (eds), *After the Boom: The Politics of Generation X*, Totowa, NJ: Rowman & Littlefield.

Owen, D. (1997b) 'Talk Radio and Evaluations of President Clinton', *Political Communication* 14: 333–353.

Owen, D. (2001) 'Media Mayhem: Performance of the Press in Election 2000', in Sabato, L.J. (ed.), *Overtime! The Election 2000 Thriller*, New York: Longman.

Owen, Diana and Davis, Richard (2004) 'The Georgetown University/Brigham Young University Online Election Study', Washington, DC and Provo, UT, October.

Pew Internet and American Life Project (2000) 'Parents, Kids, and the Internet', Washington, DC: Pew Internet and American Life Project, October.

Pew Internet and American Life Project (2001) 'Longitudinal Tracking Survey', Washington, DC: Pew Internet and American Life Project, March.

Pew Internet and American Life Project (2004a) 'Internet Activities', Washington, DC: Pew Internet and American Life Project, May–June.

Pew Internet and American Life Project (2004b) 'The Internet and Democratic Debate', Washington, DC: Pew Internet and American Life Project, 27 October.

Pew Research Center for the People and the Press (2000) 'Internet Election News Audience Seeks Convenience, Familiar Names: Youth Vote Influenced by Online Information', Washington, DC: Pew Research Center, 3 December.

Pew Research Center for the People and the Press (2002) 'Public's News Habits Little Changed by September 11', Washington, DC: Pew Research Center, 9 June.

Pew Research Center for the People and the Press (2003) 'Political Sites Gain, but Major News Sites Still Dominant', Washington, DC: Pew Research Center, 5 January.

Pew Research Center for the People and the Press (2004) 'Young People More Engaged, More Uncertain', Washington, DC: Pew Research Center, 30 September.

Putnam, Robert (2001) *Bowling Alone: The Collapse and Revival of American Community*, New York: Touchstone.

Radio and Television Director's Association (2001) 'The American Radio News Audience Survey', www.rtnda.org/radio.

Rainie, L. (2002) 'College Students and the Web', Washington, DC: Pew Internet and American Life Project, September.

Rheingold, H. (2002) *Smart Mobs: The New Social Revolution*, New York: Perseus Press.

Schudson, M. (1998) *The Good Citizen*, New York: Free Press.

Tierney, J. (2003) 'An Antiwar Demonstration That Does Not Take to the Streets', *New York Times*, 26 February online.

Verba, S., Schlozman, K.L. and Brady, H. (1995) *Voice and Equality: Civic Volunteerism in American Politics*, Cambridge, MA: Harvard University Press.

3 The Minnesota E-democracy project

Mobilising the mobilised?

Jakob Linaa Jensen

The Internet plays an increasingly larger role in daily and political life. There have been widespread hopes that the new technology will help break down barriers, reduce hierarchies, facilitate easier access to the political field as well as motivate new groups for civic involvement and political action. As such the Internet has been associated with a renewal and strengthening of civil society (Dyson, 1998: 45–46; Graham, 1999: 66–70). Recently we have seen an upsurge of campaigns for human rights, petitions, political chat rooms, city networks and various other kinds of political activity, all mediated via the Internet. Many of these activities have undoubtedly proved quite successful and have demonstrated that political influence certainly can be achieved via online action. The examples of this include various human rights and privacy petitions against censorship and control; lively debate forums such as The Well and Minnesota E-democracy; and new social movements such as the international anti-globalisation forum ATTAC that to a large extent are mobilising new members via the Internet.

However, so far the identity of online activists remains an open question. This study will address the following research questions: How does online political participation differ from more traditional forms of political involvement? Are the participants new actors on the political scene who used to be marginalised in the 'physical' political world due to the lack of adequate resources or are they rather the usual 'gladiators' who have found yet another battle of politics in which to engage?[1] Further, which factors determine online participation compared to those that determine more traditional participation? The investigation of these questions is based on a survey of participants in the Minnesota E-democracy programme. A non-profit organisation, Minnesota E-democracy (www.e-democracy.org) was founded in 1994 and aims to promote 'the use of the Internet to improve citizen participation and real world governance through online discussions and information and knowledge exchange'. E-Democracy sponsors election-year online partnerships 'to promote citizen access to election information and interaction'. The organisation is now branching out into democracy initiatives beyond Minnesota. The project is generally considered to be among the most successful attempts to create democratic dialogue within a given regional area. It is probably the longest on-going initiative on electronic democracy. In 2003, it involved about 2,000 participants, among those many leading politicians, civil servants and media people.[2]

This chapter begins by briefly discussing theories of political participation and the specific potential of the Internet. Here, the chapter presents a theory developed by French sociologist Pierre Bourdieu, who claims that various personal resources that form a type of capital are crucial factors behind political participation. Then, the chapter investigates the capital available to participants in Minnesota E-democracy and discusses whether these participants are a representative sample of the US and Minnesota population in general. The analysis then turns to the political activities of the participants and compares them with general data on political participation in the US to examine whether these individuals are new political actors, gladiators or something in between. This should allow one to conclude whether personal resources matter as much for online participation as they do for more traditional forms of political involvement. Lastly, the chapter turns to the question of whether online participation requires specific characteristics or competences. Access to the Internet is an obvious prerequisite, but it is also worth investigating whether the location of access, amount of time spent online or media competence in general have any effect on online political participation. In other words, are there any remarkable differences within the groups of participants on Minnesota E-democracy? This will enable conclusions to be drawn about the barriers for online political participation.

Political participation online and in 'real' life

The concept of political participation is heavily debated and contested. There is no basic agreement on the ideal character of political participation. Concerning the rationale behind political participation, developmental views emphasise the educational and enlightening aspects of political participation, whereas instrumental views claim that the purpose of political participation is the representation of citizens' interests and values (Bogdanor, 1993: 461). Most scholars agree that extensive political participation is a prerequisite of modern democracy. Advocates of the instrumental view often have stressed that modern democracy works well as long as there are no formal barriers to political participation (Dahl, 1973). Thinkers inspired by the developmental view emphasise that democracy is something more than formal procedures and that democratic debates and public discourse are necessary elements in achieving a democracy that works well (Habermas, 1975).

Whatever the views on the ideal form of democratic participation, many observers have focused on the 'participation crisis' experienced in Western democracies during the last 40 years. Among the characteristics are political apathy and a decline in party membership as well as a lack of civic involvement (Putnam, 2001). The condition has been labelled a democracy of spectatorship rather than one of participation. The media, especially television, have been accused of turning citizens into observers rather than participants of the political process (Hart, 1994). Among other explanations are the many barriers between citizens and the political establishment; the complexity of modern society; and the scarce resources available to ordinary citizens. In this context, it has been suggested that the Internet is a powerful tool for increasing political participation and strengthening the links between civil society and the political establishment. The Internet is characterised by being non-hierarchical, having the capability of instantaneous response and being relatively cheap compared with other media. These factors make it well suited to break down old barriers. The immense amount of information, it is argued, can empower citizens and diminish the information asymmetry between citizens and decision makers. On the Internet, physical resources lose significance and the importance of social status diminishes as participants can remain anonymous (Rheingold, 1993; Dyson, 1998; Graham, 1999).

These arguments are interesting, as scholars have for years discussed how personal characteristics determine the level of political participation. They have focused on specific competences or personal motivation to account for differences in participation among apparently similar people (Verba *et al.*, 1995). Others, among them Bourdieu, emphasise the significance of personal resources, most notably socio-economic status and level of education, for political participation. Bourdieu notes the personal resources 'capital'; for him, the amount and composition of capital determines an individual's position and possibilities within certain social fields such as politics (Bourdieu, 1984). Bourdieu distinguishes between three forms of capital: economic, cultural and social. Economic capital refers to material resources such as income; cultural capital to formation and education; and social capital to the relative position and societal status of the individual (Järvinen, 2000: 349). He adds a fourth form, symbolic capital, which is an aggregate of the three and determines which position an individual has within a given field. For Bourdieu, the overall social space (society) can be subdivided into various fields, e.g. the political field, the art field and the religious field. The relative importance of a given form of capital varies for different fields. For example, according to Bourdieu, there is a close relation between economic and cultural capital and these hold dominant positions within the political field (Bourdieu, 1984: 451–453). Bourdieu is mainly occupied with analysing political preferences, but concludes that people with high cultural and/or economic capital tend to dominate the political field.

Bourdieu's framework is used in this study to investigate whether there is a correspondence between the 'normal' political field and the online political field. Are the same forms of capital necessary in the online field or do new factors show up as paramount to participation? At this point, it should be noted that this chapter uses the work of Bourdieu as a heuristic device in order to investigate the claims of the Internet's equalising effects on political participation. A straight adherence to the theories and methods of Bourdieu would have included the 'correspondence analysis' described by Bourdieu.[3]

However, the method is quite complicated and the results are not particularly easy to communicate. Thus, the analysis is based on more common statistical procedures and the chapter uses the framework of Bourdieu to elaborate the overall points of the proceedings.

The case study and method

To investigate the research questions outlined above, it is natural to look at a case such as the Minnesota E-democracy project, in which the democratic process seems to work relatively well and where there are several examples of online discussions that have led to or changed political decisions. The participants had not previously been surveyed to elucidate whether Minnesota E-democracy also fulfils the Internet's promises of democratic inclusion and mobilisation of new groups.

People participate in Minnesota E-democracy by subscribing to one or more of four email lists: Minneapolis Issues List, St Paul Issues List, Winona Online Democracy and Minnesota Politics Discussions. A total of 1,834 people subscribed when the survey was launched. A proportional random sample of 50 per cent of the subscribers was taken from each list. This totalled 917 participants. Of this sample, 89 were duplicates (subscribing to several lists), 51 of the email addresses were invalid, and 9 stated actively that they did not want to participate. Of the remaining 768 respondents, 256 chose to participate, leaving us with 33.3 per cent. Of the 256 replies, 14 were incomplete, leaving the valid number of responses as 242.

At this point, it is important to discuss a major methodological challenge in online surveys, namely the issue of representativeness. Participants in Internet debates are not representative of the population in general. The purpose of this investigation is to describe some of the differences that might exist. In this survey, it is important to ensure a representative sample of the participants on Minnesota E-democracy. There was an attempt to make sure the sample was representative by using proportional random sampling, but one can argue that the most active participants are also those who tend to answer surveys. However, the statistics suggest that the survey captured many 'lurkers', i.e. those not actively participating in the debates: 47.5 per cent of the respondents rarely post and 19 per cent never post. This suggests that the sample is fairly representative.

Minnesota E-democracy participants: capital and other resources

This section examines the participants and their capital. The aim is to describe whether and how the participants on Minnesota E-democracy differ from the population in general, and the figures are therefore compared with similar demographics for the US and Minnesotan populations.[4] This makes it possible to sketch the participants' position in the general social field to describe how they might differ from the population in general. We are also able to regard Minnesota E-democracy as a social field in itself. Which forms of capital seem to be important within that field? The next section examines the Internet, represented by Minnesota E-democracy, as a political field compared with the traditional political field. Considering the practical operationalisation of Bourdieu's capital forms, economic capital is defined as income; cultural capital as educational level; and social capital as the respondents' self-identification of citizen status.

Economic capital

The income level of Minnesota E-democracy users is higher than that of the population of Minnesota and the US in general. Figure 3.1 shows that among the participants there are more people within the four upper-income categories than in both the Minnesotan or the US populations overall. Further, we see that the average household income in Minnesota is about 25 per cent higher than the national average ($52,681 versus $42,228).[5]

Cultural capital

The concept of cultural capital is measured using the highest level of education attained by the participants. The frequencies are presented in Table 3.1 and compared with the general education level in Minnesota. People with

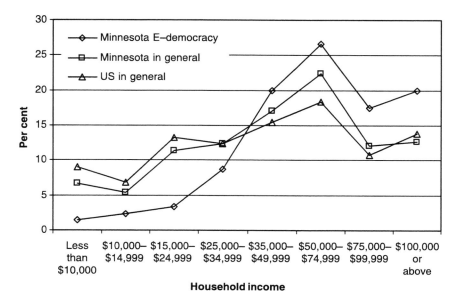

Figure 3.1 Income distribution for participants of Minnesota E-democracy versus Minnesotan and US population in general.

Table 3.1 The educational background of the participants

	Minnesota E-democracy %	Minnesota in general %
11 years of schooling or less	0	12.0
Vocational education	1.3	—
High school/merchant school	0.4	28.8
Advanced studies, 1–2 years	17.6	24.0
Advanced studies, 3–4 years	35.6	26.8
Advanced studies, 5 years or more	45.1	8.3
Number of respondents (N)	233	—

college degrees are remarkably over-represented among the Minnesota E-democracy participants. More than 80 per cent hold degrees and 45 per cent have post-graduate or professional degrees, compared to 35 and 8 per cent respectively for the state of Minnesota.[6] Almost no one holds just a high school diploma or less. The table confirms that the participants are extremely well educated, even compared to the Minnesota population, whose education level is higher than that in the US in general. There is evidence that this trend is not specific to the Minnesota E-democracy participants, but is characteristic of online participants in other Western democracies in general. A study of Danish online participants reveals similar findings (Linaa Jensen, 2003a: 367). Thus, it would appear that a high level of cultural capital is a fundamental prerequisite for political participation online.

Social capital

It is quite difficult to devise a comprehensive measure of social capital as the measurement should account for many different, often highly subjective factors. However, as we are dealing with the political field, it seems natural to define social capital in terms of status and competences related to that area. One could argue that the employed concept of social capital is somehow tautological as 'activist citizens' are defined in terms of political participation. However, the important element here is how they perceive themselves rather than how they are objectively defined. Thus, the respondents are asked to estimate their own status in the political system, as either activist or average citizens or participating as a 'professional'. Seventy-four per cent of the participants identify themselves as citizens, 45 per cent as activists and 29 per cent as average citizens. Many politicians, civil servants and journalists participate in the forums of Minnesota E-democracy alongside the citizens.[7] Twenty-six per cent of the participants identify themselves with other positions. Within that group, 2 per cent are elected politicians and officials whereas the vast majority are civil servants: 9 per cent are employed at city level, 4 per cent at county level and 4 per cent at state level. Finally, 7 per cent are journalists.

The figures tell us that Minnesota E-democracy attracts a large share of activist citizens while at the same time average citizens participate as well. Even though similar data are unavailable for Minnesota or the US in general, it seems fair to assume that activist citizens are heavily over-represented among Minnesota E-democracy participants. Interesting as well, a fair share of city, county or state employees follow the debates and even some elected politicians are active. Their mere presence indicates that Minnesota E-democracy is more than just a 'virtual coffee house' for internal debates among citizens with no contact to the political establishment. In sum, social capital in the form of political activity and experience seems to be an important factor for participation in Minnesota E-democracy. Participants here possess more capital than the general population. In particular, cultural capital defined as education really seems to matter, a finding that does not come as a big surprise in view of existing literature on political participation (Verba *et al.*, 1995). Figure 3.2 portrays these tendencies graphically by plotting the participants on Minnesota E-democracy into a model of the general social field.

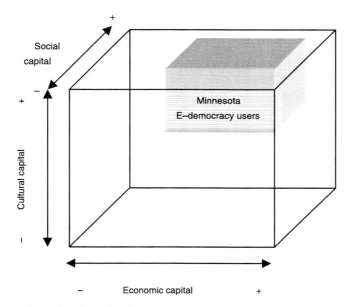

Figure 3.2 The situation of Minnesota E-democracy participants within the general social field.

Other demographic characteristics of Minnesota
E-democracy participants

The picture of the economic, cultural and social capital of the participants can be broadened by looking at factors such as gender, age and race. Thereby it is possible to determine if there is a trend toward engaging a more diverse segment of the population than was the case in the earlier days of the Internet. A much proclaimed bias of the Internet is the user gender gap. Up to the mid-1990s, the typical Internet user was a highly educated, white male. As these differences tend to diminish as especially more and more women go online, it is natural to ask whether these trends apply to online participation as well. The gender distribution on Minnesota E-democracy is 57.7 per cent male and 42.3 per cent female versus 49.5 per cent and 50.5 per cent for the Minnesotans in general. As a comparison, a similar Danish debate attracted 71 per cent men and 29 per cent women (Linaa Jensen, 2003b: 44). The figures indicate an equalising effect on gender distribution over time, as the debate in Minnesota has been online for eight years while online debates in Denmark are a relatively novel phenomenon. Hence, online participation seems to follow the trend of Internet activity in general.

The median age of Minnesota E-democracy users is 42.8 years versus 44.9 for the Minnesotan voter population in general.[8] Thus, the participants are only slightly younger than the average voter. Finally, turning to race, it should be noted that 96 per cent of the participants are white while the equivalent figure for Minnesota in general is 89 per cent.[9] Among other races specifically, African Americans and Hispanics are under-represented. If not dominated by white males, Minnesota E-democracy is definitely dominated by whites. The immediate impression of Minnesota E-democracy is that marginalised groups and those with poor resources are not mobilised politically as some Internet advocates would claim. Rather, it seems that the forum is dominated by the gladiators – those rich on capital – who also dominate other areas of political life. In order to go deeper into these questions, it is necessary to regard Minnesota E-democracy as a political field by comparing it with the field of traditional political participation.

Traditional versus online political participation

Previous sporadic studies of participants in online political discussions have often focused on the material resources of participants, and based on general demographics it has been shown that only 'the chosen few' join in.[10] So far, however, few analyses have touched upon whether the participants are active in other ways than via the Internet and very few relevant data exist. By comparing data on the wider political activity level of participants with figures on political participation in general, we should be able to further qualify our conclusions on the characteristics of the E-democracy participants and the mobilising effects of the Internet in general. In order to look at this aspect of participation, this study compares the political interests, traditional participation and online participation of Minnesota E-democracy users with available data on political participation in society in general.

Political interests

First and foremost it is natural to ask whether Minnesota E-democracy is dominated by people who are especially interested in politics. Unsurprisingly, 96 per cent of the Minnesota E-democracy participants are 'very' or 'to some extent' interested in politics. This trend is probably general for online political participation, as the equivalent figure from a Danish study is 98 per cent (Linaa Jensen, 2003c: 83). For comparison purposes, index scores for political interest are calculated.[11] For Minnesota E-democracy the score is 7.3 and for the Danish Usenet group dk.politik it is 7.2. This is remarkably higher than a similar average score at 5.8 for the US population in general (Verba *et al.*, 1995: 349, 353).

It is no surprise that participants in a political activity are more politically interested than the average voter. In order to really grasp how Minnesota E-democracy participants differ, if at all, from other politically active citizens, we move on to investigate their patterns of political participation. Scholars have argued that in the past 30 to 40 years there has been a decline in formal forms of participation and a rise in informal ones (Bogdanor, 1993: 461–462). The distinction between formal and informal participation is used here as well. In the study, the type of participation that includes more binding commitment (membership etc.) and constitutionally defined forms is considered formal. These activities include voting, party or organisation membership as well as candidacy for electoral office. Among the informal forms of participation are discussing politics with others, writing letters to the editor as well as attending town meetings. Table 3.2 seeks to give an overview of different forms of political participation among Minnesota E-democracy participants and compare them to available data for the US in general.

The obvious trend is that the Minnesota E-democracy users are extremely active within formal forms of participation. Ninety-three per cent voted in the 2000 presidential election, while nationwide only about half of the eligible voters cast ballots. Sixty-three per cent are affiliated with political parties while the best estimate for the remainder of the population is 30 per cent. Finally, 45 per cent are members of organisations or grassroots movements, a figure three times higher than for people outside Minnesota E-democracy. The participants are no less active in more informal types of political engagement. Almost three-quarters have attended town meetings or other political meetings and a similar number have consulted politicians or civil servants regarding a political matter. Again, among Minnesotan E-democracy participants, political activity is three to four times higher than in the US population.

The overall impression when comparing online and 'real-life' participation

Table 3.2 The political activity of the participants

Question asked: In which ways have you been politically active during the last 12 months?	Minnesota E-democracy* %	USA** %
Formal political participation:		
Voted in the most recent election	93	53–59
Member of a political party	63	5
Member of organisation, grassroots movement, etc.	45	14
Member of users' councils etc.	31	31
Member of or candidate for parliament, county council or city council	8	—
Informal political participation:		
Discussing politics with friends, family and colleagues	93	—
Participating in town meetings, hearings and other political meetings	71	18
Contacting a politician or a civil servant regarding a political matter	74	27
Writing a letter to the editor	41	—
Other political activities online	66	—
	N=241	

* Each respondent was asked to 'check all that apply'. Total percentage is hence more than 100.
** Data from Ranney (2000: 750) and Verba *et al.* (1995: 63–76).

is that the two fields are highly interdependent. It seems to be the same gladiators from existing forms of political participation who flock to the new medium as they see it as yet another opportunity to be heard and achieve influence. We cannot confirm the often-heard claim that marginalised groups normally alien to political participation will use the Internet as a new and more accessible way of becoming involved in political matters. The traditional economic, educational and social effects on political participation seem to be carried over to online participation.

The political fields online and in 'real' life

As we have seen, there is a close correspondence between the online and 'real' life political fields. A last topic to be addressed is the scope of the online political field compared to the total political field. Two questions have to be asked: First, what is the correspondence between online participation and more 'traditional' political participation? Second, does online participation tend to replace traditional participation forms? The participants in Minnesota E-democracy were asked whether they had participated in ten traditional and ten online political activities during the last 12 months. To summarise the answers, two descriptive indices were constructed, one for traditional participation and one for online participation. For each index, the participants score between 0 and 10, depending on the number of participation forms. The relationship between the two forms of participation is shown in Figure 3.3. There is a statistically significant correlation between online and traditional political participation, as the latter tends to determine the former. The correlation persists when controlling for age as an intervening variable. As traditional political activity rises, so does online political activity among the participants. The beta coefficient of 0.174 indicates the relationship as well. However, traditional political participation is only a small factor of explaining online political participation. The r^2 is 0.057, indicating that it accounts for about 6 per cent of the explanation behind online participation.

The degree of online participation thus seems to follow the patterns for traditional political participation, which tells us that even on the Internet it is mainly the 'chosen few' or the 'gladiators' who participate. Further, traditional political activities are only to a limited extent replaced by online political involvement. The participants' average number of traditional activities is almost four times higher than the corresponding number for online involvement, 5.82 versus 1.58. Instead of a substitution, online political involvement seems to supplement a steady, high level of political activity in general.

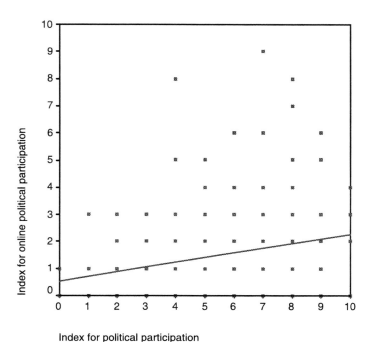

Figure 3.3 Traditional versus online participation among participants.

How does one summarise these findings in terms of Bourdieu? According to the literature, the position of an individual within the political field is determined by mainly cultural capital, but other factors also play a role. Thus, we have to imagine the political field as situated in the upper part of the general social field where cultural capital is either high or very high. Within that political field, the online political field is (still) only a limited subfield in which cultural and social capital matter in particular, as we have seen in this section (see Figure 3.4).

Inside the field of online participation

We have seen that most participants on Minnesota E-democracy fall into the category of political gladiators. However, within the group, participation in Minnesota E-democracy seems to enhance political interest and activity. Sixty-eight per cent say that it has made them more interested in political or community issues; 91 per cent that their knowledge of political or community issues has increased; and 46 per cent believe that Minnesota E-democracy has had a positive effect on their overall civic involvement. Eighty-six per cent feel they have gained increased knowledge of other people's opinions and, as a result, 53 per cent now have more respect for those whose opinions differ from their own. In other words, participation in Minnesota E-democracy

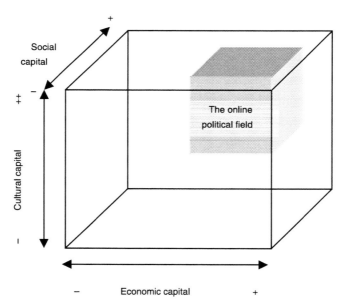

Figure 3.4 The political field and the 'online political' subfield.

seems to be a highly developmental activity, contributing to the political enlightenment and education of participants. Finding such effects on a group of mainly politically active, interested and knowledgeable people is undoubtedly an indication that online democracy projects might have a similar effect on those less politically interested and informed. It makes the question of mobilisation even more interesting.

What specific competences determine online participation? Do different resources and competences affect the activity level even for online participants? All participants obviously have access to the Internet, but it is also interesting to determine where and how they access it as well as how much, and in what ways, they use it. Not surprisingly, a vast majority of the participants (more than 90 per cent) use the Internet on a daily basis. Further, more than 75 per cent indicate that they use the Internet several times a day. As other surveys have documented, email is the most popular activity among Internet users:[12] 93 per cent of the participants check their email every day, 77 per cent several times a day. Browsing websites is another popular activity performed by 90 per cent of the participants on a daily basis and 66 per cent of them several times a day. The use of instant messaging is much less frequent: 58 per cent never use it and only 14 per cent use it on a daily basis. The figures indicate that extensive and daily Internet use is a prerequisite for participating in online political discussions. The impression that the E-democracy participants are in fact 'super users' is confirmed by the numbers in Table 3.3, which lists where the Internet is accessed. Almost 72 per cent are 'super users' who are online from home as well as from work, school or similar venues. The equivalent figure for US Internet users overall is 45.5 per cent and only 24.5 per cent for the US population in general. Moreover, 52 per cent of the participants on Minnesota E-democracy access the Internet via a broadband connection and hence have fast access to all the wonders of the web. According to figures from the Pew Internet and American Life Project, the equivalent figure for all US households is only 21 per cent.[13]

As the participants are clearly well used to navigating on the Internet, it

Table 3.3 Types of users based on places of access for Minnesota E-democracy users and the US

	Minnesota E-democracy %	US Internet users* %	US population %
No access	0	0	46.1
Out-of-home user	12.0	19.1	10.3
Home user	16.3	35.4	19.1
Home and out-of-home user	71.7	45.5	24.5
	N=233		

* Data from US Department of Commerce (2002) (accessed 27 August 2004).

is interesting to survey their general media competence. Surprisingly for the US, television is not the most popular medium. Radio and newspapers attract 93 and 91 per cent of the participants on a weekly basis, whereas television comes in third at 82 per cent. Finally, 74 per cent state that they read magazines and 15 per cent use other media. In general, participants make frequent use of media other than the Internet. Sixty-five per cent use four or more different media every week. Interestingly, no one answered that they used only the Internet. Once again, it does not seem as if the Internet replaces more traditional activities.

Explaining differences in online participation

In the preceding sections, we have seen how participants in online activities differ from the population in general and how, to a large extent, they follow the patterns of traditional political participation. Yet, are there any differences within the group of online participants? Which factors determine how much they engage in online activities in general and in Minnesota E-democracy in particular? Further, as a group within the online subfield of the political field, which factors determine their political interest and participation rates?

To explore these questions, this study uses an MCA multivariate analysis on four different dependent variables: participants' political interest, traditional political participation, online political participation and use of Minnesota E-democracy. For the two participation variables, the number of political activities in which the participants are involved (0–10) is used as an index. For political interest, the index is constructed to measure the participants' interest on a scale from 0 to 10 and, finally, the variable 'use of Minnesota E-democracy' is composed of three other variables: how often they access the forums in total, how often they participate actively and how many forms of activities they have engaged in. The first two together and the last variable each account for half the index, which again has a range from 0 to 10. The exogenous variables are income, education and social status (see Table 3.4).

Table 3.4 reports the adjusted and unadjusted means within each group and in total for each dependent variable. However, there are almost no major differences between the two measures in any one field, indicating that there is little or no interplay among the independent variables. An exception is the group of participants with non-college education, but the low number of respondents in this group (three) rather than hidden interactions most likely accounts for the variation. It makes good sense, then, to regard income, education and status as non-related factors, each contributing to explaining the dependent variables. It would seem that the largest variations for all four dependent variables are explained by status. Activist citizens score higher on all indices than do average citizens. Civil servants and journalists follow the same trend, although not as markedly as activist citizens. An examination of

Table 3.4 MCA analysis of the importance of resources for political participation

	Political interest		Political participation		Political participation online		Use of Minnesota E-democracy		N
	Unadj.	Adj.	Unadj.	Adj.	Unadj.	Adj.	Unadj.	Adj.	
Income:									
<$24,999	9.73	9.70	6.00	6.00	1.67	1.55	6.03	6.02	15
$25,000–$49,999	9.27	9.24	5.63	5.57	1.75	1.68	6.04	6.02	55
$50,000 or more	9.33	9.35	5.88	5.91	1.49	1.53	5.97	5.97	128
Education:									
Non-college	8.67	9.16	4.33	5.09	.00	.36	6.33	6.65	3
College	9.32	9.31	5.88	5.94	1.68	1.64	6.00	5.98	106
Post-graduate	9.39	9.39	5.80	5.70	1.51	1.54	5.97	5.98	89
Status:									
Average citizen	8.55	8.56	4.40	4.40	1.09	1.11	5.59	5.57	58
Journalist	9.69	9.69	4.38	4.35	2.46	2.40	6.00	6.00	13
Civil servant/politician	9.45	9.44	6.10	6.13	1.53	1.56	5.93	5.92	40
Activist citizen	9.77	9.77	6.84	6.83	1.79	1.77	6.28	6.29	87
Grand mean	9.34		5.82		1.58		5.99		198

the standardised beta coefficients makes it clear that status is statistically significant for political interest, participation and use of Minnesota E-democracy on a 99 per cent level and for online participation on a 95 per cent level.

Education matters as well. On all dependent variables except use of Minnesota E-democracy, participants with college and post-graduate degrees score higher than those without college education. Again, the differences must not be overestimated as there are only three participants within the category 'non-college'.[14] There are no obvious differences across income categories, although the lowest income category's average in general is slightly higher than the other. One could claim that, once online, some of the participants with lower incomes become more involved than they do offline, although the tendency is not statistically significant.

We now turn to whether competences matter for activity among participants. The figures presented in Table 3.5 are calculated in much the same way as those above. The three independent variables are now location of Internet access, Internet use and media competence. Again, the average values within each group are presented uncontrolled as well as controlled for the other independent variables. The almost total lack of differences tells us that there are no significant interactions among the independent variables. Table 3.5 reveals no clear tendencies for political interest and political participation. Interestingly, though, there is a statistically significant relationship between Internet use and online political participation. Although the tendency is not replicated for Minnesota E-democracy specifically, it tells us that the single most explanatory factor of online involvement is the degree of Internet use. In addition, the place of Internet access contributes to explaining the degree of political participation and use of Minnesota E-democracy. Once again, 'super users' with access and use at home as well as at school or work are more active than the rest.

Conclusions

The study of online participants does not confirm the democratic promise that the Internet would mobilise new groups of people. Rather, the gladiators now have yet another platform for political involvement and influence. Online participation, however, seems to have positive effect by strengthening political interest and involvement. The participants in Minnesota E-democracy generally have more resources than the average American. More specifically, they are extremely well educated compared to the rest of the population. The demographic patterns of online participation follow the same trends as those of more traditional forms of political participation. The online participants show a high level of activity within traditional forms of activities as well. It does not seem that online participation replaces more traditional forms, and, as such, the online political field can be regarded as a subfield within the general political field.

Table 3.5 MCA analysis of the importance of competences for political participation

	Political interest		Political participation		Political participation online		Use of Minnesota E-democracy		N
	Unadj.	Adj.	Unadj.	Adj.	Unadj.	Adj.	Unadj.	Adj.	
Income access:									
Work/school user	9.59	9.59	5.55	5.56	1.10	1.13	5.93	5.95	29
Home user	9.30	9.24	5.54	5.44	1.46	1.58	5.82	5.80	37
'Super user'	9.29	9.30	5.86	5.88	1.67	1.64	6.02	6.02	167
Internet use:									
Occasional	10.00	9.97	7.00	6.95	.40	.20	6.70	6.67	5
Frequent	9.34	9.34	5.83	5.86	1.19	1.21	5.90	5.91	145
Intensive	9.28	9.27	5.59	5.55	2.30	2.27	6.06	6.04	83
Media competence:									
Occasional	9.50	9.47	6.00	6.07	1.50	1.66	6.13	6.18	4
Frequent	9.12	9.13	5.52	5.52	1.22	1.24	5.80	5.81	73
Intensive	9.42	9.42	5.88	5.89	1.73	1.72	6.05	6.05	156
Grand mean	9.33		5.77		1.57		5.97		233

Whereas analyses of traditional political participation such as those carried out by Verba *et al.* (1995) and Bourdieu (1984) often emphasise cultural capital as the most determinant factor of political participation, this study finds that that social capital, i.e. self-defined citizen status, is the single most important factor.[15] Among other resources that determine whether citizens become involved in political activities online, Internet use seems especially to affect online participation. The vast majority of the participants are 'super users' who access the Internet both at home and at work or school. We can conclude by setting up four steps to determine whether an individual chooses to become involved in online participation:

1   Internet access;
2   resources, mainly education and social capital;
3   level of existing political participation;
4   general competences and motivation for using new media.

Even though it is obvious that the online possibilities make political involvement easier, online participation seems to be determined by the same factors as traditional political participation. Further, some new 'digital factors' such as access and media competence provide even more obstacles for online political involvement.

Notes

1 The term 'gladiators' originates from Milbrath (1965: 20) who claimed that political participation is hierarchical. The politically active (gladiators) engage in all parts of the political games and the rest of the citizens (spectators) are reduced to a passive or even apathetic role.
2 For an earlier account on Minnesota E-democracy, see Dahlberg (2001).
3 For example, as described and developed by Greenacre (1993).
4 Where possible, the comparisons are made with Minnesota data as the composition of the Minnesotan population differs from the general US population. Minnesotans are generally better educated and have the fourth-highest average income in the United States, according to the US census of 2002.
5 Based on US census data. Available online at http://www.census.gov/prod/ 2002pubs/p60–218.pdf and http://censtats.census.gov/data/MN/04027.pdf (accessed 20 February 2003).
6 For comparison purposes, the term 'advanced studies' is used within the table.
7 Many participate as citizens as well as officials. Participants are asked directly how they identify themselves. As such, the answers point to the role in which they mostly participate.
8 The figures are compared to the voter population because they are the potentially politically active. Very few under the age of 18 could be potential participants of the forums. Data are extracted from US census 2000 for Minnesota. Available online at http://censtats.census.gov/data/MN/04027.pdf (accessed 27 August 2004).
9 Based on US census data 2000 for Minnesota. Available online at http:// censtats.census.gov/data/MN/04027.pdf (accessed 27 August 2004).
10 Some examples include Hoff, Löfgren and Torpe (2003) with an investigation of

the use of the Internet in Danish politics as well as Hill and Hughes (1998) with a study of participants in American online political life.

11 The average score is calculated in order to compare the respondents' political interest with available scores for general political interest in the US. The categories from 'yes, very much' to 'not at all' are given values 8, 6, 4 and 2 and the weighted average is computed.

12 See US Department of Commerce (2002) Available online at http: //www.ntia. doc.gov/ntiahome/dn/html/Chapter 3.htm.

13 Available online at http://www.pewinternet.org/reports/pdfs/PIP_Broadband_ Report.pdf (accessed 19 February 2003).

14 It was difficult to collapse categories to show a range of educational levels and still get a sufficiently large sample within each group for statistical analyses. Once again, the very high educational level of the participants explains the low variance.

15 One could argue that the construction of the variable tends to be somewhat tautological as, for example, 'activist citizens' tend to be very active. However, the categories are not constructed on the basis of participation but on the basis of self-experience of the participants within the political realm. This is probably one of the most precise and adequate single measures when investigating relative positions within the political field.

References

Bogdanor, V. (ed.) (1993) *The Blackwell Encyclopaedia of Political Science*, London: Blackwell.

Bourdieu, P. (1984) *Distinction*, Cambridge, MA: Harvard University Press.

Dahl, R.A. (1973) *Who Governs*, New Haven, CT: Yale University Press.

Dahlberg, L. (2001) 'Extending the Public Sphere through Cyberspace: The Case of Minnesota E-Democracy', *First Monday* 6(3). Online. Available http:// www.firstmonday.org/issues/issue6_3/dahlberg/index.html (accessed 27 August 2004).

Dyson, E. (1998) *Internettet og vores liv [Release 2.0]*, Copenhagen: Munksgaard – Rosinante.

Graham, G. (1999) *The Internet:// A Philosophical Inquiry*, London: Routledge.

Greenacre, M. (1993) *Correspondence Analysis in Practice*, London: Academic Press.

Habermas, J. (1975) *Borgerlig offentlighet – dens framvekst og forfal: henimot en teori om det borgerlige samfunn*, Oslo: Fremad.

Hart, R.P. (1994) *Seducing America: How Television Charms the Modern Voter*, New York: Oxford University Press.

Hill, K.A. and Hughes, J.E. (1998) *Cyberpolitics: Citizen Activism in the Age of the Internet*, Lanham, MD: Rowman & Littlefield.

Hoff, J., Löfgren, K. and Torpe, L. (2003) 'The State We Are In: E-democracy in Denmark', *Information Polity* 8 (1–2): 49–66.

Järvinen, M. (2000) 'Pierre Bourdieu', in Andersen, H. and Kaspersen, L., *Klassisk og moderne samfundsteori*, 2nd edn, Copenhagen: Hans Reitzels Forlag.

Linaa Jensen, J. (2003a) 'Public Spheres on the Internet: Anarchic or Government-sponsored – a Comparison', *Scandinavian Political Studies* 26 (4): 349–374.

Linaa Jensen, J. (2003b) 'Virtual Democratic Dialogue? Bringing together Citizens and Politicians', *Information Polity* 8 (1–2): 29–48.

Linaa Jensen, J. (2003c) *Den digitale demokratiske dialog*, Aarhus: Systime.

Milbrath, L. (1965) *Political Participation*, Chicago, IL: Rand McNally.

Putnam, R. D. (2001) *Bowling Alone: The Collapse and Revival of American Community*, New York: Touchstone.

Ranney, A. (2000) 'Politics in the United States', in Almond, G., Bingham Powell, G., Strøom, K. and Dalton, R.J. (eds), *Comparative Politics Today: A World View*, New York: Longman.

Rheingold, H. (1993) *The Virtual Community: Homesteading on the Electronic Frontier*, Reading, MA: Addison-Wesley.

US Department of Commerce (2002) *A Nation Online*, February, Washington, DC: US Department of Commerce. Online. Available http://www.ntia.doc.gov/ntiahome/dn/html/chapter4.htm.

Verba, S., Schlozman, K.L. and Brady, H.E. (1995) *Voice and Equality: Civic Voluntarism in American Politics*, Cambridge, MA: Harvard University Press.

4 Hunting protestors

Mobilisation, participation and protest online in the Countryside Alliance

Wainer Lusoli and Stephen Ward

Introduction

Over the past decade, there has been considerable interest in the apparent upsurge of protest activity, especially as traditional representative organisations such as parties and trade unions appear to be in decline in many liberal democracies. A number of accounts have highlighted the importance of the Internet and other new media in the mobilisation of several mass protests and in the activity of campaigning organisations generally (Cisler, 1999; Jordan, 2001; Scott and Street, 2000).[1] There has been considerable speculation as to whether new information and communication technologies (ICTs) can provide a catalyst for political participation and a more active citizenry and, if so, what types of political organisation are likely to benefit (Diani, 2000; Bimber, 1998). However, whilst there has been a growing amount of evidence examining the online strategies of political organisations from a top-down perspective, there has been little evidence emerging from the grass roots about the role of ICTs in participation.

This chapter attempts to partially fill this empirical gap through a survey of members of the Countryside Alliance (CA) in the United Kingdom. The alliance has come to prominence over the past six years in opposing government proposals to ban hunting with dogs, most notably with its large 'Liberty and Livelihood' protest march in London in September 2002. While the Countryside Alliance has a reputation of representing an ageing, conservative, rural, middle-class membership – unpromising ground for ICT campaigning – the organisation has devoted considerable resources to use ICTs for mobilisation purposes. Consequently, the survey examines the profile of members online, the use of the Internet and the attitudes of members towards new ICTs and participation. In short, it assesses what difference ICTs make in the context of Countryside Alliance participation and activism. Under a *widening participation* rubric, we are interested in the importance of the Internet for organisational reach and for a wider social profile of the membership. We find evidence that the Countryside Alliance is reaching out to a slightly wider constituency with quite different socio-demographic traits than the traditional membership: younger, professional and less likely to use traditional media. As concerns *deepening participation*, we are interested in the effects of ICTs on members' general levels of activism and more specific mobilisation in the London march. We find solid evidence that new media are a very effective campaign mobilisation tool, though they are less useful in fostering intra-organisational democracy.

Mobilisation, participation and protest online

The value of ICTs for organisations in terms of mobilisation and participation can be assessed in two areas: (1) widening participation through the inclusion of a greater number and diversity of citizens into the participatory process; and (2) deepening or extending the range and efficacy of participatory activity.

Widening participation?

At one level, the Internet can be used by organisations for recruitment purposes to increase and maintain membership numbers. From a rational choice perspective, the Internet lowers the barriers (costs) to participation for individuals from more marginal and excluded groups. Political activity such as information gathering, joining organisations or directly contacting political institutions and organisations could become far easier (Bonchek, 1995). The arrival of set-top boxes and Internet TV could allow the housebound, such as the elderly, single parents and the disabled, to participate more easily from their homes. ICTs also could be employed to recruit new members from sections of the community that are less attracted through traditional media and less likely to join political organisations, such as younger citizens who have wider ICT access via educational establishments (Gibson *et al.*, 2002; Lupia and Philpot, 2002).

In contrast to this positive outlook, some have suggested that the Internet is unlikely to make much difference and may indeed widen participation gaps (Norris, 1999, 2000; Katz and Rice, 2002). Firstly, access to the technology is still restricted. A digital divide exists where the poor and elderly, in particular, lack the resources and skills to use the technology. Often these are the very people who already are disengaged from the political process. The Internet may provide additional resources for those already participating. Secondly, although the technology may provide the means to engage with political organisations and institutions, it does not provide the motivation to do so. Without wider reforms in the overall structure of political opportunities, i.e. the increased willingness of organisations to provide engagement opportunities, the technology alone is unlikely to make people more interested in politics or engage with political organisations (Lusoli *et al.*, 2002).

Deepening participation?

Aside from simply increasing the number of participants, the Internet could both extend participatory activity and deepen the quality of the participatory experience (Ward *et al.*, 2003; Rheingold, 2002). The speed and convenience of ICTs may encourage participants to supplement and extend their range of participatory experiences. The interactivity of the Internet, in the form of email, discussion fora and live chat rooms, provides the public with a range of additional channels to voice their opinions on issues. In theory, ICTs make it possible to participate 24 hours a day, seven days a week, 52 weeks a year (Washbourne, 1999). The Internet also provides greater possibilities for organisational members to network both vertically and horizontally. Vertically, it is now easier for individual members to advance their views directly to organisational elites via electronic means. Political organisations can post online large amounts of policy information/documents and encourage feedback directly from members, supporters and the wider public. Similarly, leading figures from political organisations can now engage in online debate and question-and-answer sessions with members much more directly than through traditional media. Horizontally, the net can further online community building or networking and increase member-to-member contacts via email lists, discussion groups and hyperlinks on websites. Studies of traditional forms of participation indicate the importance of regular contact with an organisation for maintaining members' interest and rates of participation. Theoretically, this should be easier via application of ICTs. The interactivity, speed and networking potential of ICT participation could actually enhance the quality of participatory experiences.

Pessimists, however, are sceptical of the ability of electronic forms of participation to deepen participation activities or produce meaningful political deliberation. In the first place, they question whether ICTs can really foster networking and community building online, arguing that most ICT communication is a relatively passive and solitary experience that is unlikely to link participants together and develop collective ties. Face-to-face networking, Diani suggests, is far more effective in generating activism and increased levels of social capital (2000). Secondly, critics contend that the individualistic push-button mode of participation will actually render participation less meaningful and erode citizen interest, making collective action harder and elites less accountable (Lipow and Seyd, 1996; Barber *et al.*, 1997; Street, 1997). Participation through electronic referenda and the like may become no more than registering individual preferences (McLean, 1989). Whilst citizens may have access to large amounts of information online, they may either become overloaded and switch off, or avoid it and insulate themselves from alternative opinions by selecting only a narrow range of online information sources (Shapiro, 1999; Sunstein, 2001).

The rise of rural protest

The growth of the Countryside Alliance

Over the past decade or so, a number of countries have witnessed the rise of protest groups and movements focused around a rural agenda (Woods, 2003, 2004). Prominent amongst this trend in the United Kingdom has been the growth of the Countryside Alliance. While it is a relative newcomer to protest politics (1997), the Countryside Alliance has well-established roots, having been formed from an amalgamation of three established pressure groups – the British Field Sports Society (BFSS), the Countryside Movement and the Countryside Business Group. Although the Countryside Alliance's agenda covers a broad range of rural issues, critics argue that the alliance is still primarily a pro-hunting organisation with only an opportunistic interest in other rural issues.[2] Yet, whilst hunting is clearly at the core of the alliance's agenda, many involved in its formation and early direction saw the need for the organisation to represent a broader constituency (Woods, 1998). Certainly, the Countryside Alliance has been sustained over the past six years by a variety of rural crises and emerging issues, which have provided ammunition in its fight with the current British Labour Government. These have included: an ongoing crisis in the agricultural sector most notably highlighted by the foot-and-mouth epidemic in 2001; the fuel protests in autumn 2001 highlighting that increasing government petrol duties have a disproportionate impact on the car-reliant rural public; the government proposals for increasing access to the countryside through its 'right to roam' legislation; and apparent reductions in a range of rural public services, notably proposals to close rural post offices. It is noticeable also that the Countryside Alliance has drawn on anti-Labour feeling among traditionally Conservative rural voters (Ward, 2002). Though the pro-hunting cause is by far the most prominent issue, the Countryside Alliance has tapped into and encouraged the perception of a growing urban–rural divide in the United Kingdom, arguing that rural issues and countryside pursuits have been misunderstood and discriminated against by an urban political class. Richard Burge, the CA's Chief Executive, encapsulated this view when he claimed that the purpose of the Liberty and Livelihood march was 'about country mindedness, and country minded people who feel disenfranchised by the system [and] feel like a colony in their own nation. . . . The march is about them demanding to be heard.'[3] In short, Woods (1998) characterises the Countryside Alliance approach as one of reactive ruralism to 'a perceived challenge from ill-informed urban intervention'.

Organisational and member profile

Organisationally, the Countryside Alliance is a combination of a traditional pressure group and a social movement organisation. It is perhaps most akin to what Diani and Donati (1999: 17) describe as a professional protest organisation, which combines professional activism, mobilisation of financial resources and confrontational tactics amongst its tactical options. The Countryside Alliance has a professional staff of around 100 people (including policy and campaigns staff, communications and press officials and regional directors) based mainly in offices in London and Worcestershire. Although membership income is important for the organisation, it is supported by a considerable number of wealthy backers. The Countryside Alliance operates under a partial internal democracy with regional and county branches that are able to organise their own activities. Individual members elect the executive board by postal ballot and can contribute to annual general meetings.

The Countryside Alliance combines traditional lobbying, research, petitions and letter-writing campaigns, along with a series of national marches and rallies. The Countryside Alliance is probably best known for the three large-scale London marches it organised in July 1997, March 1998 and September 2002. The most recent 'Liberty and Livelihood' demonstration was one of the biggest protest events ever seen in the United Kingdom. Such events were important not only in attracting considerable media coverage[4] but also in symbolic terms, building the image of the Countryside Alliance as a wider rural protest organisation. It is clear that the alliance has drawn on the example of large environmental organisations such as Greenpeace and Friends of the Earth, but also more radically on the activities of direct-action protest networks (Doherty *et al.*, 2003; Woods, 2003, 2004).

There are few statistics on the socio-demographic or political profile of the CA membership or their participatory activities. The stereotypical picture portrayed by its opponents is of wealthy, middle-aged/elderly, middle-class Conservative members obsessed by hunting, fishing and shooting (Norton, 2002). The Countryside Alliance has countered this line by stressing that its membership extends beyond the hunting fraternity and covers a wide range of social backgrounds from agricultural labourers to country landowners.[5] Limited evidence comes from three MORI surveys of participants in various countryside rallies and marches, who are not necessarily alliance members. All three surveys indicate a similar supporter base with a very high proportion of middle-class, relatively affluent, overwhelmingly Conservative voters. They are particularly from southern England with hunting acting as the main stimulus for participation on the marches.[6] Strikingly, this profile is very dissimilar from the typecast of the traditional protestor – young, politically unaffiliated and progressive.

The Countryside Alliance and online campaigning[7]

Given the traditional membership profile of the Countryside Alliance, there is a surprising degree of technological development within the organisation as well as considerable investment in staff and resources.[8] The nucleus of the organisation's communication infrastructure is the Rural Communication

Network (RCN), which is located in rural Hagley. The RCN move to a larger, more modern estate in summer 2002 reflects the growth in importance of communication within the organisation. The communication strategy of the Countryside Alliance has been increasingly decentralised, though coordinated centrally via the RNC, with more power given to regional directors to communicate with the media. The IT unit at the RNC is reported to benefit from extensive freedom of action within the organisation. Three staff at the Countryside Alliance RCN worked permanently on the web.

The Countryside Alliance website (www.countryside-alliance.org) was first set up in May 1998. It was restructured in 2001, when it moved from an ISP type of website aimed at servicing a limited number of stakeholders to a higher-profile corporate design. An online joining facility was then added in August 2002 to sustain the membership drives of the organisations involved in the alliance. The website claims over '100,000 full ordinary members plus some 250,000 associate members through affiliated clubs and societies'.[9] The Countryside Alliance operates with two main databases, one for the management of the emailing list, the second including data on membership and email contact details for a small minority (12 per cent) of the membership. There is an on-going attempt to consolidate the two databases into a single, functional unit. The *Grass-E-Route* is the weekly electronic newsletter of the Countryside Alliance. Circulation is estimated at 250,000 as it is posted on around 500 websites (November 2002) and circulated via several mailing lists. In addition, 14 regional e-newsletters – with targeted local information – are distributed every fortnight. Membership of the mailing list is in the region of 35,000. Overall, the Countryside Alliance seems to have invested considerable time and thought to the development of an IT structure. The Countryside Alliance web manager has stated they believe that 'the Internet has enabled us to reach out to a larger audience by providing a portal to our campaigns which is updated every day'.[10]

Research design

In assessing the participatory potential of ICTs for the Countryside Alliance, we undertook a survey of its membership and set out to explore and analyse the use of ICTs by alliance members. Data were gathered in two main areas. The first area is descriptive and exploratory, the second more hypothesis-based. We first asked about the demographic composition and patterns of Internet use of the alliance online membership as compared to traditional alliance members. Then, we investigated the political profile and the online political behaviours of different categories of Countryside Alliance supporters: offliners, onliners and site visitors who are not formally members. In reporting online connectedness, we wanted to understand whether ICTs *widen* and *deepen* membership participation. Specifically, four research questions are drawn from the debate on the changing nature of the organisation presented above and addressed in the context of ICT use by the organisation's membership:

1   *Organisational reach:* Do ICTs widen the Countryside Alliance's organisational reach?
2   *Diverse membership:* Do ICTs balance the social profile of the membership?
3   *Increasing levels of activism:* Do ICTs increase members' organisational activism?
4   *Effective mobilisation:* Do ICTs favour mobilisation, and who is mobilised?

Data were collected using both a postal and an online survey that were agreed to by the Countryside Alliance webmaster and endorsed by the organisation. The online and postal questionnaires were identical, except that the online version made a (positive) assumption about the respondents' use of the Internet. The postal questionnaire was sent to 1,969 randomly selected members. To ensure representativeness, the sample was geographically stratified across the 17 administrative regions of the alliance. The questionnaire and a cover letter from the alliance were sent out on 6 December 2002. Two weeks after the closing date (20 December) the response rate for the postal survey was 21.3 per cent.

The online survey was active for three weeks, from 13 December 2002 to 6 January 2003. The Countryside Alliance sent a 'cover' email with a link to the online questionnaire to the 38,000 subscribers to the *Grass-E-Route* mailing list. Additionally, the cover email was posted on the home page of the Countryside Alliance website (13 December). After the screening for genuine duplicates, 1,476 unique questionnaires from both the postal and the online survey were processed and analysed using SPSS.

Unless otherwise specified, results are based only on members from the postal survey (valid N = 411).[11] Online and offline respondents were similar in terms of socio-economic status and general political orientations, but online respondents were considerably younger and slightly better off. The online method appears to reduce the well-known self-selection biases of postal surveys related to age, education level and occupation. Results for political attitudes and behaviour of both samples are remarkably similar. Onliners are very similar across the two modes of administration, and represent a progressive element for the re-balancing of the response bias.

Data analysis

Socio-demographic profile and general political attitudes

Our survey's results on the socio-demographic profile of respondents corroborate the stereotypical picture of Countryside Alliance members. Alliance membership is predominantly male – two in three members – and drawn from the eldest segment of the population, as 63 per cent are at least 50 years old. Just 3 per cent of members are under the age of 26. Income levels are also relatively high. Only 21 per cent report earnings below £15,000 per year, whereas 40 per cent report earnings in excess of £35,000. Occupational patterns and education levels reflect the age profile of membership. Almost 40 per cent are retired, while only 2 per cent are students. One in three hold a university degree, while an additional one in six members have attained A levels. Those members in active employment include 20 per cent in professional and higher technical work, whilst small business owners represent 13 per cent of the membership.

Our data profile the political attitudes of alliance members more precisely than anecdotal media reports. Countryside Alliance membership is constituted by a core of politically moderate members – in terms of both ideology and activism – and a large subgroup of conservative, politically active members. In terms of political interest, numbers decrease along the ideological slopes of political activism and apathy, with a robust predominance of neutral attitudes towards politics: 53 per cent of members report an 'average' interest in politics. The political views of Countryside Alliance members lean clearly to the centre-right of the political spectrum. On a left–right scale (range: 0–6), the average CA member scores 4.3, which is located approximately between the centre and the right extreme (mode = 4). The very low variance (standard deviation = 1.1) suggests that the group is ideologically homogeneous, at least on the traditional left–right dimension. We also found that Countryside Alliance members who are also Conservative Party members are significantly more interested in politics ($\gamma = 0.43***$, N = 1,168) and further on the right than non-party-affiliated members ($\gamma = 0.33***$, N = 1,118).

Many of the respondents are long-term Countryside Alliance supporters, having first joined the British Field Sports Society (49 per cent), which provides qualified support for the claim that the Countryside Alliance has the interests of the hunting fraternity at its core. Of the remaining half of the membership, one in six have been members for a year or less, one in five joined two to three years ago, while only one in ten joined four to five years ago. However, we found no significant difference in political orientations between old and new members. The profile of the growth in membership tentatively suggests that the Countryside Alliance has succeeded in their aim of widening their membership base.

Finally, respondents report high levels of organisational activity (see Table 4.1). Low-engagement activities are quite common among the membership. Three in four members regularly read Countryside Alliance literature, while two in four talk to colleagues and friends about the alliance and donate money to it. Respondents report similarly high levels of campaign engagement of different types. Around 60 per cent of the membership attends political rallies and demonstrations, with 35 per cent also attending fairs and social/organisational events. An additional 10 per cent claim to campaign for the alliance. 'Sub-elite' organisational behaviours record considerably smaller numbers. A proportion ranging from 1.5 per cent to 2.5 per cent hold official

Table 4.1 Organisational involvement of CA members

	Overall	*Online*	*Postal*	*Difference*
Read CA's literature	73%	72%	74%	−0.02
Attend rallies/demonstrations	60%	67%	47%	−0.20***
Talk to colleagues/friends about the CA	51%	56%	42%	−0.13***
Donate money	49%	46%	54%	0.07*
Attend fairs/social events	36%	39%	29%	−0.10**
Meet with other members	14%	17%	11%	−0.08**
Campaign for the CA	10%	14%	3%	−0.18***
Official position	2.5%	4%	1%	−0.10***
Visit CA offices	2%	3%	—	−0.09**
Volunteer clerical work	1.5%	2%	—	−0.08**
N	1,190	779	411	

Difference is measured with γ. * = sig. p. < 0.05, ** = sig. p. < 0.01, *** = sig. p. ≤ 0.001.

positions; visit Countryside Alliance offices and headquarters; or perform volunteer clerical work for the organisation.

Internet adoption and use

Countryside Alliance members report remarkably high levels of Internet access and use, especially given the age profile of the membership. Fifty-seven per cent of the membership has accessed email, the web or intranet systems (N = 411). This roughly corresponds to the British average, as individual access to the Internet was recorded at 52 per cent in October 2002 (ONS, 2002). Ninety-six per cent of online members have used email, 90 per cent have accessed the World Wide Web, while 32 per cent have used an Intranet/ closed-access communication system. Access from home exceeds access at work, for both the online and the offline respondents.

Despite relatively high levels of Internet access, 45 per cent of members responding to the postal survey have never accessed the Countryside Alliance website, 10 per cent have done so once, and an additional 25 per cent have accessed the site irregularly in relation to specific events. Thus, one in five of online members use their organisation's site regularly – only one in nine overall. These figures are comparable with those relative to use of traditional technologies to keep in touch with the alliance – phone (45 per cent), letter (48 per cent) and face-to-face meetings (44 per cent). The only notable exception is 'print material from the organisation' (76 per cent), which does not require members' initiative.

The site is accessed mainly for information purposes (see Table 4.2). The most frequently accessed features include seeking information on current events, alliance campaigns and policy. The *Grass-E-Route* (the alliance email bulletin) is received by 84 per cent of online members, and the alliance newsletter and magazine on the site by 83 per cent. Information is also the most

Table 4.2 Access to and usefulness of CA website features

	Access %	Mean usefulness	SD
Information on current events	93	4.7	1.2
Information on CA campaigns	89	4.6	1.2
Information on policy	86	4.7	1.3
Grass-E-Route	84	5.1	1.2
Newsletter/magazine	83	4.3	1.3
Information on CA structure	73	3.6	1.6
Links to related sites	66	3.9	1.6
Feedback (e.g. email)	56	3.7	1.8
Membership application/renewal	52	3.6	1.7
Internet trade directory	47	2.8	1.7
Educational section	44	3.3	1.7
CA Internet auction	44	2.7	1.8
Discussion point	42	3.0	1.7

N = 858 (both online and postal). Includes members who have visited the CA website. Usefulness of site features is measured on a 0–6 scale.

highly valued feature of the site. Organisational information and feedback scores lower, in terms of both access and usefulness. In terms of the attractiveness of online joining or recruitment possibilities, it is interesting to note that the online membership application/renewal has been accessed by half of the online members, and rated just above average ($\mu = 3.6$, standard deviation = 1.7).

People are less drawn to the new interactive 'community' features afforded by new media. The online trade directory, the discussion point and online auction are least popular. This result is confirmed by the type of features 'members would like to see on the CA site'. The ability to sign petitions online was rated highest at 5.1 on a 0–6 scale of desirability, followed by a range of traditional political activities *qua* the Internet. Access to a local branch website scored an average of 4.3, email details of leadership 3.9. Online voting for both Countryside Alliance policies and elected officials also were reported as highly desirable features. However, the more innovative, online features – such as online discussion forums and the members-only area of the site – scored lower averages, had higher variances and higher 'don't know' rates (see Table 4.3).[12]

Expanding organisational reach?

Overall, the Countryside Alliance seems to reach online an audience that is different from its traditional field-sports base. Zero-order correlation results suggest that the Internet-using member is significantly younger than the average member, from a higher educational background and, partly as a consequence, has higher income levels than the average for alliance members

Table 4.3 Desirability of CA website features

	Mean	*SD*	*DK%*
Online petitions to sign	5.1	1.5	4
Website of local branch	4.3	1.8	3
Online voting for policy issues	4.0	1.9	5
Email details of leadership	3.9	1.8	6
Online voting for elected officials	3.8	1.9	5
List of members in my area	3.7	2.0	4
Members-only area of the site	3.5	2.1	9
Online discussion forums	2.9	1.8	9

N = 948. Members who are Internet users. Both online and postal surveys.

(see Table 4.4). Internet users tend to be employed in professional/higher technical/managerial jobs, significantly more so than their non-user counterparts. This partly depends on the rate of retired members in the two groups, as only one in five members who are Internet users are retired, compared to two in three amongst non-users. Internet users reside principally in London's southeast, while they are under-represented in Scotland, especially in east Scotland. Internet users tend to be recent recruits to the alliance, and they report significantly higher levels of interest in politics (especially online respondents as compared with postal survey respondents). Finally, slightly more members are male than female among Internet users as compared to non-users.[13]

The strength and extent of the expansion hypothesis was tested using three sets of results from our survey. First, we asked about the profile of those members, specifically Internet users, who have visited the Countryside Alliance website. Data suggest that site visitors come equally from different socio-economic and political interest categories, except for age, as younger member-users tend to visit the site more often than any other category of members. In general then, the alliance site attracts younger-than-average members who are otherwise quite similar to the membership at large. Secondly, within the wide range of methods members might use to keep in touch with the Countryside Alliance – letter, fax, phone, face-to-face meetings and printed material – we have identified a significant negative effect of Internet use on letter writing. Members who are Internet users tend to write to the alliance considerably less frequently that the average member ($\gamma = 0.24**$, N = 420). Third, we asked about (online) survey respondents who are not members, although they use the alliance site and *Grass-E-Route* to keep in touch with the organisation. Twenty-five per cent of online respondents are not Countryside Alliance members. This figure is telling about the capacity of the Internet to reach beyond the boundaries of the 'institutional' organisation. When we check the media consumption habits of this group,[14] we find that they are considerably less likely to use any traditional media to keep in touch

Table 4.4 Socio-demographic characteristics of CA members

	Non-users	*Users*
Gender:		
Female	43%	31%
Age:		
18–25	1%	4%
26–35	2%	12%
36–49	10%	33%
Above 70	44%	7%
Income:		
£ 25,000 to £ 34,999	13%	20%
£ 35,000 to £ 49,999	10%	15%
£ 50,000 or more	15%	26%
Education:		
No qualifications	15%	1%
Professional qualification	12%	7%
GCSE/O levels	29%	17%
A levels	13%	20%
Undergraduate degree (e.g. BA)	17%	31%
Post-graduate degree (e.g. MA)	4%	13%
Residence:		
Scotland east	5%	2%
London	3%	8%
Wessex	4%	8%
Occupation:		
Professional or higher technical work	5%	32%
Manager or senior administrator	4%	14%
Small business owner	10%	18%
Student	—	2%
Retired	64%	19%
N	175	1,115

Figures reported are column percentages. Only category values where differences between users and non-users are significant at p. < 0.05 are reported.

with the alliance (γ ranges from 0.41*** to 0.84***, N = 1,008). They are younger (γ = 0.24***, N = 1,039) and have lower income levels (γ = 0.17***, N = 1,033). Hence, both the *Grass-E-Route* and the Countryside Alliance site may serve to both numerically expand membership and diversify the profile of that membership.

Increasing engagement?

Both email and the World Wide Web have an important role for increasing levels of activism among members, especially in relation to campaign activities. The possibility of signing online petitions is the single most important feature members would like to see on the alliance site. We asked members whether the CA website and emails from the organisation led them to engage in a range of organisational activities. The results suggest that both media play an important role in mobilising supporters. The most significant results are indeed in the areas of campaigning and contacting (see Table 4.5). In fact, 29 per cent of members who use the Internet claimed that use of the Countryside Alliance websites led them to participate in the London march. Surprisingly, 45 per cent of non-member users of the site report the web as a main influence (not reported in Table 4.5). Similarly, 15 per cent and 13 per cent of the members respectively claimed that the web led them to attend another rally/demonstration or participate in a specific campaign. Hence, web mobilisation is strong and concerns mostly audiences that, at least in theory, are supposedly less suitable for a 'net effect'. Furthermore, the web is an important stimulus for individualised forms of political participation, such as writing letters to political representatives (18 per cent) and to the media (12 per cent). Finally, the web is much less functional for engaging members in routine collective organisational activities: volunteering time/work, attending branch meetings or purchasing services. Email is reportedly at least as important as the web in facilitating campaign participation. Almost every other respondent claims that email led them to attend the London march; in addition, one in three report attending another rally and one in four report participating in a specific campaign due to email communication from the alliance. Email has also an extremely important function in stimulating contact with others on alliance issues. Almost 42 per cent report that email led them to write to a representative, and 47 per cent forwarded the information received. Additionally, 25 per cent have contacted the media after receiving an email from the alliance. Finally, email seems marginally more effective than the web in drawing people into routine activities. Conversely, the website is relatively more effective in eliciting donations and encouraging people to join the organisation.

The results of this study challenge the received view that email is the 'killer application' in online campaigning, a powerful activation tool for newcomers to politics on the net. Our data suggest that email is a powerful mobilisation tool for members who are already engaged online. Conversely, the World Wide Web has a wider impact on less frequent and less active Internet users. While email clearly emerged as an important activation factor for online respondents, including non-members, the web is slightly more important for those who responded offline. That the web is mainly an entry point for subsequent, higher-level engagement with a political organisation is in line with the results of previous studies about the use of the Internet to mobilise supporters (Ward *et al.*, 2003).

Table 4.5 Web and email activation

	Website			Email		
	Postal members	*Online members*	*All members*	*Postal members*	*Online members*	*All members*
Campaign activities:						
Attend the London march	31	28	29	22	50	45
Attend other rally or demonstration	11	16	15	8	42	34
Participate in a specific campaign	9	14	13	7	34	27
Contact activities:						
Write to an elected representative	17	20	18	13	53	42
Write to the media	9	13	12	8	34	25
Forward information to a friend (non-member)	14	17	16	16	56	47
Contact the CA with views/ comments	6	10	9	7	27	22
Contact other members	2	5	4	5	24	19
Money-related activities:						
Donate money to CA	14	16	16	8	27	22
Join the CA	11	13	12	2	11	10
Institutional activities:						
Attend a social event	5	7	16	6	19	16
Volunteer some time/work	4	4	4	3	16	13
Attend a local branch meeting	3	4	4	4	16	13
Purchase services	3	9	6	2	7	6
N	242	759	1,001	242	759	1,001

Source: Q8 'Has use of the Countryside Alliance website or email information from the Countryside Alliance ever led you to undertake any of the following activities?'

Note: Results reported are percentages, and refer to Internet users only.

Mobilisation: the march on London

The march in London on 22 September 2002 created a considerable degree of public interest around the Countryside Alliance. The march was announced on 22 April, capitalising on the interest created the previous year by the foot-and-mouth epidemic.[15] The march was attended by 63 per cent of the membership. The consequences in terms of traffic on the Countryside Alliance site were significant. The average number of monthly visitors increased from some 40,000 visits per month to 57,000 in August and 160,000 in September. A special march website was set up roughly three months before the march to help coordinate activities (http://www.march-info.org). The site attracted some 120,000 visits over the time span of its existence (as of December 2004, it still existed, only as a historical marker). It further prompted the subsequent development of an 'activism' section on the CA main site, which allows members to get more involved with the organisation. The *Grass-E-Route* email list grew from an average of 20,000 over 2002 to a peak of 40,000 in the run-up to the London march. In terms of resources, two additional staff were employed at the time of the protest to manage the march website and coordinate online activities. Two special emails were sent out in the fortnight preceding the march with details of small-scale action around the country.

Within this framework of reference, we tried to assess more precisely the importance of the Internet for march participants. We specifically asked members about attendance at the march, sources of information used to keep informed about the event, and frequency of access to the special march site. Printed material from the alliance is the highest-rated media for information about the march, followed by the national press (see Table 4.6). However, different types of respondents relied on different sources. Online media, such as the alliance mailing list and the two websites, were much more important for online respondents than for postal respondents. This is hardly surprising, even though knowledge about the websites negatively biases the results, i.e. the low score depends mainly on a lack of visibility rather than a negative assessment of the service. Indeed, the high standard deviation value for postal respondents shows that, once the sites or email service were accessed, the evaluations are substantially higher, even higher than the value attributed to traditional media.

We employed logistic regression analysis to assess the importance of the web as a mobilising factor for the London march on the range of socio-economic, attitudinal and information-seeking behaviours discussed above. It is worth remembering that 31 per cent of members who use the Internet reported the web as an important stimulus for them to join in the march (see Table 4.6). The results of our final logistic model are quite telling (see Table 4.7). The web seems to be especially important for recent CA members, and members who are less likely to have contact with their fellow members. Mobilised members are habitual users of the web, and have frequently

Table 4.6 Importance of the Internet for march participants

Importance of march media		Internet use and administration mode		
		Non-users	Users – postal	Users – online
National press	Mean	4.1	4.0	3.4
	Standard deviation	2.2	2.0	2.1
Local press	Mean	2.7	2.6	1.9
	Standard deviation	2.5	2.4	2.1
Printed material from CA	Mean	4.6	4.8	4.3
	Standard deviation	2.0	1.6	1.9
Word of mouth	Mean	3.3	3.8	3.9
	Standard deviation	2.5	2.2	2.1
Website of the march	Mean		2.7	4.5
	Standard deviation		2.5	1.9
CA national site	Mean		2.4	4.1
	Standard deviation		2.4	2.1
Grass-E-Route mailing list	Mean		3.0	5.2
	Standard deviation		2.6	1.6

Results are based on the entire sample.

Table 4.7 Determinants of web activation for the march

Length of CA membership	0.67	***
Frequency of access to the march site	1.58	***
Frequency of use of the WWW	1.27	**
Frequency of access to the CA site	1.26	**
Importance of the press for information about the march	1.23	***
Meet with other members (yes)	0.50	**
Online survey (yes)	0.52	*
Constant	0.09	***

N = 713. Chi ^{2}(7df) = 111 ***. Cases correctly classified = 74.2%.
Results refer to members who have attended the march. Results reported are standardised log coefficients * = sig. p. < 0.05, ** = sig. p. < 0.01, *** = sig. p. < 0.001.

accessed both the march site and the alliance main site. Web-activated respondents also are more likely to have followed the campaign in the press, which indicates a reinforcement effect between printed and new media. The same does not apply to television. Furthermore, it is interesting to note that online respondents are more likely to report web activation than postal respondents.

The most conspicuous finding is that traditional socio-economic variables – high income, younger age and higher education – have insignificant and weak relations with web mobilisation in both the zero-order correlations and the multivariate model. Similarly, the level of respondents' political interest and left–right orientations seem to have no effect on online mobilisation.

Online mobilisation seems to be embedded in online dynamics, i.e. general web habits and activities, and does not follow pre-existing, traditional patterns of political socialisation. In other words, online mobilisation builds more on the familiarity with information technologies than on a personal history of political engagement – or the lack thereof.

If the question is whether the Internet is mobilising a new constituency, the answer is probably yes. Yet, if we ask whether the Internet has mobilised the previously engaged (existing activists) or the disengaged (politically uninterested), our data suggest the answer is a resounding 'neither'. The constituency reached by the web is very new to issue politics, has average levels of political activism and no specific socio-demographic traits. This group may have latent sympathies for the issue or organisation but it is the ICTs that make them an 'engageable' constituency. This possibly supports early claims of political dis-intermediation via ICTs, albeit in the context of a political organisation rather than a polity at large (Becker, 1981; Poster, 1996; for a critique see also Coleman, 1999). The question remains, however, whether the mobilising importance of ICTs remains once they are exposed to 'real' life political events. Further research is needed to explore the changing patterns of mutual relationship between the virtual and the real in the domain of political mobilisation.

Conclusions

Contrary to increasing scepticism about whether ICTs can really *widen* participation, our survey results indicate they have significant *widening potential*. Of course, this is not a uniform process – certain groups are more susceptible to online mobilisation than others. This study of the Countryside Alliance underscores the importance of organisations in the mobilisation process and more specifically the organisational context and culture. Despite the hype about ICTs fostering a more direct form of democracy, organisations still have key roles to play in the participatory politics. If ICTs are to be used to widen political participation, then they need to be linked to a wider communication strategy. In our study, ICTs were embedded into the alliance's broader organisational strategy of widening its general profile, in both issue and membership terms. ICTs were successfully employed by the Countryside Alliance to achieve this broader organisational goal.

We also found evidence of *deepening* in our study. Members were engaging in new activities online, especially those who were already the most active in the alliance and generally members who saw ICTs as a valuable resource in this respect. Again, this was not a uniform process. When we look at the types of participation most undertaken and valued, it is generally the more passive and individualised forms of activity that have increased, notably receiving and reading information. Whilst much of the academic and media focus of e-participation has been on e-enabled interactive discussion, i.e bulletin boards, chat rooms, etc., these types of e-participation are the ones less favoured by participants. For professional protest movements such as the Countryside Alliance, the technology is beneficial in the context of mobilisation via top-down information and political marketing rather than as a networking or discussion tool. This reiterates the point that political organisations will use the technologies in ways that bolster their pre-existing organisational culture. Professional protest organisations that have less of a commitment to grassroots democracy are likely to use them for information dissemination and as occasional mobilising tools.

The survey also provided evidence of how people are activated. While we do not dispute the standard story of the reinforcement effect, where offline activists extend their activity online, our survey intriguingly found some evidence of a possible Internet effect as mobilisation was engendered by virtual, rather than traditional, triggers. The survey uncovered a group of people, who had an average interest in politics and were inactive offline, who *were* mobilised through the net. As yet we have no way of knowing whether this is a novelty factor or how such a group will be socialised over time. As concerns directly new media, the view of ICTs as a total package reduces different types of technologies to one category with apparently uniform effects. The research here supports other organisational surveys we have conducted (Ward *et al.*, 2003) that the use of different types of ICT may well produce different participatory results. It appears from an organisational perspective that websites are more useful for initial recruitment and information dissemination purposes while email is then more useful for activating members.

The survey here cannot claim to be representative of the pressure group and social movement world as a whole. What is now required is long-term tracking of activist groups in different organisational contexts and additional qualitative data – interviews, online diaries, etc. – on whether 'virtual' mobilisation then turns into 'real' political activity. Do people activated online with little or no previous political history gradually become politicised and engaged both online and offline over time? If this were to be the case, then new ICTs may well be offering something novel to participatory politics. However, the study does add additional evidence to claims about the relationship between the new media and participation in a specific organisational context. In particular, it sheds additional light on questions of who participates online (the widening question), what types of participation they are engaged in (the deepening question) as well as how and why people participate – and the role of new ICTs in this process.

Notes

1 For example, see the discussion of the Stop the War campaign online in 'A Revolution for Revolt', Alistair Alexander, *Guardian*, 20 February 2003.
2 Corporate Watch's Report (2002) 'The Countryside Alliance – Voice of the Rural Dispossessed?!', http://www.corporatewatch.org.uk/pages/Countryside_Alliance.html; 'Hunters Accused of Hijacking Protest', John Vidal, *Guardian*, 21 September 2002.

3 Interview with Epolitix.com, 20 September 2002.
4 Both broadsheets and mid-range newspapers carried the march as front-page news. The *Daily Telegraph*, a staunch supporter of CA's hunting stance, carried five pages of coverage.
5 See Countryside Alliance press release, 25 October 2002, 'Countryside Alliance Membership Breaks 100,000', http://www.countryside-alliance.org/news/02/021025tat.htm.
6 See the following surveys: 'The Countryside March – Who Was Really There?', MORI 1997, http://www.mori.com/polls/1998/hunting3.shtml; 'The Edinburgh Countryside March Poll', MORI 2001, http://www.mori.com/polls/2001/edinburgh.shtml; 'Hunting March Unrepresentative of the Countryside', League Against Cruel Sports press release, 22 September 2002, http://www.league.uk.com/news/media_briefings/2002/september_2002/22_sep_02_hunting_march_unrepresentative.htm.
7 This section is based on information gathered from several interviews with CA staff.
8 A *Guardian* report claimed that the CA has extremely sophisticated database records on supporters and some of its opponents ('Hunt Lobby Holds Personal Files on Thousands', 1 November 2002).
9 http://www.countryside-alliance.org/The_Alliance/about_us/about_us/, accessed 7 December 2004.
10 See article 'Anti-Government Activism' at http://www.globalprofile.co.uk.
11 Standard notation is used for statistical significance, $* =$ sig. $p. < 0.05$, $** =$ sig. $p. < 0.01$, $*** =$ sig. $p. \leq 0.001$.
12 A further question on 'comfort using the Internet rather than traditional media' was asked of Internet users and non-users alike for a range of organisational activities. Results corroborate the findings reported in the text.
13 Several alternative logistic regression models were run with Internet use as a dependent variable. We included socio-economic status and political attitudes variables having significant zero-order correlations as independents. In all models occupation, income and age were the main predictors, while betas for political orientations and political engagement were either non-significant or small.
14 Here, members responding online are the contrast group: $N = 1,039$, members $N = 779$, non-members $N = 260$.
15 This highly contagious disease among animals led to the mass cull of livestock, with severe consequences for farmers who lost breeding stock. Although the farmers were compensated, feelings ran high over the government's approach to the problem.

References

Barber, B., Mattson, K. and Peterson, J. (1997) 'The State of Electronically Enhanced Democracy: A Survey of the Internet', Report for the Markle Foundation, Walt Whitman Center for Culture and Politics of Democracy, New Brunswick, NJ.
Becker, T. (1981) 'Teledemocracy: Bringing Back Power to the People', *Futurist*, December: 6–9.
Bimber, B. (1998) 'The Internet and Political Transformation: Populism, Community and Accelerated Pluralism', *Polity* 31 (1): 133–160.
Bonchek, M.S. (1995), 'Grassroots in Cyberspace: Using Computer Networks to Facilitate Political Participation', Paper presented to the 53rd annual meeting of the Midwest Political Science Association, 6 April, Chicago, IL. Online. Available at http://www.ai.mit.edu/people/msb/pubs/grassroots.html.

Cisler, S. (1999) 'Showdown in Seattle: Turtles, Teamsters and Tear Gas', *First Monday* 4 (2), http://www.firstmonday.dk/issues/issue4_12/cisler/index.html.

Coleman, S. (1999) 'Cutting out the Middle Man: From Virtual Representation to Direct Deliberation', in Hague, B.N. and Loader, B. (eds), *Digital Democracy: Discourse and Decision Making in the Information Age*, London: Routledge.

Diani, M. (2000) 'Social Movement Networks, Virtual and Real', *Information, Communication and Society* 3 (3), 386–401.

Diani, M. and Donati, P. (1999) 'Organisational Change in Western European Environmental Groups: A Framework for Analysis', *Environmental Politics* 8 (1): 13–34.

Doherty, B., Paterson, M., Wall, D. and Plows, A. (2003) 'Explaining the Fuel Protests', *British Journal of Politics and International Relations* 5 (1): 1–23.

Gibson, R.K., Lusoli, W. and Ward, S.J. (2002) 'UK Political Participation Online – The Public Response. A Survey of Citizens' Political Activity via the Internet', Salford: Economic and Social Research Council Report.

Jordan, T. (2001) 'Hactivism: Direct Action on the Electronic Flows of Information Societies', in Dowding, K., Hughes, J. and Margetts, H. (eds), *Challenges to Democracy: Ideas, Involvement and Institutions*, London: Palgrave.

Katz, J.E. and Rice, R.E. (2002) *Social Consequences of Internet Use*, Cambridge, MA: MIT Press.

Lipow, A. and Seyd, P. (1996) 'The Politics of Anti-Partyism', *Parliamentary Affairs* 49 (2): 273–284.

Lupia, A. and Philpot, T.S. (2002) 'More Than Kids' Stuff: Can News and Information Web Sites Mobilize Young Adults?', Paper presented at the annual meeting of the American Political Science Association, Boston, MA.

Lusoli, W., Ward, S. and Gibson, R.K. (2002) 'Political Organisations and Online Mobilisation: Different Media – Same Outcomes?', *New Review of Information Networking* 8: 89–107.

McLean, I. (1989) *Democracy and New Technology*, Cambridge: Polity Press.

Norris, P. (1999) 'Who Surfs? New Technology, Old Voters and Virtual Democracy', in Kamarck, E.C. and Nye, J.S. (eds), *Democracy.com? Governance in a Networked World*, Hollis, NH: Hollis Publishing.

Norris, P. (2000) *Virtuous Circle: Political Communication in Post Industrial Democracies*, Cambridge: Cambridge University Press.

Norton, A. (2002) 'The Relationship between Hunting and Country Life', *Countryside Recreation* 8 (1): 8–11.

Office for National Statistics (ONS) (2002) 'Internet Access: Households and Individuals', 17 December, London: ONS. Online. Available at http://www.statistics.gov.uk/pdfdir/inta1202.pdf.

Poster, M. (1996) 'Cyberdemocracy: Internet and the Public Sphere', in Porter, D.A. (ed.), *Internet Culture*, London: Routledge.

Rheingold, H. (2002) *Smart Mobs: The Next Social Revolution*, Cambridge, MA: Perseus Publishing.

Scott, A. and Street, J. (2000) 'From Media Politics to E-Protest', *Information, Communication and Society* 3 (2): 215–240.

Shapiro, A. (1999) 'The Internet', *Foreign Policy*, Summer: 14–27.

Street, J. (1997) 'Citizenship and Mass Communication', *Contemporary Political Studies*, Volume 1: 502–510, UK Political Studies Association, Belfast.

Sunstein, C. (2001) *Republic.com*, Princeton, NJ: Princeton University Press.

Ward, N. (2002) 'Representing Rurality? New Labour and the Electoral Geography of Britain', *Area* 34 (2): 171–181.

Ward, S.J., Lusoli, W. and Gibson, R.K. (2003) 'Virtually Participating: A Survey of Online Party Members', *Information Polity* 7 (4): 199–215.

Washbourne, N. (1999) 'Information Technology and New Forms of Organising? Translocalism and Networking within Friends of the Earth', in Webster, F. (ed.), *Culture and Politics in the Information Age: A New Politics?*, London: Routledge.

Woods, M. (1998) 'The People of England Speak? Rurality, Nationalism and Countryside Protest', Paper presented to the Rural Economy and Society Study Group Conference, Aberystwyth, Wales, September.

Woods, M (2003) 'Deconstructing Rural Protest: The Emergence of a New Social Movement', *Journal of Rural Studies* 19 (3): 309–325.

Woods, M. (2004) 'Politics and Protest in the Contemporary Countryside', in Kneafsey, M. and Holloway, L. (eds), *Geographies of Rural Cultures and Societies*, Aldershot: Ashgate.

5 Design matters

The political efficacy of government-run discussion boards

Scott Wright

The British government has become concerned about decreasing popular interest in local government decision making highlighted by low turnouts at elections and the detachment of people from decision makers more generally. Turnout in local elections dropped from an average of 41 per cent between 1976 and 1996 to less than 27 per cent in 2000, and this was 'perilously close to removing the claim of any local authority to speak with legitimacy as the authentic voice of its community' (Kearns *et al.*, 2002: 13). In response to these problems, British Prime Minister Tony Blair has said that he wants to 'redraw the boundaries between what is done in the name of the people and what is done by the people themselves' (Blair, 1996: 320). One of the methods advocated in the drive to achieve this new relationship is electronic democracy.

There are a number of strings to the government's bow in terms of electronic democracy, including:

- electoral pilot schemes to make voting easier;
- help for councils to develop their arrangements for participation and consultation;
- more frequent elections and the right to hold referenda;
- money to invest in e-government and e-democracy infrastructure;
- a consultation to help develop a concrete e-democracy policy.

In effect, the British government is using a variety of institutional techniques in an attempt to both encourage and shape political participation at the local level. Yet, the extent of central government influence on local e-democracy initiatives is contested. For example, Peri 6 *et al.* (2002: 99) argue that the centre believes 'only the most relentless regime of inspection, incentive, sanction and discipline will produce effective action'. Pratchett and Leach (2004: 367) take a more nuanced approach, characterising the central–local relationship as one of 'choice within constraint', arguing that this was not merely a top-down process as 'significant scope remains for choice within it' as typified by Best Value Performance Indicator 157.[1] There is no central prescription in the United Kingdom for the use of online discussion boards; rather, the decision to include one is locally made.

The development of policies and tools that are intended to encourage participation is only one side of the coin though. The flip side is how will these policies be received? Will people actually take advantage of these new opportunities? These arguments fit within a broader debate between how social capital and institutional design affect political participation. To provide answers to this question, this chapter uses a case study analysis of two local government Internet discussion boards with different designs. The first, from Cumbria County Council in the north of England, was an asynchronous discussion board with a threaded arrangement of messages. This highlights the relationships between messages and was designed to facilitate debate. The second, from Suffolk County Council in the east of England, was a message or bulletin board in which posts were piled one on top of the other with no visible linkages between messages. This arguably makes it much more difficult to hold and follow discussions.

This chapter will argue that there are a number of factors that shape how, if at all, people participate on discussion boards and that the relationship between institutional design and social capital is a two-way one (Lowndes and Wilson, 2001: 631). There remains, though, a need to account for how institutional – or in this case website – design can affect the nature of discussion on a micro level, that is, at the interface between government and citizen.

Social capital and institutional design

The social capital thesis as espoused most famously by Robert Putnam (1993, 2001) is predominantly society-centred and based on human agency – and how this is important to good governance and political participation. Putnam's basic argument is that dense networks of civic engagement produce a capacity for trust, reciprocity and cooperation, which in turn produces a healthy democracy in a virtuous circle. He analysed a series of case studies for characteristics associated with social capital and examined how they had evolved. Putnam's work has been a subject for considerable debate (Lowndes and Wilson, 2001; Levi, 1996; Newton, 1999). Accusations have been made that Putnam has a 'bottom-up' bias (Newton, 1999); that his work is too society-centred (Levi, 1996); and that he has undervalued the role that state agency and institutional design can have in facilitating, shaping and promoting social capital, which in turn has led Putnam to be too fatalistic (Lowndes and Wilson, 2001).

Institutional design emphasises how the design of institutional structures, such as their capacity for allowing or listening to the participation of citizens, affects the likelihood and the nature of how people will participate (Goodin, 1996). Vivien Lowndes and David Wilson have analysed how the relationship between institutional design and social capital shaped the development and success of the current British Labour government's local government modernisation agenda. They argue that Putnam has, by assuming that the design of institutions was constant throughout his case studies in *Making Democracy Work*, underplayed the role that this has in the creation of social capital and political participation. For Lowndes and Wilson, the 'roles of social capital may be better understood in the context of a two-way relationship between civil society and government' (2001: 631).[2]

This chapter supports this point but takes issue with Lowndes and Wilson's framework for analysing the relationship between institutional design and social capital. The framework has four interacting dimensions that they believe shape the creation and mobilisation of social capital at the local level: relationships with the voluntary sector; opportunities for public participation; the responsiveness of decision making; and arrangements for democratic leadership and social inclusion. It is argued here that Lowndes and Wilson's framework does not sufficiently account for how the design of the interface between government and citizens affects public participation and the ability of such facilities to generate social capital.[3] This is because design, here, is working on a micro rather than just a macro level. The power of the design principle as outlined by Lowndes and Wilson needs to be developed further. It is not just the provision of participatory facilities and whether they are responsive that is important in encouraging participation and shaping the production of social capital; rather, it is the design of these facilities and the extent to which the design allows and encourages participation as well as facilitates the production of social capital. As regards discussion boards, it is critical to examine the ease of use of the interface between government and citizen, and whether that interface encourages discussion and deliberation. The interface can facilitate debate in the following ways: by arranging the messages in a coherent, structured manner, with clearly framed debates; providing explanatory notes at the beginning of new debates; and having well-designed and transparent moderation policies.

Although within the e-democracy debate there has been significant talk of how it may be possible to facilitate a deliberative form of democracy through discussion boards, very little empirical testing of these claims has been undertaken to date. Moreover, these studies have concentrated on Usenet (Unix User Network), an Internet communications medium in which users read and post textual messages to a network of distributed bulletin boards known as newsgroups. Usenet is highly decentralised, being sustained by a large number of servers, which store and forward messages to one another. Two recent empirical studies of Usenet were conducted by Richard Davis in *The Web of American Politics* in 1999 and by Anthony Wilhelm in 2000 in *Democracy in the Digital Age* (also see Schneider, 1997; Hill and Hughes, 1998). They both posed a number of questions about the nature of discussion – based on James Fishkin's (1991) conception of deliberative democracy[4] – and set out to answer them empirically. Their findings suggest that discussion boards may not be up to the task at hand, as they were not deliberative. For example, Davis's analysis found high levels of 'flaming', in which people posted aggressive or derogatory messages; a reinforcement rather than exchange of views;

and that the forums were unrepresentative.[5] This led Davis to conclude that: 'the promise of Usenet is a hollow one. It turns out that even the Internet's most democratic corner is not as democratic as it appears' (1999: 167).

Usenet groups, however, are a particular form of discussion board. They are not linked formally to government, and Usenet groups have a vast arrangement of often highly politicised and polarised threads. The framing of debates (for example alt.politics.clinton and alt.politics.white-power) may – through design – lead to a polarisation of debate with pro-Clinton supporters rallying around each other to defend themselves against the flaming of anti-Clinton users. This problem is exacerbated because Usenet forums are typically un-moderated and this means that it is difficult to rein in abusive posters.[6] Thus, the problems that Wilhelm and Davis found may be a consequence of the design of the interface. Although both authors note the role of design – Wilhelm even made design his fourth feature of virtual political life – neither really analyses in detail how the particular design of Usenet groups may have affected their empirical findings. In the light of this, Wilhelm and Davis may have been too pessimistic about the chances for Internet-based discussion and we must take great care in generalising their findings into a broader commentary of the nature of online political discussion. Different types of discussion-board interface must be analysed to see what effect these have on the nature of discussion. Hence, the case studies in this chapter were chosen, in part, because their contrasting designs enabled comparisons to be drawn.

Generating discussion through design

There is a long-standing belief that the structure of a democracy will affect the results – be they top-down and results-driven, or bottom-up and input-led. There has been a particularly lengthy discussion about how the design of parliament buildings, council chambers and the like affects the quality of the discussion and the nature of the debate. For example, the structure of the British Houses of Parliament, with the government on one side and the opposition facing them across the chamber, is thought to create arguments and hullabaloo politics, while rounded chambers lead to more open debate and less vitriol. The design of the Scottish Parliament's new debating chamber, opened in October 2004, was the subject of much debate between those who preferred the Westminster system and those (including the architect) who favoured a European-style semi-circle.[7] Furthermore, the importance of design was highlighted by a competition, held in October 2002, which explored 'the role that design can play in deepening democracy and promoting citizen engagement in local decision making'.[8] This was based on the premise that the shape of meeting places affects discussion and democracy: 'Sensitively planned auditoriums can facilitate debate and foster consensus.'[9]

Discussion boards can be conceived as democratic meeting places – a kind of virtual agora. Indeed, we have seen much discussion and a variety of 'e-conceptualisations' such as virtual Habermasian public spheres (Sassi,

2001; Keane, 2000; Tsagarousianou, 1998; Wilhelm, 2000), electronic Athens (Mulgan and Adonis, 1997) and electronic commons (Abramson, 1988). The discussion boards analysed here worked on the assumption that design affects discussion as they were both 'designed' to meet the specific aims ascribed to them. Suffolk County Council's Graffiti Wall was left relatively unstructured with no threads as it was intended to be a free-thinking space, while Cumbria County Council's discussion board had a structured threading system designed to focus discussion into specific policy areas. These arguments go to the heart of the debate between institutional (website) design and social capital. Is it possible to structure through design how (and arguably if) people discuss matters? To what extent is possessing social capital the key factor? Or are yet more forces at play? It is instructive to cross-analyse different types of discussion board design to see what type and level of interactivity they generate, and where these differences come from.

The 'ownership'[10] and design of websites are important factors in determining the participatory facilities offered. Typically, county council website structures or frames are designed by a private company who then pass this over to the council to fill out, maintain and update. This has led to considerable standardisation within an overall picture of diversity. A Northumbrian company, Tagish Ltd, for example, is responsible for the design of all or part of numerous county council websites. Their client list includes Bedfordshire County Council, Norfolk County Council, Cambridgeshire County Council, Suffolk County Council, Durham County Council, Lincolnshire County Council, Nottinghamshire County Council and Surrey County Council.[11] According to Tagish, there is a 'consistency of requirements between councils that enables the use of standardised packages'.[12] It is particularly important to note that Tagish believes these services 'will be increased in breadth and depth as [the] requirements of Councils change'.[13] Thus, technological design is still reactive to the demands of councils: if councils want a discussion board on their site, Tagish will be more than happy to provide one – but there has been relatively little demand. This is supported by a survey conducted for this chapter that found that only 15 per cent of county councils had discussion boards.[14] Furthermore, a survey by the Institute for Public Policy Research in the United Kingdom found that only 10 per cent of local authorities encouraged moderated forums as a form of communication with citizens and that only 7 per cent encouraged citizens to use such forums as a tool for consultation (Kearns *et al.*, 2002: 20, 22).

Having discussed how the design of a forum can affect the nature of discussion, and the forces that are at play behind this, the chapter next turns to results from the case studies in Cumbria and Suffolk.

Methodology

The methodology adopted for this research was primarily a quantitative analysis of the content of government-run discussion boards. Quantitative analysis of websites has many advantages.[15] Nevertheless, the Internet provides specific problems for researchers, as it changes rapidly (McMillan, 2000). The basic methodology outlined below can, nevertheless, be applied to most discussion boards, although arguably discussion boards differ in style to a degree that different methodologies may also be needed to take account of this fact. The two case studies were chosen because the contrasting formats of the discussion boards enabled comparisons that were necessary to show how design affects the nature of discussion. Suffolk's was the only county council site in Britain at that time to feature a bulletin board and was thus self-selecting, while Cumbria County Council was chosen because of a desire to see how usage changed during the foot-and-mouth crisis.[16]

The first step was to analyse how people were communicating through government-run discussion boards – if they were communicating at all. This was done through a mixture of analysing the overall usage statistics for each site with specific statistics for usage of the discussion board. In particular, the number of posts, replies to posts, replies to replies and so on was analysed. This gives a richer understanding of the nature of the discussions, and builds on the work of both Davis and Wilhelm. Though one might have expected diffidence from officials in gaining website usage statistics, people were generally helpful. Of course, the figures may have been manipulated to present the councils in a favourable light but as they normally went to councillors and other senior figures such manipulation was unlikely.

The bigger problem with this form of quantitative analysis is that baseline statistics, though helpful in giving an overall picture, do not represent the complexity that exists within the figures as there are great differences in the quality of websites. For example, one website may provide a very basic feedback mechanism such as giving a general email and postal address while others have online forms from which people can choose the recipient and whether they want to make a complaint or a compliment. However, for this analysis of discussion boards, a descriptive account of the structure of the board combined with an in-depth quantitative analysis of the number of posts, as well as the way in which they relate to each other, allows us to get behind the baseline statistics into a richer picture of the nature of the discussion.

Cumbria County Council discussion board

The Cumbria County Council discussion board was set up on 15 September 1999. It was hoped that it would enable the council to create a dialogue with citizens, and this desire shaped the decision to choose a threaded discussion forum. The discussion board was initially a 'freeware' tool downloadable at no cost from the Internet through a company called DiscusWare. However, the council upgraded the discussion board to the company's Professional Forum, which offers more features (for a fee), on 5 February 2001. Between its inception and September 2002, the board received 2,414 posts.

Each discussion topic had a separate topic moderator or moderators. This was intended to speed up response times and take the pressure off individual moderators. Each moderator was a civil servant with a direct link to the subject at hand. The rules and guidelines for moderators were posted on the Internet and this enabled users to see the rules by which moderators should have been acting. They also provided training and advice for moderators on how to respond to messages, such as the 'netiquette' of discussion forums.

Although the administrator had to activate a new discussion topic, once this had been done all responsibility lay with the moderators. This included setting the subject of the debate (although citizens could have suggested new topics, the ultimate decision lay with the moderators); generating a message that explained what the topic was about; creating relevant sub-topics; and monitoring the discussions. Moderators also were tasked with keeping the discussions on topic; responding to any questions that required official responses within two working days; splitting new topics within threads into separate threads; closing old discussions and threads; and ensuring that any abusive posters/postings were removed. It was stated that this option must be used with 'caution',[17] and that only messages 'deemed to be offensive or in any way wholly inappropriate to the nature of the discussion' would be removed.[18] Where a message was deleted, the moderator was required to replace it with his or her own explaining why the post had been removed.[19] It is assumed that this system was adopted because of the use of post-moderation and was intended to explain to all users why a message had been removed.

The threads themselves were structured to generate discussion on specific policy areas. Generally, there was an introductory post from the council detailing information about the subject, any areas of particular interest for the council and sometimes how the comments were to be used. This system did give users some basic information before they posted their own comments. The downside, though, is that it gave the council the power to set the agenda. This power is somewhat counterbalanced by the general discussion thread in which people could set their own topics.

According to Kevin Paulisse, the designer of the DiscusWare software, its most unique user/interface feature was the combination of a linear messaging style (see Figure 5.1) combined with the 'add message' box on the same page itself, 'which implies to the reader that a contribution is expected, and obviates the need to hunt around for a "Reply" button'.[20] Interestingly, Paulisse believed that site administrators were 'more likely to be motivated by an attractive interface than the quality of the debate it will inspire'.[21] This is intriguing because it suggests that a key factor shaping the development of discussion forums is technical capacity and aesthetics rather than the quality of the debate that the software will help to produce.[22]

Of the 2,414 posts made, 126 (5.2 per cent) were made by forum moderators, who often passed users on to the relevant people or reported information back from the relevant section.[23] By far the most significant block of messages related to the foot-and-mouth enquiry. In total, this topic received

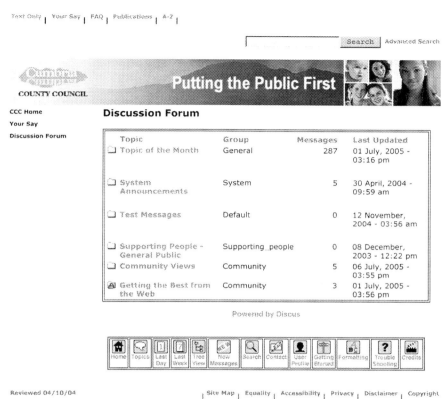

Figure 5.1 Screen shot of the Cumbria County Council discussion forum.

Source: www.cumbriacc.gov.uk. Permission granted by Cumbria County Council for reproduction.

1,458 messages or 60.4 per cent of the total number of messages with 34 (3.6 per cent) responses from moderators. The 1.6 per cent difference in response rate, though small, suggests that the increased traffic did affect the ability of civil servants to keep pace with forum usage. However, a further 26 posts were made by the 'Access Team', primarily answering questions about open and closed footpaths – this meant that 4.1 per cent of posts were official responses and thus the effects of increased usage were negligible.

This left only 956 messages in total for other discussions. Thus, considerably more than half of all the posts were on the single subject of the foot-and-mouth crisis. Before the crisis, the Cumbria County Council website was receiving an average 600,000 hits per month, but during the crisis this rose greatly, reaching 1.6 million hits in June 2001 before falling gradually back to the 600,000 average again by November 2001.[24] The most active parts of the site during the crisis were the discussion forum, latest news and a section detailing information on open and closed footpaths (a subject that also was widely discussed in the forum). These figures suggest that people – and very significant numbers at that – will make use of interactive website-based facilities if they feel they have a need to do so. This suggestion can be made because there were no other apparent differences, such as a new access centre opening, a redesigning of the website or a publicity campaign, to explain the increased usage of this local government website.[25] The only apparent factor to explain the increased postings was that this was an issue about which people felt strongly and were actively seeking information. Some people were coming across the site for the first time and then using the discussion board while others had known about the site before but not bothered to post a message.[26] These findings support Lowndes *et al.*'s focus group analysis of citizens' attitudes, which suggested that 'people would participate in consultations on "the issues that mattered" ' (Lowndes *et al.*, 2001: 446).

The evidence suggests that there is a complex interplay of factors that determine whether people will participate in a web-based civil forum. An easy-to-use interface is important as it removes a potential barrier and can affect the nature of discussion. However, it was the strength of feeling about the issue that was the key determinant of whether people participated in Cumbria. Some have suggested that this amounts to a latent political activism: people are willing to participate but only on an issue-by-issue basis (Beetham, 2002; Parry *et al.*, 1992).

The primary use of the discussion board was to find out information in a fast-changing environment. What could be described as a grassroots activist network developed, with people posting that footpaths were open and closed, and which had been closed illegally. This generated some animosity between the limited number of farmers who used the site and the more numerous ramblers, fell walkers and dog walkers (as well as tourist businesses that relied on their custom).[27] According to posts on the site, the ramblers worked together to provide accurate information on what footpaths should be open and what were open, with many local businesses encouraging people to keep visiting. Users were both residents of Cumbria and visiting tourists (or people hoping to visit the area). The results do not completely match those found by Wilhelm and Davis: people apparently were influencing policy and significant debate (if not discussion) was occurring.

However, there did appear to be the formation of 'gangs' and there was very little evidence of people listening to opposing views and coming to considered decisions. Furthermore, the forum was dominated by a small number of active users who posted regularly. Numerous people made more than 20 posts, with the most active users being: 'Cumbrian Rambler' with 42 posts; 'Chris from Penrith' with 41 posts; and 'Jon from Copeland' with 37 posts. Thus, the three most active posters accounted for 5 per cent of all the messages. This is not necessarily a bad thing, however, as, without these active users, irregular ones might see a lack of activity and decide not to post.

Thus, in the short to medium term, active users may play a useful rather than detrimental role in the establishment of a discussion board.

The discussion board was a particularly useful tool in facilitating discussion and providing information because of the geographical diversity of users. Aside from the national and international queries (primarily tourists), many parts of Cumbria itself are isolated and it is not easy to arrange group meetings. Furthermore, during the foot-and-mouth crisis many roads and footpaths were closed, and people were encouraged not to use their cars for fear of spreading the disease – factors that may have encouraged people to use the website. Thus, we can conclude that the discussion board was a good method to use in these particular circumstances as it allowed geographically diverse people to read and update one central hub of information in their locale. Postings were virtually real-time, and comparatively cheap to make. From this we can surmise that discussion boards are most likely to be used in situations in which the advantages of virtual meetings over physical meetings come to the fore.

The Cumbria County Council discussion board was quite unusual in that people could post messages without having to register; though the council did encourage people to give their details, it was not compulsory. Although there were 'significant advantages' if people registered,[28] the reality is that most users did not. Typically, there were fewer than 30 people registered at any one time and the majority of posts were made by non-registered users.[29] However, only 132 posts were made by people posting without leaving a name at the top of their post (entitled anonymous), suggesting that many people were prepared to leave some details, but did not take the time to register. They may have failed to register not only because it was not required, but also because they perceived the actual benefits to be minimal.[30] The decision not to make registration or membership compulsory was taken because when the council initially encouraged membership it generated a lot of suspicion from users; people were fearful of some form of Big Brother surveillance of messages.[31]

To give an idea of the degree of interactivity, an in-depth analysis of the e-government topic was undertaken. This had three threads, of which only two received replies. A thread on video conferencing had received one initial response, followed by an official reply, then a further response and official reply. All were, broadly speaking, focused on the subject. The more general 'Other Comments' thread received 40 messages with nine separate sub-topics. These generated 17 replies from members of the public, four responses from the original poster and seven official responses. Of the nine sub-topics, only three related to e-government. In fact, 77.5 per cent of all the messages were unrelated to the topic at hand.[32] Digression and/or completely ignoring the thread subject are recurring problems on discussion boards. It would appear that the title of the thread as 'Other Comments' encouraged this digression. Thus, giving discussion threads a specific topic – while at the same time offering a separate area for general comments and questions – is advisable to maintain focus. Nevertheless, each and every new topic received a response, and the level of discussion and interactivity among citizens as well as between citizens and civil servants was high compared to similar discussion boards (Wright, 2002).

The site did not generate discussions between citizens and their representatives as no representatives had used the message board.[33] It is also worth noting that, of the 84 county councillors listed at the time, six did not give an email address.[34] This would appear to be a personal choice because generative email addresses (i.e. John.Doe@cumbriacc.gov.uk) were available for every councillor and Internet access was provided at Cumbria's County Hall. Obviously, this is a human rather than technological problem. It partially limits the democratic usefulness of the site and shows that there is considerable difficulty in achieving the 'ideal' of citizen–representative communication through discussion boards. Though there appeared to be demand from citizens for these services, the lack of usage by councillors suggested that they were not all receptive to this form of communication. Nevertheless, even without citizen–representative communication, the forum was still used. Owing to the comparatively high level of responses from moderators, much democratic good – be it pushing people in the direction of requested information or to debates about specific issues – was achieved.

Suffolk County Council

Let us now look at the second case study – Suffolk County Council and its Graffiti Wall. Suffolk County Council has initiated a number of schemes in recent years to encourage citizen participation.[35] The council believes that 'democracy is made healthier and stronger' by 'involving people in all aspects of our work' and that this should be 'a cornerstone of the county council's approach to delivering high quality services'.[36] The council claims that it will try to listen to people's views on what services are needed and how these services should be provided; that it will allow people to express opinions; and that it will be involved in monitoring the quality of services.[37] Furthermore, responses will be fed back to citizens wherever possible.

A strong (but not sole) emphasis was placed on the potential for encouraging interaction and communication with citizens through the council's website. This was based on findings from the council's Citizen Panel. In 2002, Suffolk was found to have a greater degree of Internet penetration (a total of 64 per cent) than the national average and that some 37 per cent of residents were interested in participating in online consultations.[38] Furthermore, a not insignificant number of the panel suggested that they were likely to use the Internet to communicate with the council. For example, 54 per cent said they were likely to use the Internet to find out about public services; 34 per cent to enquire about or change personal details; and 22 per cent to make transactions.[39] However, only 4 per cent said their main way of being kept informed about public services was over the Internet, with 7 per cent suggesting this will be the main way in the future. However, some 16 per cent said they used the Internet as their main source if they needed *more* information, with 24 per cent saying this will be their main source of more information in the future. If the drive toward Internet-based communication is to be successful, the Suffolk County Citizen Panel results suggest that more work needs to be done to make people aware that the website exists: only 20 per cent of respondents had heard of the county council website and only 9 per cent had visited it.[40] Although in their infancy, the policy mechanisms and overall standpoint of Suffolk County Council in relation to electronic democracy are worth analysing in detail.

Suffolkcc.gov.uk

The Suffolk County Council website was redesigned in October 2002 to make it more user-friendly and to meet corporate goals on increasing access to council facilities. Chris Kitchener, Corporate Information Manager for Suffolk County Council, also cited a number of other factors for the redesign, such as image; a progressively minded council; a desire to not lose marks for their website during corporate performance assessment; and that county councillors were keen to see the site improved.[41] The old website mapped the structure of the council itself, with information following departmental structures. This meant that users had to understand the logic and structure of the council to find the desired information. The new site was designed internally and related information was posted across departmental boundaries to make it easier for users to find the information they wanted. However, Kitchener was keen to stress that the site was information-led rather than technology-led. The biggest design constraints were money and the need to fit work into existing schedules.

Graffiti Wall

The Graffiti Wall was launched on 23 June 2001 as part of a national initiative by the County Council Network to give children a means to express their views on council policy making. The council does not own the Graffiti Wall concept.[42] This meant that the council could not redesign the Graffiti Wall when it modernised the broader website. However, the council had no plans to change the format and merely extended the initial goal to include the broader populace. The Graffiti Wall was subsequently intended to be 'a free thinking place' where people could 'express themselves' and was not necessarily results-driven, according to Kitchener.[43] This matched one of the initial aims cited above, and registration was not required in order to increase access.[44] Moreover, the freedom complemented the structured format of the 'Have Your Say' consultation section and it was suggested that the two facilities could be used jointly.[45]

A second reason for not having threads was that the council felt this would be simpler for people to use. Kitchener was 'quite anxious that we keep something that is very simple to use and people can let off steam or make comments without having any knowledge of how to use a forum'.[46] In practice, she thought that 'it seems to be used for anything that is topical, which is very good. There have been a lot of comments about the firemen's strike and feelings have run very high at certain points. [. . .] It is a discussion forum that might not be available anywhere else.'[47] This suggests that it did meet its aims. However, on the downside, the open structure facilitated some problems of abuse, and inflammatory posts about US citizens and Microsoft were removed.

The Graffiti Wall was an un-moderated message board, except for 'obscene, illegal and unacceptable messages'.[48] Although no promise was made on the web page about such input having an effect on decisions, civil servants did take the time to respond to posts. In fact, the Communications Unit read each message on a daily basis, picked off the ones it felt needed a reply, and sent them to the relevant directorate for response. Of course, receiving a response does not automatically mean that posts are affecting policy, though Kitchener felt that the Graffiti Wall did influence decision making. There was one example in which posts did lead to a change, and that was on the layout of the message board itself. One person made a series of complaints about how the brick background of the board made reading posts very difficult, and this was changed.

As of midnight on 20 February 2002, there were 1,615 posts.[49] The 'discussions' were a mixture of both youth and adult comments and questions.[50] There were many people who regularly posted on the site and a significant number of these were non-Suffolk residents. It is particularly interesting to note that civil servants regularly participated in the debates and answered questions – to much praise.[51] There were, however, a minority of people who argued strongly (if somewhat confusingly) against the site. 'Smiley', for example, stated that: 'i have decided that this is a waisted opportunity 4 everyone like me and you wrecked by the makers of this pittyfull site'.[52] 'Lok', in Ipswich, provided more serious criticism: 'This site is dead. If you aren't getting at least one hit a day then this is a wasted resource. Oh, I forgot – this is Suffolk Council, the home of wasted resources. Keep it then, just up everyones Council Tax again and that'll cover it. Good old council.'[53]

While it could be argued that political persuasions were at play here, the degree of usage, or increasingly lack thereof, has significant implications for the initiative's 'success'. An analysis of the period between 1 January and 20 February 2002 can examine these claims in more detail. While the findings from this period cannot be said to be representative of the whole message board, they nevertheless provide an interesting insight into how much, and exactly how, the message board was used. In this period, there were only 19 posts, including one repeated post and one apparently aborted post, leaving 17 'proper' posts. Of these, five were about the message board itself (or part of a discussion about this); six were related to road safety issues – of which two were responses from the council;[54] three were related to enquiries about the existence of a cycle route map on the website; two were a combination of these discussions; and one was apparently from a professor of juridical and countable sciences in Buenos Aires who wanted council memorabilia to add to his collection. By responding to people's comments and enquiries, Suffolk County Council was fulfilling its desire to increase communication between itself and the public. However, there appeared to be very little policy-related debate occurring – and this was dominated by a small group of people.[55] Instead, the board operated more as a service through which people could get their questions answered.

But is this a problem? The Graffiti Wall was designed, after all, for any citizen to openly express anything they wanted to, and for this to be available to anyone who wished to access it. In this sense, it was designed to be more of a sounding board than a discussion forum. With such an open aim, it appears that the best measure is not so much what is being debated, but how much, as people were encouraged to post on any subject. To determine this, the ratio of new posts to responses was measured. In this same period, there were 15 replies (some were replies to posts that pre-dated the period under examination), with only three posts starting new subjects. Analysed in this way it is clear that significant interaction was occurring, even if on a small scale. Secondly, and as has already been shown, this interaction took place between citizens and civil servants as well as among citizens themselves. It is arguable that such 'debate' was largely irrelevant and did not affect decision making. However, the Graffiti Wall was designed to meet its aim as a free and open space for comments, and not necessarily to promote discussion in the same way as the Cumbria County Council discussion board. Thus, it can be argued, at least in this small study, that the design of the message board succeeded in meeting its aims. It is open to question whether these aims were correct, and whether such a forum was the best way to attain them.

The council believed that, overall, the Graffiti Wall had received 'a good response with some very lively feedback' and for this reason they did not see the need to promote it.[56] However, the number of messages left on the Graffiti Wall has continued to decline (in the context of the high usage levels generated during the school initiative).[57] This suggests that once such a project is initiated it cannot be allowed to rest; local governments must continue to promote these activities if such sites are to remain active. One possible mechanism for encouraging use is by linking these services in with public information points in libraries, schools and similar institutions. In Suffolk, there is potential for this, as three electronic on-street information kiosks have been installed in Ipswich, Bury St Edmunds and Lowestoft.[58] This 'aftercare' is an often-misunderstood yet crucial ingredient for the success of electronic democracy.

To suggest that there was a lack of commitment from Suffolk County Council in using the Internet to expand public participation would be harsh. Civil servants did respond to the posts made by citizens – no matter how few or how trivial the enquiries. Of course, the lack of usage may have actually encouraged civil servants to interact, as they did not fear being swamped by a deluge of enquiries. Nevertheless, the commitment seemed to be there. The problem was an apparent lack of commitment to the site from ordinary citizens, showing that apathy persists online. There was no apparent major issue that might have encouraged people to participate, such as the impact of the foot-and-mouth crisis on the more rural Cumbria. In fact, the majority of posts were made by school children effectively 'forced' to have their say during lesson time. This suggests that, if opportunities are made available for citizens to participate, design can affect the nature of discussions. However, design of and by itself does not guarantee participation.

Conclusions

There is a complex range of factors that influence whether people will participate, and the form in which they will choose to do so. The necessary prerequisites are institutionally provided opportunities for participation and a reasonable level of social capital. Lowndes and Wilson are right to suggest that the relationship between them is two-way: institutional design can influence the development of social capital. It has been argued here that design also works on a micro level at the interface between government and citizen. The analysis has suggested that the design of the web-based discussion forums did influence the nature of the subsequent debate, which is widely considered to be important (Fishkin, 1991, 1992, 1995). It is by these criteria that online discussion is often judged (Wilhelm, 2000: 87). However, little or no emphasis has been placed on how such deliberative 'ideals' can be designed into the structure of online discussion boards to improve the quality of the debate. This is necessary if discussion boards are to successfully meet the goals of theoreticians or policy makers. Wilhelm is right, however, to note that improved designs, by themselves, will not automatically increase the volume of participation because, although this may reduce the costs of involvement, 'it does not get to the heart of what motivates citizens to move from the state of disengagement to one of salutary involvement in civic life' (Wilhelm, 2000: 87). Motivation was shown to be particularly important by the increased usage during the foot-and-mouth crisis. These are timely reminders that design is but one factor at play in the question of why and how people participate – though one which must not be underestimated.

Notes

1 Best Value Performance Indicator (BVPI) 157 was drawn up by central government and measures the percentage of types of interaction that are enabled for electronic delivery out of the total that could be delivered electronically. However, as electronic can mean telephone, email and even face-to-face contact, the extent to which councils meet this target through more experimental Internet-based facilities is left open.

2 See also Margaret Levi's (1996) wide-ranging critique of Putnam's work, but particularly that she notes how 'Policy performance can be a source of trust, not just a result' and that, although Putnam realises that government can be a source of social capital in *Bowling Alone*, he does not account for this in *Making Democracy Work*.

3 There is still relatively little written on how the interface affects usage from a social science perspective. For a brief discussion of interfaces, see part two of Negroponte (1996).

4 Fishkin's basic argument is that there are three necessary conditions for a fully functioning democracy. First is deliberation, i.e. the chance for considered reflection over time, tempered by the need to come to a decision. Second is political equality, by which Fishkin means an institutionalised system that gives equal consideration to people's preferences and which gives everyone approximately equal opportunities to formulate preferences. The third condition is non-tyranny whereby decisions that cause severe deprivation for the minority are avoided. In face-to-face deliberation, three further conditions are important: political messages of substance exchanged at length; the opportunity to reflect on messages; and interactive exchanges and the testing of rival arguments.

5 Similarly, Wilhelm (2000: 97) found that only 15.5 per cent of messages replied; that 27.9 per cent sought information from others; and that 67.8 per cent validated their arguments in some way.

6 Some Usenet forums are moderated by human intervention. However, the most common form of moderation is computerised 'kill-bots'. This refers to software that automatically moderates the content of messages against pre-set criteria. For example, they can analyse for repetitiousness both within and across forums as well as for the use of swear words (Leug and Fisher, 2003).

7 http://www.scottish.parliament.uk/nmCentre/news/news–99/pa0032.htm

8 The competition was run by the Institute for Public Policy Research in association with the Design Council, the Commission for Architecture and the Built Environment and the *Architects' Journal*: http://www.designsondemocracy.org.uk/resources/StageOneBrief.pdf.

9 http://www.designsondemocracy.org.uk/resources/StageOneBrief.pdf

10 On a technical level, websites can be owned by either outsourced website developers, by one centralised IT department or by individual departments. The ownership can affect the content of websites because both funds and cultural factors shape what is, and is not, offered.

11 For a complete list with explanations of the services provided see: http://www2.tagish.co.uk/clients. It is also interesting to note that Tagish have worked for a variety of other political and government websites such as the European Commission, Norwich City Council, yougov.com, the Cabinet Office and the Central IT Office.

12 http://www.tagish.co.uk/isite2.htm

13 http://www.tagish.co.uk/NonStopGov/

14 This survey of 34 county councils was undertaken from 13 March to 15 March 2002.

15 http://www.swiftinteractive.com/white1.asp

16 Foot-and-mouth is a highly contagious virus spread between animals and, though not necessarily fatal for them, causes severe economic disruption to farmers, as all infected animals have to be culled. To try to limit the spread of the disease, a number of restrictions were put in place, including footpath and road closures around infected areas.

17 http://www.cumbria.gov.uk/forum/modnotes.html

18 http://www.cumbriacc.gov.uk/forum/legal.html

19 http://www.cumbria.gov.uk/forum/modnotes.html

20 Email from Kevin Paulisse, co-creator and owner of DiscusWare. Reply received 28 May 2003.
21 Email from Paulisse.
22 Email from Paulisse.
23 This figure only includes posts made by moderators who used their titles. They may have posted using other titles when adding their own input into discussions in an unofficial capacity.
24 Figures from Kevin Maxwell, Business Manager, Infrastructure and Development, Corporate Information Systems.
25 No direct evidence was found of the website being advertised or highlighted in local or national media. There was a link to the discussion forum on the home page, but this pre-dated the foot-and-mouth crisis.
26 http://www.cumbriacc.gov.uk/forum/messages/96/120.html?998989310, 'Old Hutton', Wednesday 18 July 2001.
27 Post by Roger, Leeds, Wednesday 18 July 2001, 10 a.m., http://www.cumbriacc. gov.uk/forum/messages/96/120.html?998989310. This post has since been removed.
28 See http://www.cumbria.gov.uk/forum/register.html. The stated advantages included a personal email address; the ability to create user profiles; the ability to post bigger messages and attachments; notification when new posts were made to topics of interest; simplified identification measures for posting messages; and that certain forums created by moderators were only open to registered members.
29 Data from Maxwell.
30 One potential advantage of registering, outside of the physical advantages the site gave to members, is that it can help create a sense of community.
31 Data and analysis/opinion from Maxwell.
32 Analysis conducted: 21 August 2002, 2 p.m.
33 As of 4 p.m. on 20 August 2002. To find this statistic, each councillor's surname was run through the site's search engine as well as other key words such as 'councillor'. It is possible that councillors posted under different names, but, if this were the case and they were not obviously councillors, this really negates the idea that people could hold discussions with their councillors. One post was made from a 'Councillor Denis Graham' from Wigton on 10 October 2001, but there were no records of a Councillor Graham.
34 Records from Cumbria County Council website at 4.19 p.m., 20 August 2002.
35 These included telephone surveys, face-to-face surveys, postal surveys, citizen panels, stakeholder surveys, the distribution of door-to-door publications, community workshops, providing opportunities for participation through the website, discussion forums, public meetings, conferences, exhibitions, distributing comment /compliment/complaint sheets, direct contact through councillors and holding Best Value Reviews. See *Policy and Performance Plan 2002/2003: Listening to You, Learning From You*, Suffolk: Suffolk County Council, for more details.
36 *Policy and Performance Plan 2002/2003*, p. 3.
37 *Policy and Performance Plan 2002/2003*, p. 4.
38 *Policy and Performance Plan 2002/2003*, pp. 12, 17.
39 *Policy and Performance Plan 2002/2003*, p. 13.
40 http://www.suffolkcc.gov.uk/documents/Consultation_and_Feedback/Suffolk_ Speaks_Final_report.doc
41 Interview with Chris Kitchener, Corporate Information Manager, Suffolk County Council, 15 September 2002.
42 http://www.suffolkcc.gov.uk/consultation/graffiti/report.pdf
43 Interview with Kitchener.
44 This can be interpreted as either highly democratic (anonymity) or undemocratic (potential for subversion). It did lead to some problems as users could create false identities. In fact, one respondent claimed to be the moderator and admonished

someone for his or her use of language and then another 'moderator' admonished the 'moderator'. The point is: how can we know if either was really a moderator?

45 Interview with Kitchener.

46 Interview with Kitchener.

47 Interview with Kitchener.

48 http://www.suffolkcc.gov.uk/consultation/graffiti/index.html. No attempt was made to define unacceptable, obscene or illegal – or how this was determined. However, as the Graffiti Wall encouraged children to have their say, and as postings suggested that they were making use of the opportunity, it would perhaps be expected for the moderator to take a strong line on such issues.

49 The system for displaying posts was quite confusing. It started with the most recent posts and worked backwards. This was confusing because the last five posts from the previous page were carried forward. Thus, when people clicked for the 'next 15 posts' they were greeted by the five posts they had just read. Furthermore, this meant that there were actually 20 posts on each page rather than the 15 stated. This was done to achieve continuity in discussion from page to page. However, there was no facility to pick out a particular page in the archive, so people had to search through the records.

50 See the debate about the A14 corridor raised by GO (31 December 2001 and before) as an example of adult discussions and a rap posted by 'The Orwell Crew' about what the council could do for them (2 November 2001).

51 See, for example, a response from GO in Suffolk referring to surprise that the 'grey suits' had taken the time to respond to an earlier question (31 December 2001, 11.29 a.m.).

52 28 November 2001, 2.48 p.m. Original spelling and grammar.

53 27 November 2001, 9.36 a.m. Original spelling and grammar.

54 It would appear that more posts were from council employees but that they did not always identify themselves as such. For example, 'Andrew from Suffolk' was apparently responsible for changing the design of the site – and if this was the case (it could of course be a hoax) we could expect him to be employed by the council.

55 Eleven separate people posted in total. Of these, two made three posts and two made two each.

56 Interview with Kitchener.

57 Since this research was conducted, usage levels have remained low. Between 1 January 2004 and 29 September 2004, the forum received just 44 messages. This figure includes a number of repeated posts, aborted posts and a message from one person in Suffolk, New York.

58 This was part of the Pathfinder project. It was intended that the kiosks would promote joined-up government, and they have been funded through the Local Transport Plan. The kiosks allowed people to send free emails, check the weather and even pay their television licence fee.

References

6, P., Seltzer, K., Leat, D. and Stoker, G. (2002) *Toward Holistic Governance: The New Agenda in Government Reform*, Basingstoke: Palgrave.

Abramson, J. (1988) *The Electronic Commonwealth: The Impact of New Media Technologies on Democratic Politics*, New York: Basic Books.

Beetham, D. (ed.) (2002) *Democracy under Blair: A Democratic Audit of the United Kingdom*, London: Politico's Publishing.

Blair, T. (1996) *New Britain: My Vision of a Young Country*, London: Fourth Estate.

Davis, R. (1999) *The Web of American Politics: The Internet's Impact on the American Political System*, Oxford: Oxford University Press.

Fishkin, J. (1991) *Democracy and Deliberation: New Directions for Democratic Reform*, New Haven, CT: Yale University Press.

Fishkin, J. (1992) 'Beyond Teledemocracy: "America on the Line" ', *Responsive Community*, 2 (3): 13–19.

Fishkin, J. (1995) *The Voice of the People: Public Opinion and Democracy*, New Haven, CT: Yale University Press.

Goodin, R. (1996) *The Theory of Institutional Design*, Cambridge: Cambridge University Press.

Hill, K. and Hughes, J. (1998) *Cyberpolitics: Citizen Activism in the Age of the Internet*, Oxford: Rowman & Littlefield.

Keane, J. (2000) 'Structural Transformations of the Public Sphere', in Hacker, K. and van Dijk, J. (eds), *Digital Democracy: Issues of Theory and Practice*, London: Sage.

Kearns, I., Bend, J. and Stern, B. (2002) *E-participation in Local Government*, London: Institute for Public Policy Research.

Leug, C. and Fisher, D. (eds) (2003) *From Usenet to CoWebs: Interacting with Social Information Spaces*, London: Springer.

Levi, M. (1996) 'Social and Unsocial Capital: A Review Essay of Robert Putnam's *Making Democracy Work*', *Politics and Society* 24 (1): 45–55.

Lowndes, V. and Wilson, D. (2001) 'Social Capital and Local Governance: Exploring the Institutional Design Variable', *Political Studies* 49 (4): 629–647.

Lowndes, V., Pratchett, L. and Stoker, G. (2001) 'Trends in Public Participation: Part 2 – Citizens' Perspectives', *Public Administration* 79 (2): 445–455.

McMillan, S.J. (2000) 'The Microscope and the Moving Target: The Challenge of Applying Content Analysis to the World Wide Web', *Journal of Mass Media and Communication Quarterly* 77 (1): 80–98.

Mulgan, G. and Adonis, A. (1997) 'Back to Greece: The Scope for Direct Democracy', in Mulgan, G. (ed.), *Life after Politics: New Thinking for the Twenty-First Century*, London: Fontana Press.

Negroponte, N. (1996) *Being Digital*, London: Hodder & Stoughton.

Newton, K. (1999) 'Social Capital and Democracy in Modern Europe', in van Deth, J., Maraffi, M., Whiteley, P. and Keman, H. (eds), *Social Capital and European Democracy*, London: Routledge.

Parry, G., Moyser, G. and Day, N. (1992) *Political Participation and Democracy in Britain*, Cambridge: Cambridge University Press.

Pratchett, L. and Leach, S. (2004) 'Local Government: Choice within Constraint', *Parliamentary Affairs* 57 (2): 366–379.

Putnam, R. (1993) *Making Democracy Work*, Princeton, NJ: Princeton University Press.

Putnam, R. (2001) *Bowling Alone: The Collapse and Revival of American Community*, London: Simon & Schuster.

Sassi, S. (2001) 'The Transformation of the Public Sphere? The Internet as a New Medium of Civic Engagement', in Axford, B. and Huggins, R. (eds), *New Media and Politics*, London: Sage.

Schneider, S. (1997) 'Expanding the Public Sphere through Computer-Mediated Communication: Political Discussion about Abortion in a Usenet Newsgroup', Ph.D. thesis, Massachusetts Institute of Technology, Boston, MA. Online. Available http://www.sunyit.edu/~steve/main.pdf.

Tsagarousianou, R. (1998) 'Electronic Democracy and the Public Sphere: Opportunities and Challenges', in Tsagarousianou, R., Tambini, D. and Bryan, C. (eds), *Cyberdemocracy: Technology, Cities and Networks*, London: Routledge.

Wilhelm, A. (2000) *Democracy in the Digital Age: Challenges to Political Life in Cyberspace*, London: Routledge.

Wright, S. (2002) 'Dogma or Dialogue? The Politics of the Downing Street Website', *Politics* 22 (3): 135–142.

Websites:

http://www.cumbriacc.gov.uk/
http://www.designsondemocracy.org.uk/resources/StageOneBrief.pdf
http://www.suffolkcc.gov.uk/
http://www.sunyit.edu/~steve/main.pdf
http://www.swiftinteractive.com/white1.asp
http://www.tagish.co.uk/

Interviews and email correspondence

Kitchener, C., Corporate Information Manager, Suffolk County Council, 15 September 2002.

Maxwell, K., Business Manager, Infrastructure and Development, Corporate Information Systems, Cumbria County Council. Email reply received 12 August 2002.

Paulisse, K., Co-creator and owner of DiscusWare. Email reply received 28 May 2003.

6 Cybercortical warfare

Hizbollah's Internet strategy

Maura Conway

The acceleration of the historical tempo and the move from hierarchical to networked conceptions of power are disintegrating the mechanisms of control and political representation at the disposal of the state. The upshot of this is that 'resistance confronts domination, empowerment reacts against powerlessness, and alternative projects challenge the logic embedded in the new global order' (Castells, 1997: 69). These reactions and mobilisations, often take 'unusual formats and proceed through unexpected ways' (Castells, 1997: 69). This chapter deals with one such alternative project. It is a preliminary empirical analysis of the adoption by the Lebanese-based terrorist group Hizbollah (Party of God)[1] of a strategy of cybercortical warfare. In his introduction to the Vintage edition of *Covering Islam* (1997), Edward Said refers to the 'information wars that have gone on since 1948 around the whole question of the Middle East' (p. xxi). He is particularly concerned with the way in which Hizbollah 'who identify themselves and are perceived locally as resistance fighters' are 'commonly referred to in the American media as terrorists' (p. xiii). Hizbollah are one of a number of groups that have utilised the Internet 'to produce and articulate a conscious and forceful self-image' (Said, 1997: 66) of themselves not as terrorists, but as resistance fighters and statesmen.

The major focus of this chapter is the way in which Hizbollah have wielded the Internet as a weapon in their information war. As will be demonstrated, the group's collection of websites is targeted not at Lebanese or Palestinian audiences, but at the Israeli population and global publics. For this reason, the chapter represents a case study of the possibilities of the new technology, discussed and defined by this chapter as 'cybercortical warfare'.

Szafranski's neocortical warfare

Neocortical warfare 'attaches more importance to communicating with other minds than to targeting objects' (Szafranski, 1997: 396). It points to the reframing of conflict as warfare against minds and envisions its weapons as any means used to change the enemy's will (Szafranski, 1997: 404). It is founded on the belief that at base politics is the pursuit and eventual exercise of power, and that 'power' is 'the ability to influence people who otherwise might not choose to be influenced' (p. 397). The concept of neocortical warfare originated with Richard Szafranski in his article entitled 'Neocortical Warfare: The Acme of Skill?', which first appeared in 1994 in the *Military Review*, a publication of the US Army Command and General Staff College. Szafranski quoted Sun Tzu to the effect that 'To subdue the enemy without fighting is the acme of skill' (p. 399).

Neocortical warfare may be conceived of as a species of Perception Management, which is generally held to include the disciplines of Public Affairs, Public Diplomacy, Psychological Operations, Deception and Covert Action (Dearth, 2002: 1). Perception Management may be defined as:

> Actions to convey and/or deny selected information and indicators to foreign audiences to influence their emotions, motives and objective reasoning; and to intelligence systems and leaders at all levels to influence official estimates, ultimately resulting in foreign behaviors and official actions favorable to the originator's objectives.
>
> (Dearth, 2002: 2)

This chapter is concerned more with the conveyance of information than its denial, and focuses on its effects upon foreign publics rather than intelligence systems and leaders. Its focus is therefore Public Diplomacy, rather than the other disciplines that compose Perception Management. The practice of Public Diplomacy has undergone significant change as a result of the information revolution.

The new Public Diplomacy

Diplomacy has traditionally been thought of as the development and implementation of foreign policy by diplomats. However, states and their representatives are no longer the only actors in diplomatic relations. There is an increasing emphasis on the role of non-state actors and publics in diplomacy, not only as recipients of diplomacy – the traditional understanding of 'public diplomacy' as a government's process of communicating with the public of another nation in order to influence its opinion – but also as diplomatic actors. Put simply, the public dimension of diplomacy has been increasing in importance. While there was a time when diplomats were the sole interlocutors between countries, now unmediated dialogue and information exchange between citizens from around the globe occurs 24 hours a day, seven days a week. The theory and conduct of diplomacy is undergoing a radical rethink as a result. There have been repeated calls for diplomacy to be 'reinvented' to take account of the information revolution and a welter of analyses published suggesting how this might be accomplished (Vickers, 2001). This chapter is concerned with just such a reinvention, albeit a reinvention outside the purview of a majority of the research undertaken to date.

In the past, Public Diplomacy was often seen as irrelevant and unimportant. However, there is a growing movement to give Public Diplomacy a greater prominence in the conduct and study of international relations. This interest follows from an emergent view that the practice of world politics is changing; that things are being done in a new way; that new actors are important. Rather than a realist world composed purely of states acting militarily to maximise their power positions, this consensus points to a world in which international politics can be thought of in terms of an 'informational pluralism'. On the one hand this is a world with a variety of agents at work, but where the operation of this pluralism is shaped by the impact of the information or communications revolution. These processes can be summarised in the idea that we are seeing the development of a 'new Public Diplomacy'. This idea has a double meaning: firstly, that we are seeing diplomacy – understood in the broad sense as the practice of international relations – taking place in public and the public being involved; and secondly, that the central instrument of this new diplomacy is actually Public Diplomacy, that is communication and communications technologies (Brown, 2001a; White, 2001: 317–330).

Soft Power

Brown (2001a) suggests that the new Public Diplomacy entails a change in the nature of power, but it also helps us to understand how power is utilised in international affairs. The most widely discussed alternative conceptualisation is the idea of Soft Power developed by Joseph Nye. Nye first put forward his thesis in *Bound to Lead* (1990), but has returned to the idea on several occasions, most notably in two contributions to the journal *Foreign Affairs*. In 1996, in an article with William Owens, Nye defined Soft Power as 'the ability to achieve desired outcomes in international affairs through attraction rather than coercion' (Nye and Owens, 1996: 21). In a 1998 article with Robert Keohane, Nye returned to this theme to draw a distinction between free information (such as scientific data, advertising, political propaganda), commercial information (information that is sold) and strategic information (information that is useful because it is possessed by one actor, but not others). They argue that:

> Politically . . . the most important shift has concerned free information. The ability to disseminate free information increases the potential for persuasion in world politics. NGOs [non-governmental organisations] and states can more readily influence the beliefs of people in other jurisdictions. . . . Soft power and free information can, if sufficiently persuasive, change perceptions of self-interest and thereby alter how hard power and strategic information are used.
>
> (Keohane and Nye, 1998: 89–92)

As Brown has pointed out, one major consequence of this new environment is the importance of credibility as a source of power (Brown, 2001b: 11).

Although there have been many guerrilla groups fighting as oppressed national minorities, only five groups have had the credibility that allowed them to become significant diplomatic actors in the last two decades. In the mid-1970s, the Palestinian Liberation Organization (PLO) and South West African People's Organization (SWAPO) achieved membership of the Non-Aligned Movement and the Group of 77, along with observer status in the United Nations General Assembly and at all UN conferences. Three other groups – the African National Congress, the Pan-African Congress, and the Patriotic Front of Zimbabwe – obtained the right to attend UN conferences (Willetts, 2001: 368). However, world politics today transcends simple international relations and intergovernmental organisation, and much of the change has taken place as a result of the spread of information infrastructures. Diplomacy is no longer the sole province of states and their representatives. Instead, the Internet offers the opportunity for non-state actors and marginalised groups to engage in what has been called 'virtual diplomacy' (Smith, 2000) or 'cyber-diplomacy' (Potter, 2002), essentially the practice of Public Diplomacy via the Internet.

Cybercortical warfare

'Neocortical warfare is warfare that strives to control or shape the behavior of enemy organisms, but without destroying the organisms' (Szafranski, 1997: 404); it 'uses language, images and information to assault the mind, hurt morale and change the will' (Szafranski, 1997: 407). In other words, neocortical warfare is the conduct of Public Diplomacy in an explicit conflict situation. 'Cybercortical warfare' is therefore an apposite term to describe the conduct of Public Diplomacy *via the Internet* in the same situation. In the broadest sense, cybercortical warfare is about offensively shaping the information environment, particularly the 'conflict space' (Dearth, 2002: 8). To do this successfully, one must possess credible political and military power in order to command attention and convincingly project information power. In the realm of Public Diplomacy, for example, all Arab states have launched their own websites and many have several such sites. These sites are designed to get information about their countries out to the rest of the world, and to counter or balance information provided on the web by Israel, Iran and other states (Franda, 2002: 81). States are not the only actors to establish a presence on the Internet, however. Worldwide, recent years have seen more and more groups that are engaged in militancy and political violence – the representatives of 'uncivil society', if you like – establish an online presence. A comprehensive list of all such sites, both official and unofficial, is maintained by an individual in the United States and is available online.[2] An overview of the background to and purpose of these sites is provided below.

Terrorism and mass communication

In their study of terrorism and the media, *Violence as Communication*, Alex Schmid and Janny De Graaf point out that:

> Before technology made possible the amplification and multiplication of speech, the maximum number of people that could be reached simultaneously was determined by the range of the human voice and was around 20,000 people. In the nineteenth century, within one lifetime, the size of an audience was expanded twenty-five to fifty times. In 1839 the *New York Sun* published a record 39,000 copies; in 1896, on the occasion of President McKinley's election, two U.S. papers, belonging to Pulitzer and Hearst, for the first time printed a million copies. William McKinley paid dearly for this publicity. In 1901 he was killed by an anarchist, Leon Czolgosz, who explained his deed with the words: 'For a man should not claim so much attention, while others receive none.'
>
> (Schmid and De Graaf, 1982: 10)

Historically, access to the communication structure was intimately related to power (Crelinsten, 1987: 443). With the growth of the press, and later television, a situation arose that gave unequal chances of expression to different people. This connection between power and free expression was summed up by A.J. Liebling who observed that 'Freedom of the press is limited to those who own one' (quoted in Schmid and De Graaf, 1982: 177).

Terrorism has always been about communication. In fact, scholars argue that 'without communication there can be no terrorism' (Schmid and De Graaf, 1982: 9). Each new advancement in communication technology has resulted in new opportunities for terrorists to publicise their positions, from Marxist revolutionaries such as Brazil's Carlos Marighela's advice to his comrades to use photocopying machines to produce large numbers of pamphlets and manifestos to Hizbollah's establishment of its Al Manar television station in the early 1990s. While seeking to convey a message through their 'propaganda of the deed', terrorists also must employ written and spoken language in an effort to legitimise, rationalise and, ultimately, advertise their actions. Now, thanks to the new communications technologies, particularly the Internet, for the first time terrorists are equal communication partners in the electronic agora.

In the space of 30 years, the Internet has metamorphosed from a US Department of Defense command-and-control network consisting of fewer than 100 computers to a network that crosses the globe. Today, the Internet is made up of tens of thousands of nodes (i.e. linkage points) with over 105 million hosts spanning more than 200 countries. With a current estimated population of regular users of just under 1 billion people, the Internet has become a near-ubiquitous presence in many world regions (Clickz Stats, 2004). That ubiquity is due in large part to the release in 1991 of the World

Wide Web. In 1993 the web consisted of a mere 130 sites; by 2004 it boasted more than 1 billion (Dunnigan, 2003: 37).

Media have for decades been attributed with considerable significance in processes of cultural and political transformation. The Internet is daily heralded as a new media technology of enormous and increasing significance; it is the first many-to-many communication system and the instrument of a political power shift. The ability to communicate words, images and sounds, which underlies the power to persuade, inform, witness, debate and discuss (not to mention the power to slander, propagandise, engage in misinformation and/or disinformation, etc.), is no longer the sole province of those who own or control printing presses, radio stations or television networks. Every machine connected to the Internet, from laptop computers to mobile phones, is potentially a printing press, a broadcasting station, a place of assembly. And in the twenty-first century, terrorists are availing themselves of this opportunity to connect.

It is the unmediated nature of the Internet, in conjunction with high levels of connectivity, which renders it a communications medium unlike any other. There is a tendency in newspapers and on television for the primary sources of political information to be those who represent authority or who are members of the existing power structure. The British scholar Stuart Hall distinguishes between these 'primary definers' (politicians, police spokesmen, government officials) and what he calls 'secondary definers' (political or social activists, 'reformers', terrorists) who reside outside of the existing power structure. The latter are used much less frequently by the media than are primary definers, according to Hall (Crelinsten, 1987: 420). So while modern terrorists can manipulate the media into devoting newsprint and airtime to their activities, political claims and demands, the media in turn manipulate the terrorists: 'The insurgent terrorist messages are transported to the public mainly by the media and the message is thereby almost invariably abbreviated, distorted or even transformed' (Schmid and De Graaf, 1982: 110). Journalists and TV presenters achieve this by playing up the violent spectacle at the expense of analysis, in order to attract consumers, thus undermining the terrorists' claim to legitimacy by depicting them as merely violent, often irrational and even psychotic, and not political (Crelinsten, 1987: 421). With the advent of the Internet, however, the same groups can disseminate their information undiluted by the media and untouched by government censors. In 1998 it was reported that 12 of the 30 terrorist organisations identified by the US State Department had their own websites. Today, a majority of the 36 groups on the same list maintain an official online presence (see Conway, 2002: Table 1).

The state of the research on the Internet and terrorism

In 1979 Nathan Leites recognised that, although much work of a varied nature had been undertaken on what terrorists do and a smaller amount on what makes them do it, very little research considered 'what they thought they were doing' or more precisely 'what good they thought it would do' (Cordes, 1988: 151). Since then, large amounts of research have been devoted to describing and analysing what terrorists have done in the past and to identifying trends in order to gauge what they might do in the future. However, much less attention has been focused upon terrorist motivations, mindsets or self-perceptions. Leites' analysis is therefore as relevant today as it was more than two decades ago, which is surprising given the easily accessible primary materials provided by modern terrorists (in the form of their websites) from which much information can be gleaned. These websites, however, have not yet been the subject of any sustained academic investigation. A majority of the research and analysis pertaining to the Internet and websites as political tools has focused on the power of transnational advocacy groups, such as Greenpeace, Amnesty International and other civil society actors, and their ability to harness the power of international communications technologies to forward their goals (Bennett, 2003; Cleaver, 1998; Couldry and Curran, 2003; Van De Donk *et al.*, 2003; Hajnal, 2002; Kahney, 2003; Leizerov, 2000; Lin and Dutton, 2003). Much less attention has been paid to those groups that compose 'uncivil society', particularly terrorist groups. This may be due to a number of factors, including the difficulty associated with fitting groups that employ violence into the various frameworks devised to categorise social movements, and a certain 'feel-good factor' that imbues the work of scholars concerned with issues of transnationalism, international advocacy, etc.

An alternative reason why the academic community has essentially ignored websites maintained by terrorist organisations may be that scholars doubt the efficacy of the Internet as a political tool. Walter Laqueur, a respected figure in terrorism studies, made the following observation in 1999 (p. 262):

> No amount of e-mail sent from the Baka Valley to Tel Aviv, from Kurdistan to Turkey, from the Jaffna peninsula to Colombo, or from India to Pakistan will have the slightest political effect. Nor can one envisage how in these conditions virtual power will translate into real power.

This statement is particularly startling when one considers that a few lines previously Laqueur admits that audiocassettes smuggled into Iran played a key role in the Khomeini revolution. In more recent times, numerous civil society actors have conducted successful campaigns via the Internet that have had significant political effects. For example, email was credited with halting a US banking plan aimed at combating money laundering. The Nobel Prize-winning International Campaign to Ban Landmines, which successfully lobbied for a treaty stopping the use, production, stockpiling and transfer of anti-personnel mines, coordinated its activities via the net. The website MoveOn.org, best known today for its efforts to mobilise opponents of both George W. Bush and the Iraq war, has attracted over 2 million subscribers to join its email list and has instituted a US television advertising campaign paid for by online donations. In each case 'virtual' or 'soft' power was translated into 'real' power, whether financial, legal or otherwise. It is the ability of such 'soft' power to bring about 'real' effects that is the subject of the remainder of this chapter, which describes Hizbollah's strategy of cybercortical warfare and analyses its effects.

Hizbollah: some background information

Hizbollah[3] has been described as 'one of the most significant terrorist organisations operating today' (Whittaker, 2001: 41). The US government has maintained a list of foreign terrorist organisations since October 1997 when former US Secretary of State Madeline Albright approved the designation of the first 30 groups under the Immigration and Nationality Act (as amended by the Antiterrorism and Effective Death Penalty Act 1996). Hizbollah appeared on the original list and has remained on it to the present time. Groups officially designated as foreign terrorist organisations by the US Secretary of State (in consultation with the Attorney General and the Secretary of the Treasury) are subject to a number of legal restrictions. It is unlawful, for example, for a person in the United States or subject to the jurisdiction of the United States to provide any kind of financial or material support to such organisations. Both representatives and members of these groups may be denied visas or excluded from the United States, and US financial institutions must block the funds of these groups and report the blockage to the Office of Foreign Assets Control of the US Department of the Treasury.

Hizbollah was established in 1982 in response to the Israeli invasion of Lebanon. The group is composed of radical Shias and takes its ideological inspiration from the Iranian revolution and the teachings of the Ayatollah Khomeini. The Majlis al-Shura, or Consultative Council, is the group's highest governing body and is presided over by Secretary General Hassan Nasrallah. Hizbollah advocates the establishment of Islamic rule in Lebanon and the liberation of all occupied Arab lands, including Jerusalem. It has expressed as a goal the elimination of Israel (Saad-Ghorayeb, 2002: 134–167). The group refused to work within Lebanon's established political system until 1992, when it fielded candidates in parliamentary elections (Palmer Harik, 2004: 95–110). Although closely allied with and often directed by Iran, the group is thought to have conducted operations that were not approved by the Iranian leadership. While Hizbollah does not share the Syrian regime's secular orientation, the group has been a strong tactical ally in helping Syria advance its political objectives in the region (see Palmer Harik, 2004: 29–41). In addition to political, diplomatic and organisational aid, Hizbollah receives substantial amounts of money, training, weapons and explosives from both Iran and Syria (US Department of State, 2003).

The group has thousands of supporters, but only a few hundred terrorist operatives. These operate in the Bekaa Valley, the southern suburbs of Beirut, and southern Lebanon. According to US experts, the group also has established cells in Europe, Africa, South America, North America and Asia, and is suspected to have been involved in numerous anti-US terrorist attacks, including the suicide truck bombings of the US Embassy in Beirut in April 1983, the US Marine barracks in Beirut in October 1983 and the US Embassy annexe in Beirut in September 1984. Three members of Hizbollah are on the FBI's list of 'Most Wanted Terrorists' for the hijacking in 1985 of TWA Flight 847 during which a US Navy diver was murdered. Elements of the group were responsible for the kidnapping and detention of US and other Western hostages in Lebanon in the 1980s (see Jaber, 1997: 97–144; Ranstorp, 1997). The group also attacked the Israeli Embassy in Argentina in 1992 and is a suspect in the 1994 bombing of an Israeli cultural centre in Buenos Aires (US Department of State, 2003; Saad-Ghorayeb, 2002: 88–111).

Hizbollah was among the few groups that President Bush mentioned by name in his January 2002 State of the Union address:

> Our military has put the terror training camps of Afghanistan out of business, yet camps still exist in at least a dozen countries. A terrorist underworld – including groups like Hamas, Hezbollah, Islamic Jihad, Jaish-i-Mohammed – operates in remote jungles and deserts, and hides in the centers of large cities.
>
> (Bush, 2002a)

Bush also condemned the group as terrorists in his June 2002 speech on the Middle East:

> I've said in the past that nations are either with us or against us in the war on terror. To be counted on the side of peace, nations must act. Every leader actually committed to peace will end incitement to violence in official media and publicly denounce homicide bombings. Every nation actually committed to peace will stop the flow of money, equipment and recruits to terrorist groups seeking the destruction of Israel, including Hamas, Islamic Jihad and Hezbollah.
>
> (Bush, 2002b)

Hizbollah's cyber capabilities

The issue of Hizbollah's cyber capabilities was discussed as early as 1996. In that year, John Deutch, former director of the US Central Intelligence Agency, testified before a Senate committee that international terrorist groups had the capability to attack the critical information infrastructure of the United States. Deutch said the methods used could range from such traditional terrorist methods as a vehicle-delivered bomb – such as one directed against a telephone switching centre or other communications node – to electronic attacks relying on paid computer hackers. He identified Hizbollah as one of a number of terrorist groups who used the Internet for their communications and might therefore have both the inclination and the ability to launch such an attack (Deutch, 1996).

More recently, a CIA report to the US Senate Intelligence Committee identified a number of terrorist organisations, Hizbollah among them, that 'have both the intentions and the desire to develop some of the cyberskills necessary to forge an effective cyberattack modus operandi' (McCullagh, 2002). There is ample evidence confirming that 'terrorists who fight modernity and its perceived evils in the name of defending traditional values and religious principles do not shy away from enlisting advanced technology for their holy wars or secular fights to enforce their agendas' (Nacos, 2002: 108). For example, the leadership of Hizbollah wear traditional dress and adhere to Islamic custom in the way they live their daily lives and in their preaching. But like other similar fundamentalist and anti-modern groups, they rely heavily on the predominantly younger members of their organisation that are trained in modern communication technologies. Members of Hizbollah and other terrorist groups are known to be computer-literate. There is evidence that they compose training manuals on their laptop computers, distribute them on CD-ROMs or transmit their files via email to trusted operatives (Whine, 1999: 236). This chapter is concerned neither with the ability nor the desire of Hizbollah to carry out a cyber attack on the United States, which is a matter for further research. Rather, this chapter seeks to describe and analyse the effect of the group's strategy of cybercortical warfare, carried out via its collection of websites, on the citizens of Israel and Western publics more generally.

Hizbollah's Internet strategy

The websites

Autonomous communication is a paramount objective for Hizbollah. The group first went online in early 1996. The Central Press Office site, or Hizbollah.org, is the group's official home page, and is available in both English and Arabic. Hizbollah maintains at least three other sites of an official character (all of which are available in both English and Arabic versions): http://www.moqawama.tv, known as the 'Islamic Resistance Support Association' and which describes the group's attacks on Israeli targets; http://www.manartv.com, the news and information site that is essentially the home page of Hizbollah's Al Manar Television; and http://www.nasrollah.net, the official home page of the group's leader Sayyed Hassan Nasrollah (and available in French). The sites are said to receive between 1,000 and 3,000 hits per day.

The Hizbollah websites are reasonably well designed. In recent times, both Nasrollah's personal home page and the Al Manar TV site have been redesigned to a fairly high standard. Although the Central Press Office and Moqawama sites are the group's flagship sites in their campaign of cybercortical warfare, they are beginning to look slightly dated. Both sites are, however, densely packed with information. The top English-language page of the Central Press Office site provides links to sections entitled 'In the Press', 'Statements of the Resistance', 'Political Declarations', 'Speeches of the Secretary General' and others. The site contains an extensive photographic archive, sound recordings (in Arabic only) and over 100 video clips for viewing or download. The latter are divided into four categories: 'Aggressions', 'Operations', 'Intifada' and 'Miscellaneous'. The top English-language page of the Moqawama site provides links to sections entitled 'Reality', 'Background', 'Features', 'Views in Zionism', 'Cartoons' and 'Readers Letters', amongst others. The sections entitled 'Military Operations', 'Martyrs' and 'Israeli Aggressions' are updated on an almost daily basis. The 'Military Operations' section, for example, provides a day-to-day accounting of Hizbollah operations from 1997 to the present, while the section entitled 'Israeli Aggressions' contains hundreds of pages – over 700,000 words – detailing what appears to be every perceived act of Israeli aggression against the Lebanese since 1998. The Moqawama site also contains a gallery of photographs of dead 'martyrs' numbering over 150. The Al Manar TV site, designed in grey and gold, contains information about the station's programming, and extensive television footage drawn from the same. The Secretary General's home page contains a biography of Nasrollah, updated news, an archive of speeches and interviews, a photographic archive and more. There is a 'Contributions' button located on the top page of the Moqawama site, but this is not operational. A request for financial contributions was at one time included on the Al Manar TV site and was accompanied by an account number for a bank in Beirut, Lebanon. However, all such requests for contributions now appear to have been deleted from Hizbollah's English-language websites. None of the Hizbollah sites offer items for sale.

A study published in November 1997, over a year after the establishment of the Hizbollah sites, found that the total number of Internet users in the Arab world (excluding Israel) as of July 1997 was 215,500. Of a population of over 3.5 million people, there were just 35,520 Internet users in Lebanon (Nua, 1997).[4] Hizbollah maintained their sites in both Arabic and English from the outset, despite the low number of Internet users in the whole of the Middle East and the fact that a 1998 study found that Arabic sites with Arabic text received many more visitors from within the Arab world than Arabic sites with English text (Nua, 1998). Further, Pippa Norris has shown that in societies where the online population is not large there is minimal incentive for groups to develop websites, and the lack of infrastructure hinders their development (Norris, 2001). This indicates that Hizbollah were interested in targeting a non-Lebanese and non-Middle Eastern audience from the outset. Their targeted audiences were the citizens of Israel and English-speaking publics more generally.

In March 1997, an article in Beirut's *Al-Safir* newspaper drew attention to the 'psychological warfare' being employed by Hizbollah. The article is devoted to describing Hizbollah's Al Manar television station's website, which is depicted as Hizbollah's corrective to the Israelis' mis-education of Western publics:

> Psychological warfare can be used as a weapon of war to be added to the military materiel, not only to repulse the aggression, but also to confront the enemy's deceptive policy toward the world public. Although this war has many faces, it has one head only, namely the media . . . Hizballah's step is primarily aimed at refuting the fallacies Israel has been spreading abroad concerning the occupation of south Lebanon.[5]
>
> (FBIS, 1997)

The report goes on to say that the site managers regularly receive emails from Internet surfers 'some of which salute the resistance and others request information on the Lebanese–Israeli conflict' (FBIS, 1997). In addition, it is reported that some of the subscribers to the site's email list – 'who began to show sympathy with the resistance when the Qana massacre occurred' (FBIS, 1997) – transmit the information they receive across other networks and lists thus spreading these messages further than would otherwise be the case. Finally, the article also explains that Al Manar employees view Internet access as a useful educational resource due to the availability of reports and analyses produced by the Israeli Foreign Ministry and other agencies, which allow Hizbollah members to become familiar with the methods by which governments demonise terrorist organisations and thus educate the former as to how to carry out a counter-campaign. A number of employees were also said to be taking training courses via the net (FBIS, 1997).

In a September 2001 interview, Hassan Ezzieddine, the head of Hizbollah's Department of Media Relations, confirmed:

> We feel that the media can be effective in creating a special climate in public opinion on the main issues of interest. . . . We are heading toward a new sensitive security situation (in the region) which means we need to follow events very closely so that we can informatively help shape international and Arab public opinion. . . . We believe that the media has an important role in the conflict, as important as the military wing.
>
> (Blanford, 2001)

To underscore the importance of the media's role in the conflict, Hizbollah's leadership decided in 2001 to place Al Manar TV under the direct supervision of a committee composed of senior figures in the organisation and chaired by the group's secretary general, Sayyed Hassan Nasrollah. The Central Information Office, which had liaised with the press and published Hizbollah's weekly newspaper *Al-Ahed*, was abolished and replaced by the new Department of Media Relations. Ezzieddine, a member of Hizbollah's political council, was put in charge. Ezzieddine and his staff reportedly examine newspaper articles dealing with Hizbollah and follow television and radio broadcasts. The new department is also responsible for maintaining the group's official websites, which are currently in the process of a major overhaul.

Tsfati and Weimann (2002) have pointed out that almost all terrorist groups that maintain an online presence avoid presenting and detailing their violent activities: 'Although the organizations behind these sites have a record of bloodshed, they hardly ever record these activities on their sites' (p. 321). The exceptions, they point out, are Hizbollah and Hamas. Hizbollah's site contains a section ('Daily Operations') that provides updated statistical reports of its actions that 'display in minute detail all of the organization's operational successes' (p. 321). A separate page enumerates the number of dead 'martyrs' along with the number of 'Israeli enemies' and 'collaborators' killed. This is part of Hizbollah's campaign of cybercortical warfare:

> Hizbollah differs somewhat from other organizations in that it highlights its military achievements, gloating over enemy victims (showing pictures of funerals of murdered Israelis), and publishing detailed statistics about its military successes. The motive for this unique approach has been Hizbollah's attempt to influence the public debate in Israel about withdrawal from Lebanon. The organization has stated explicitly that its aim has been to exert pressure in Israel in favor of withdrawal. The organization knows that many Israelis visit the site, whose address is published in Israeli media. Hizbollah publishes its records of murdered Israelis, maintains electronic connections with Israelis, and appeals to Israeli parents whose sons serve in the Israeli army, all with the aim of causing demoralization.
>
> (Tsfati and Weimann, 2002: 325)

Cybercortical warfare: the effects

Josef Goebbels, Hitler's Minister of Propaganda, once said: 'We do not talk to say something, but to obtain a certain effect' (Schmid and De Graaf, 1982: 14). Terrorism entails the use of violence for effect, 'speaking with action' rather than words. The meaning of terrorist acts is not always clear, however. An integral part of most terrorist activity, therefore, is the explanation later provided in written and oral forms (Cordes, 1988: 164). There is an added dimension to cybercortical warfare, however. The object of the strategy adopted by Hizbollah was to understand the adversary well enough to condition or determine the choices it made: 'Using the adversary's lexicon, syntax and representational systems allows the neocortical warrior to lead the adversary through the cycle of observation, orientation, decision and action. Mastery is the result' (Szafranski, 1997: 408).

Hizbollah has succeeded in entering the homes of Israelis via the Internet, thus creating an important psychological breakthrough (see Tsfati and Weimann, 2002: 317). The group accomplished this goal in 1999 when it provided details on its website about the return of the bodies of Israeli marine commandos who had fallen in Lebanon. Hizbollah stated that the single coffin returned contained not just a single body, but the body parts of a number of the marines. The statement caused uproar among the families of the deceased and resulted in a bitter confrontation between the latter and the Israeli Defense Force (IDF) authorities. Hizbollah also has published appeals to the parents of Israeli soldiers stationed in Lebanon on their sites. A prominent example was the publication of an interview, originally aired in Israel, with four mothers of IDF soldiers entitled 'I Don't Want My Son to Die in Lebanon'. Many Israelis, particularly parents of soldiers serving in Lebanon, admit visiting the Hizbollah site to get news updates. 'I regard these sites as a legitimate source of information,' one Israeli father is reported to have said. According to Tsfati and Weimann (2002: 327), 'the Hizbollah site even offers to answer anyone who sends questions by email, and does indeed reply to Israeli questioners, sending information and news to their email addresses'.

There is no doubt that Hizbollah's leadership would also like to gain access to Western, particularly American, audiences via the Internet. It is difficult to gauge how successful they have been in this respect. They appear to have met with relatively little success in targeting the American public, despite the fact that, 'given the absence of censorship and the private ownership of most public media and the fact that "violence is as American as apple pie," the United States seems to be the country most open to terrorist uses of the media' (Schmid and De Graaf, 1982: 33). A Hizbollah spokesman was recently quoted as saying: 'The service is very important for the morale of our resistance fighters. They are always happy to know that people around the world are backing them' (Whine, 1999: 233). Considerably more evidence than this is required, however, before the group's campaign of cybercortical warfare is deemed successful outside of their immediate region.

Conclusions

Terrorists are not limiting themselves to the traditional means of communication; they increasingly employ the new media to pursue their goals. The terrorists of today, like those of yesteryear, are keen to exploit the traditional mass media while also recognising the value of more direct communication channels. As has been pointed out, 'if what matters is openness in the marketplace of ideas ... then the Web delivers an equal opportunity soapbox' (Norris, 2001: 172). As far back as 1982, Schmid and De Graaf acceded that:

> If terrorists want to send a message, they should be offered the opportunity to do so without them having to bomb and kill. Words are cheaper than lives. The public will not be instilled with terror if they see a terrorist

speak; they are afraid if they see his victims and not himself. . . . If the
terrorists believe that they have a case, they will be eager to present it to
the public. Democratic societies should not be afraid of this.

(Schmid and De Graaf, 1982: 170)

Keen to exploit the Internet, by 2004 a majority of the 36 organisations
that appear on the US list of Designated Foreign Terrorist Organizations
had established an online presence. These include not only Hizbollah,
but Aum Shinrikyo, the Tamil Tigers, Basque Fatherland and Liberty
(ETA), Lashkar-e-Tayyiba, the Kurdistan Workers Party (PKK) and
others.

The leadership of Hizbollah realised early on that establishing a meaningful virtual power base was reliant on a functioning and effective web presence.
In a recent report for the United States Institute of Peace entitled *www.
terror.net: How Modern Terrorism Uses the Internet* (2004), Gabriel Weimann
highlights the advantages offered by the Internet to terrorists: ease of access;
the ability to evade regulation, censorship and other forms of government
control; potentially huge audiences with a global spread; anonymous intra-
group communication; rapid transfer of information; inexpensive development and maintenance of websites; a multimedia environment; and the
ability to shape coverage in the traditional mass media, which increasingly
use the web as a source for reporting (p. 3). For terrorists, therefore, web-
based communication offers the potential to be a more immediate, dynamic,
in-depth, interactive and unedited process than was ever possible in conventional media. It was this realisation, along with the institution of an
extremely skilful and effective information strategy, which has ensured that
Hizbollah has been able to use the web as an additional tool for its political
aims. However, it remains to be seen whether it will be able to parlay its 'local'
success into the ability to influence international opinion in a meaningful way
with the tools of the web.

Notes

1 The 'correct' English spelling of the group's Arabic name is Hizb'Allah or
   Hizbu'llah. However, it is more usually spelled 'Hizbollah', 'Hizballah' or
   'Hezbollah'. I have chosen 'Hizbollah' because that is the spelling employed in the
   URL designating the group's official home page. However, where I have employed
   quotation, I have retained the original spelling used by the author.
2 Bob Cromwell's 'Separatist, Para-Military, Military, and Political Organisations'
   is available online at http://www.cromwell-intl.com/security/netusers.html.
3 According to the US Department of State, the group is also known as Islamic
   Jihad, Revolutionary Justice Organization, Organization of the Oppressed on
   Earth, and Islamic Jihad for the Liberation of Palestine. It is also known to refer
   to itself as the Islamic Resistance Movement.
4 The study's findings were based on actual subscription numbers to ISPs. It has
   since been shown that the average number of users per Internet account in most
   Arab countries is three. See Nua Internet Surveys (2001) 'Arab Net Population

Passes 3.5 Million'. The latter is available online at http://www.nua.com/surveys/
index.cgi?f=VSandart_id=905356603andrel=true.
5 For an alternative position on Al Manar TV, see Jorisch (2004).

References

Bennett, W.L. (2003) 'Communicating Global Activism: Strengths and Vulnerabilities
of Networked Politics', *Information, Communication and Society* 6 (2): 143–168.
Blanford, N. (2001) 'Hizbullah Steps Up Psychological Warfare: Party Believes
that the Media Plays Critical Role in Palestinian Uprising', *Daily Star* (Beirut),
8 September. Online. Available http://www.hizbollah.org/english/press/p2001/
p20010908a.htm.
Brown, R. (2001a) 'The New Public Diplomacy: Power in the Age of Mixed Media',
Paper presented at the 4th Pan-European International Relations Conference,
Canterbury, United Kingdom.
Brown, R. (2001b) 'Power and the New Public Diplomacy', Paper presented at
the British International Studies Association annual conference, University of
Edinburgh, United Kingdom.
Bush, G.W. (2002a) *State of the Union Address*, Washington, DC: White House.
Online. Available http://www.law.ou.edu/hist/state2002.shtml.
Bush, G.W. (2002b) 'Text of President Bush's Address on the Middle East', *Washington
Post*, 25 June.
Castells, M. (1997) *The Power of Identity*, Oxford: Blackwell.
Cleaver, H.M. (1998) 'The Zapatista Effect: The Internet and the Rise of an Alternative
Political Fabric', *Journal of International Affairs* 51 (2): 621–640.
Clickz Stats Staff (2004) 'Population Explosion!', *Clickz.com*, 10 May. Online. Avail-
able http://www.clickz.com/stats/big_picture/geographics/article.php/5911_151151.
Conway, M. (2002) 'Reality Bytes: Cyberterrorism and Terrorist "Use" of the Inter-
net', *First Monday* 7 (11). Online. Available http://www.firstmonday.org/issues/
issue7_11/conway/index.html.
Cordes, B. (1988) 'When Terrorists Do the Talking: Reflections on Terrorist
Literature', in Rapoport, D.C. (ed.), *Inside Terrorist Organizations*, London: Frank
Cass.
Couldry, N. and Curran, J. (2003) *Contesting Media Power*, New York: Rowman &
Littlefield.
Crelinsten, R.D. (1987) 'Power and Meaning: Terrorism as a Struggle over Access
to the Communication Structure', in Wilkinson, P. and Stewart, A.M. (eds),
Contemporary Research on Terrorism, Aberdeen: Aberdeen University Press.
Dearth, D.H. (2002) 'Shaping the "Information Space" ', *Journal of Information
Warfare* 1 (3): 1–15.
Deutch, J. (1996) *Statement before the U.S. Senate Governmental Affairs Committee*
(Permanent Subcommittee on Investigations), 25 June. Online. Available http://
www.nswc.navy.mil/ISSEC/Docs/Ref/InTheNews/fullciatext.html.
Dunnigan, J. (2003) *The Next War Zone*, New York: Citadel Press.
Foreign Broadcast Information Service (FBIS) (1997) 'Hizballah's al-Manar TV on
Internet', FBIS-NES-97-043, 3 March.
Franda, M. (2002) *Launching into Cyberspace: Internet Development and Politics in
Five World Regions*, Boulder, CO and London: Lynne Rienner.
Hajnal, P.I. (ed.) (2002) *Civil Society in the Information Age*, Aldershot: Ashgate.

Jaber, H. (1997) *Hezbollah: Born with a Vengeance*, New York: Columbia University Press.

Jorisch, A. (2004) *Beacon of Hatred: Inside Hizballah's Al-Manar Television*, Washington, DC: Washington Institute for Near East Policy.

Kahney, L. (2003) 'Internet Stokes Anti-War Movement', *Wired*, 21 January. Online. Available http://www.wired.com/news/culture/0,1284,57310,00.html?tw=wn_story_related.

Keohane, R.O. and Nye, Jr, J.S. (1998) 'Power and Interdependence in the Information Age', *Foreign Affairs* 77 (5): 81–95.

Laqueur, W. (1999) *The New Terrorism: Fanaticism and the Arms of Mass Destruction*, Oxford: Oxford University Press.

Leizerov, S. (2000) 'Privacy Advocacy Groups versus Intel: A Case Study of How Social Movements Are Tactically Using the Internet to Fight Corporations', *Social Science Computer Review* 18 (4): 461–483.

Lin, W. and Dutton, W.H. (2003) 'The "Net" Effect in Politics: The "Stop the Overlay" Campaign in Los Angeles', *Party Politics* 9 (1): 124–136.

McCullagh, D. (2002) 'CIA Warns of Net Terror Threat', *C|Net*, 29 October. Online. Available http://news.com.com/2100–1023–963771.html?tag=cd_mh.

Nacos, Brigitte (2002) *Mass-mediated Terrorism: The Central Role of the Media in Terrorism and Counterterrorism*, New York: Rowman & Littlefield.

Norris, P. (2001) *Digital Divide: Civic Engagement, Information Poverty, and the Internet Worldwide*, Cambridge: Cambridge University Press.

Nua Internet Surveys (1997) 'Middle East Internet Usage'. Online. Available http://www.nua.com/surveys/index.cgi?f=VSandart_id=878906966andrel=true.

Nua Internet Surveys (1998) 'Internet Usage in the Arab World'. Online. Available http://www.nua.com/surveys/index.cgi?f=VSandart_id=888945819andrel=true.

Nye, J.S. (1990) *Bound to Lead: The Changing Nature of American Power*, New York: Basic Books.

Nye, J.S. and Owens, W.A. (1996) 'America's Information Edge', *Foreign Affairs* 75 (2): 20–37.

Palmer Harik, J. (2004) *Hezbollah: The Changing Face of Terrorism*, London: I.B. Tauris.

Potter, E.H. (ed.) (2002) *Cyber-Diplomacy*, Montreal, Quebec: McGill-Queens University Press.

Ranstorp, M. (1997) *Hizb'Allah in Lebanon: The Politics of the Western Hostage Crisis*, London: Macmillan.

Saad-Ghorayeb, A. (2002) *Hizbu'llah: Politics and Religion*, London: Pluto Press.

Said, E. (1997 [1981]) *Covering Islam*, London: Vintage.

Schmid, A.P. and De Graaf, J. (1982) *Violence as Communication*, Minneapolis, MN: University of Minnesota Press.

Smith, G.S. (2000) 'Reinventing Diplomacy: A Virtual Necessity', *United States Institute of Peace: Virtual Diplomacy Report* (VDS6), February. Online. Available http://www.usip.org/vdi/vdr/gsmithISA99.html.

Szafranski, R. (1997 [1994]) 'Neocortical Warfare: The Acme of Skill?', in Arquilla, J. and Ronfeldt, D. (eds), *In Athena's Camp: Preparing for Conflict in the Information Age*, Santa Monica, CA: Rand Corporation. Online. Available http://www.rand.org/publications/MR/MR880.

Tsfati, Y. and Weimann, G. (2002) 'www.terrorism.com: Terror on the Internet', *Studies in Conflict and Terrorism* 25 (5): 317–332.

United States Department of State (2003) *Patterns of Global Terrorism 2001*, Washington, DC: Department of State. Online. Available http://www.state.gov/s/ct/rls/pgtrpt/2003/.

Van De Donk, W., Loader, B., Dixon, P. and Rucht, D. (eds) (2003) *Cyberprotest: New Media, Citizens, and Social Movements*, London: Routledge.

Vickers, R. (2001) 'The New Public Diplomacy in Britain and Canada', Paper presented at the British International Studies Association annual conference, Edinburgh, United Kingdom.

Weimann, G. (2004) *www.terror.net: How Modern Terrorism Uses the Internet*, Washington, DC: United States Institute of Peace. Online. Available http://www.usip.org/pubs/specialreports/sr116.html.

Whine, M. (1999) 'Cyberspace: A New Medium for Communication, Command, and Control by Extremists', *Studies in Conflict and Terrorism* 22: 231–245.

White, B. (2001) 'Diplomacy', in Baylis, J. and Smith, S. (eds), *The Globalisation of World Politics*, 2nd edn, Oxford: Oxford University Press.

Whittaker, D.J. (2001) 'Lebanon', in Whittaker, D.J. (ed.), *The Terrorism Reader*, London: Routledge.

Willetts, P. (2001) 'Transnational Actors and International Organizations in Global Politics', in Baylis, J. and Smith, S. (eds), *The Globalization of World Politics*, 2nd edn, Oxford: Oxford University Press.

7 Civil society, the Internet and terrorism

Case studies from Northern Ireland

Paul Reilly

The rapid penetration of information and communication technologies in advanced industrialised societies has created new opportunities and dangers for governments and civil society. Civil society can be defined as the 'space of uncoerced human association and also the set of relational networks formed for the sake of family, faith, interest and ideology that fill this space' (Walzer, 1995: 7). The Internet can bestow a degree of organisational coherence upon those groups outside the political establishment. These groups are often unable to orchestrate a campaign of political protest using the conventional mass media, which typically reflect the interests of larger sections of civil society. Terrorism can be defined as violence used to articulate a political message. Contemporary terrorists use the Internet like marginalised elements of 'civil' society to communicate with sympathetic diasporas, disseminate propaganda and issue statements unfettered by the ideological refractions of the mass media. This chapter will argue that terrorist utility of the Internet has two dimensions. Terrorists will use the Internet to communicate 'overtly' like other civil society actors. They will use websites to increase organisational coherence and to expound their political ideologies. Terrorist organisations may also use the Internet for 'covert communication'. They will use information and communications technologies to plan and perpetrate acts of terror. This chapter analyses several websites linked to Northern Irish terrorist organisations, to gauge whether websites related to political actors deemed 'uncivil' by many will vary significantly in form from other societal groups using the web. The study suggests that websites relating to terrorist groups not only do not differ markedly from those of 'civil' groups, but also do not seem to offer any new dimension of terrorist threat.

Cyberoptimism vs. cyberpessimism

There are three main conceptions of the relationship between civil society and information and communications technologies. The 'cyberoptimist' model argues that computer-mediated communication (often referred to as CMC in the literature) will facilitate forms of communication, interaction and organisation that undermine unequal status and power relations (Spears and Lea, 1994: 428). On the Internet, social context will be reduced in or around a message transmitted from sender to receiver (p. 431). The main beneficiaries of the reduction of social context in communication transactions would be nation-states in the developing world. The Internet can provide a degree of 'organisational coherence' to these political actors who ordinarily are incapable of 'punching above their weight' in the international community. Governments could use the databases to aid the more equitable distribution of resources in economically deprived regions. Information and communication technologies also could facilitate more sophisticated methods of democracy within advanced industrialised states. Low electoral turnouts could be partially remedied by the utility of electronic voting systems similar to the 'teledemocracy' piloted in California in the 1980s (Barber, 1984: 275). 'Dialogic' democracy, in which citizens debate political issues with those who hold diametrically opposing views, could be facilitated by electronic bulletin boards. Giddens asserts that in an ethnically divided society such as Northern Ireland, the creation of a public arena could help resolve controversial issues and constrain violence (Giddens, 1995: 16). Terrorist organisations often receive support from constituencies who feel that their perceived grievances are not recognised by their respective governments. The cyberoptimist model suggests that new technological innovations (such as bulletin boards and email) could allow these constituents to have their voices heard. This could potentially reduce the number of supporters – as well as future members – of terrorist organisations.

Inequalities in access to information and communication technologies militate against the cyberoptimist position and towards the cyberpessimist position. Cyberpessimists assert that the Internet will reinforce the gap between rich and poor as well as between activists and the disengaged (Norris, 2001: 12). Statistics from the Organization for Economic Cooperation and Development (OECD) reflect the dominance of the First World in terms of Internet usage. An estimated 54.3 per cent of Americans use the Internet regularly compared to a mere 0.4 per cent of the population in Saharan Africa (Manrique, 2002: 7). This First World hegemony is reflected in the predominance of English as the vernacular of cyberspace. This suggests that the so-called 'fourth generation rights' are being denied to developing countries in which English is not the common tongue. These rights include the right to information and the right to communicate (Council of Europe, 1997: 39). The indigenous mass media facilitate the exercise of these rights more effectively than the Internet in developing countries. The Internet has not levelled the playing field for global political actors. However, Norris asserts that the Internet retains the potential to amplify the voice of 'less resourced insurgents and challengers' (2001: 239).

The prospects for dialogic democracy using information and communications technologies would appear slim. Electronic bulletin boards devoted to political themes fail to promote deliberative political debate. People choose to post to groups that contain others with similar political ideologies to their own. This is illustrated by a survey of political Usenet groups in which only 9.3 per cent of leaders posted messages to ideologically dissonant groups (Hill and Hughes, 1997: 13). People cannot be compelled to use the Internet to increase their comprehension of complex political issues. Political activity online remains a minority interest in the shadow of popular pursuits such as entertainment and sport. Both cybersceptics and cyberpessimists project that the Internet will alter inequalities of political power and wealth. The cyber-sceptic viewpoint is perhaps the most apposite conception of how information and communications technologies have altered power relations within nation-states. Norris (2001) asserts that the potential of the Internet has not yet had a dramatic impact on the realities of 'politics as usual' (p. 13). It is too early to assess whether information and communications technologies will have a lasting effect upon patterns of political organisation and behaviour.

How do civil society actors use the Internet?

Civil society organisations have used information and communication tech-nologies in a conservative fashion to date. Environmental non-governmental organisations (NGOs) have essentially transferred their existing methods online, treating the Internet as another media tool. For example, they have chosen not to use 'electronic civil disobedience' techniques utilised by small extremist elements such as the Electro-Hippies (Denning, 2001: 73). Websites are used for recruitment, fundraising, issuing press releases and advertising the core values of environmental NGOs. Sites such as GreenNet link pressure groups across the globe through transnational advocacy networks (Green-Net, http://www.gn.apc.org/). These umbrella sites amplify the impact of smaller like-minded NGOs that might otherwise struggle to make their voices heard in the international community (Norris, 2001: 187). It could be argued that other civil society organisations have failed to realise the potential for deliberation and protest offered by the Internet. Civil rights organisations have been slow to facilitate political debate among citizens or between citizens and the government. For example, while there were already 5 million regular African American Internet users (Lekhi, 2000: 78), civil rights organ-isations such as the National Association for the Advancement of Colored People (NAACP) did not appear to be using the mobilising potential of the Internet. Rather, the NAACP maintained 'glossy' impressive websites promoting their activities (www.naacp.org). The NAACP site epitomised the hegemony of style over substance in the constitution of most civil society websites. The site provided no facility for deliberation amongst African Americans at that time (Lekhi, 2000: 85), although the site was providing a forum for discussion on the Internet by 2005. The experience of civil society groups and political parties suggests that the Internet may not live up to the hype embodied by the cyberoptimist paradigm. Only small sub-state actors at the periphery of the political establishment have used the Internet to facili-tate genuine political deliberation in the vein of the 'dialogic democracy' espoused by Anthony Giddens (1995: 16). Less institutionalised organisations such as the Cartoon Rights Network have created opportunities for political debate and participation through bulletin boards on their websites (http://www.interplus.ro/smileclub/). The Internet can have a critical multiplier effect for civil society organisations via improvements in organisational linkage, bureaucratic efficiency and the advertisement of core values to a potentially worldwide audience. However, the Internet does not provide a critical mass for these organisations. People use the Internet as a private viewing box and therefore cannot be compelled to visit the websites of transnational advocacy networks or terrorist organisations (Noveck, 1999: 30). The Internet does not increase the life expectancy of these sub-state groups. The attention of the conventional mass media, financial resources and grassroots activism are still critical to the sustenance of civil society organisations.

The Internet, civil society and semi-authoritarian states

It is in semi-authoritarian states that the Internet has precipitated tangible political change to date. The Internet can focus the attention of the international community upon the plight of oppressed sub-state actors within semi-authoritarian regimes. Oppressed groups can communicate with the Western mass media and sympathetic solidarity networks worldwide via 'mirror' sites in foreign territories. China, with the largest population on the planet, faces enormous challenges from global expansions in information and communication technologies as they increase the speed and volume of information that elites deliver to its citizens. These economies of scale might come at a high political cost for the Chinese authorities. Increased public utility of information and communication technologies will lead to increased exposure to foreign news websites, free from the ideological dogma of the Chinese political elite. An increasing number of exile groups will be able to brief their fellow citizens with information about what is really happening within the state (Noveck, 1999: 49). China has responded to this threat by erecting electronic firewalls, which block access to websites that highlight human rights abuses by the Chinese government. Citizens who wish to access the Internet have to apply to open email and Internet accounts through Public Security Bureaus (Deibert, 2002: 148). Access might be the only method through which the state can clamp down on this so-called 'cyberdissidence'. Firewalls can be easily sidestepped using proxy servers that reconnect users to sites officially blocked by the state (Deibert, 2002: 153).

The Chiapas uprising in Mexico in 1994 exemplified the potential of the Internet as a weapon against semi-authoritarian states. A group of guerrillas staged an insurrection in opposition to Mexican government discrimination against the indigenous people of the Chiapas province (Ferdinand, 2000: 13). Support for the movement and its leader, the enigmatic 'Subcomandante' Marcos, was mobilised on newsgroups such as Chiapas95 and sympathetic Internet sites hosted by US universities. This online mobilisation led to increased international scrutiny of the Mexican government and an end to their policy of repression in the region (Ferdinand, 2000: 13). While not representing a coup d'état via cyberspace, the lessons of Chiapas for the political elites of semi-authoritarian states were clear. Sub-state political activists in semi-authoritarian states can attract a multitude of sympathisers worldwide utilising the public spaces of the Internet. At the same time, NGOs can help to expose human rights violations via the Internet and, in turn, the NGOs can lobby Western decision makers to take decisive action against oppressive states. The Internet can provide information even when repression reaches extreme levels. In Zimbabwe, NGOs such as Human Rights Watch have sustained a 'drip feed' of information to Western news agencies and governments alike despite President Robert Mugabe's decision to detain and expel Western journalists from the country.[1]

Terrorist organisations and the Internet

The dichotomy of 'civil' and 'uncivil' sub-state actors on the Internet relates to the transparency of their activities. Non-governmental organisations such as GreenNet typically use information and communication technologies in a one-dimensional 'overt' manner (GreenNet, http://www.gn.apc.prg). The group uses the Internet to facilitate communication, disseminate propaganda and recruit new members. 'Uncivil' actors such as terrorists use the Internet in a two-dimensional manner. The first dimension is identical to the functions of the websites of civil society actors. Terrorists often portray themselves on websites as oppressed civil society actors, in a similar vein to the Chiapas paradigm. They rarely make reference to their 'military' campaigns, choosing instead to focus upon their perceived grievances. Terrorist organisations have an asymmetric relationship with the traditional mass media. The media can survive without terrorism and have the power to determine which atrocity is reported. The Internet allows the terrorist rather than the editors to decide whether their activities are 'newsworthy'. Terrorist organisations can issue statements free from the ideological refraction of the mass media via the Internet. In using their own vocabulary, the terrorist can attribute a degree of legitimacy to their activities. Emotive words such as 'freedom fighter' and 'state oppression' permeate solidarity sites of organisations such as the Basque separatists Euskadi Ta Askatasuna (ETA).[2] However, people cannot be compelled to visit these websites. People who access these websites are likely to be members of the organisation itself, or sympathetic to its ideology.

The second dimension of the terrorist utility is of a covert nature. Terrorists use information and communication technologies to fund, plan and execute acts of terrorism against nation-states and their citizens. The attacks on New York and the Pentagon (11 September 2001) tragically illustrated this covert utility of the Internet. Subsequent investigations into the attacks revealed that the terrorists had used email and the Internet to coordinate and plan the hijackings (Pew Internet and American Life Project, 2001). Some terrorist groups have followed the lead of transnational corporations, organising themselves into decentralised networks. Theoretically, network-based terrorist organisations should not be defeated through decapitation as they are based around the idea of 'leaderless resistance' (Tucker, 2001: 1). Network-based groups such as Hamas are gradually replacing old hierarchical groups such as the Popular Front for the Liberation of Palestine in the Middle East. However, it should be noted that network-based terrorist organisations are not a product of the information age. The Palestinian Liberation Organization (PLO) was formed as a network of smaller Palestinian groups as early as 1964. However, the restructuring of terrorist hierarchies into networks has been facilitated by technological innovations such as email. There are other examples of covert utility of these new technologies. Bomb-making instructions can be distributed in the form of CD-ROMs to members worldwide. Intelligence can be gathered using information and communications technologies. The Ulster Loyalist Information Service has provided a secure email facility enabling sympathisers to submit information about leading Republicans or rival Loyalist factions.[3] Groups such as the Ulster Freedom Fighters in Northern Ireland have used the Internet to select potential targets. In March 2001, a message on an 'Ulster Loyalist' website urged the Limavady Ulster Freedom Fighters to go to a named bar where it claimed that members of the Provisional Irish Republican Army regularly visited.[4] Although this particular example came to the attention of the press, the scale of such covert utility of the Internet is difficult to assess. Most terrorist-related Internet sites such as Red Hand Commando carry disclaimers stating that their sites are for information purposes only (http://www.freewebs.com/red-hand/, accessed 14 June 2004). It is only when terrorist operations are foiled (or exposed in the conventional mass media) that this malevolent utility of the Internet is revealed.

Information and communication technologies provide a new medium through which the terrorist can attack the nation-state. States increasingly use information and communication technologies to store and disseminate information. These information systems as manifestations of state power are potential terrorist targets. Cyberterrorism can be defined as 'the unlawful attacks and threat of attacks on computers, networks and information stored therein when done to intimidate or coerce a government or its people in furtherance of political objectives' (Denning, 2000: 1). The Liberation Tigers of Tamil Eelam (LTTE) have used 'cyber-terror' as a means of creating a new front in their conflict with the Sri Lankan authorities. In 1996, LTTE e-bombs hit several websites of Sri Lankan diplomatic missions, creating a virtual blockade (Zanini and Edwards, 2001: 44). The paralysis of the Sri Lankan missions marked a propaganda coup for the insurgent Liberation Tigers of Tamil Eelam. The methods used by 'cyber-criminals' (hackers) and 'cyber-terrorists' (terrorists on the Internet) are similar. Both hackers and terrorists manipulate the content of popular websites to spread their names to a larger audience (Denning, 2001: 72). The website www.attrition.org

contains 'mirrors' of 'hacked' official government and corporate websites (www.attrition.org, accessed 24 October 2002). However, it should be noted that statistics from the Information Warfare Database show that such incidents are more likely to be perpetrated by hackers than terrorist organisations.[5] Sites such as the Californian Republican Assembly Caucus have been defaced by cyber-vandals. Personal messages and cartoon graphics were the most popular calling cards used by the hackers (www.attrition.org). So far, terrorists have not demonstrated that they have the necessary skills to effectively hack government sites. The difference between the terrorist and hacker is usually overlooked by nation-states. It is politically expedient for nation-states to assert that all hacking incidents are perpetrated by cyber-terrorists. Internet restrictions are less likely to be resisted if the public believes that the Internet is a haven of 'perverts and terrorists' (Moore, 1999: 42). Cyber-terrorism receives more headlines in the conventional mass media than the covert utility of email or bulletin boards by terrorist organisations.

Terrorist organisations are likely to use the Internet to supplement their existing relationships with the mass media. Acts of cyber-terrorism themselves rely upon mass media reportage to permeate democratic polities. Cybercortical warfare can be defined as 'warfare' conducted against minds or to change the will of an enemy (see Chapter 6). As Maura Conway points out, Hizbollah's 'cybercortical' campaign first came to prominence in 1999, when a story about mangled remains of slain Israelis published on a Hizbollah website caused a political row between the Israeli Defence Force and the families of several slain Israeli marines.[6] However, efforts to attract an American audience to their sites have so far proved less successful, despite the provision of an English-language facility on the three main Hizbollah websites. The existence of a website does not necessarily guarantee that more people will be exposed to the message and actions of the terrorist. The reaction of the conventional mass media to the exercise of 'hard power' (or 'big spectaculars') remains a more effective means of psychological warfare. People access the mass media in a very different fashion to the Internet. Television is a low-cost public medium available in virtually every household in advanced industrialised nations. Statistics also show that newspaper penetration in advanced industrialised nations remains high. In Northern Ireland, almost two-thirds of the adult population read at least one paper daily (Wilson, 1997: 1). Media literacy can be described as a universal good in advanced industrialised democracies. Yet, while schools teach people to read and write – skills necessary to read the media – electronically mediated transactions require a new form of media literacy. The more people use information and communication technologies, the more fluent they become (Locke, 1999: 219). Once people are literate in new information and communication technologies, they are likely to use the Internet as a private viewing box. The Internet cannot replicate either the shock value or the shared experience of real-time television images beamed live to millions of viewers.

Northern Irish terrorist organisations and the Internet

This chapter now turns to an examination of websites relating to Northern Irish terrorist organisations. The websites were selected with reference to the conclusions of the Independent Monitoring Commission Report (April 2004) and the UK Terrorism Act 2000.[7] Internet search engines geared to the British audience, including Google (www.google.co.uk) and Yahoo (www.yahoo.co.uk), were utilised to locate unofficial 'solidarity' sites. Solidarity sites were selected on the basis that they issued statements in support of or on behalf of proscribed Northern Irish terrorist organisations (see Table 7.1).

Organisational linkages

Republican organisations use the Internet effectively to communicate with local party activists and the mass media.[8] Each of the Republican groups examined provided correspondence details (including email addresses) for local activists (see Table 7.2). Members (and non-members) are invited to email departments within these organisations if they require any further information. Republican organisations also offer links to both domestic and international organisations. The Irish Republican Socialist Movement provides links to such diverse groups as the Popular Front for the Liberation of Palestine, Tupac Amaru and Jaleo.[9] Sinn Fein provides an email newsletter, the *Irish Republican Media*, via its website. This service grants the subscriber access to video and audio clips, Sinn Fein archives and exclusive interviews with the leadership (www.sinnfein.ie, accessed 10 April 2004). Subscribers also are given access to downloadable copies of the Sinn Fein newspaper *An Phoblacht/Republican News*. Similarly, the Irish Republican Socialist Movement and Republican Sinn Fein provide electronic versions of their publications, the *Starry Plough* and *Saoirse*.[10] Republican groups also use their websites to issue statements targeted at the conventional mass media. All of the Republican sites examined in this study had a 'Press Releases' section. In these sections, Republican groups post comments on local and international news stories. The Irish Republican Social Movement site issues statements on diverse issues such as the dedication of local hunger strike monuments, the Swedish–Kurdish Culture Association and statements from the proscribed Irish National Liberation Army (www.irsm.org/statements/irsp/archive, accessed 12 April 2004). Republican groups use the Internet in a similar fashion to NGOs such as GreenNet. They use their sites to create more sophisticated bureaucracies, to promote solidarity with international organisations that share similar values, and to 'drip-feed' stories to the conventional mass media.

In contrast to Republican organisations, none of the Loyalist sites surveyed provide an email newsletter (see Table 7.3). Loyalist groups do not clearly identify their leadership on their websites. Loyalist organisations do

Table 7.1 Proscribed Northern Irish terrorist organisations

Group	Political orientation	Estimated strength	Year formed	Pro/anti Good Friday Agreement	Website from organisation with closest political links	Unofficial (solidarity) website
Continuity Army Council[1]	Republican	Under 50 active members	1996	Anti	Yes (as Republican Sinn Fein)	Yes
Cumann na mBan	Republican	No data available	1914	No data available	No	No
Fianna na hEireann	Republican	Unknown	1909	Anti	Yes	No
Irish National Liberation Army	Republican	Under 50 active members	1975	Anti	Yes (as Irish Republican Socialist Movement)	Yes
Irish People's Liberation Organisation[2]	Republican	No data available	1976	No data available	No	No
Irish Republican Army (also known as PIRA)	Republican	Several hundred active members	1970	Pro	Yes (as Sinn Fein)[3]	Yes
Loyalist Volunteer Force	Loyalist	50–150 active members, 300 supporters	1996	Anti	No	Yes
Orange Volunteers	Loyalist	20 active members[4]	1998	Anti	No	Yes

Red Hand Commandos	Loyalist	No data available	1972	Pro	No	Yes
Red Hand Defenders	Loyalist	Up to 20 active members	1998	Anti	No	No
Saor Eire	Republican	No data available	1931	No data available	No	No
Ulster Defence Association/Ulster Freedom Fighters	Loyalist	Few dozen active members	1971	Pro	Yes (as Ulster Political Research Group)	Yes
Ulster Volunteer Force	Loyalist	Few dozen active members	1966	Pro	Yes (as Progressive Unionist Party)	Yes

Sources: International Policy Institute (2004); Conflict Archive on the Internet, *Loyalist and Republican Groups*.

Notes:
1 Linked to Republican Sinn Fein, Continuity IRA and, according to some sources, Real IRA.
2 The Irish People's Liberation Organisation (IPLO) announced its dissolution in October 1992 following an internal feud.
3 Sinn Fein defines itself as a political organisation distinct from the IRA. However, the 2004 Independent Monitoring Commission Report found significant overlap in the two groups.
4 Security sources believe that Red Hand Defenders and Orange Volunteers are served by the same pool of volunteers.

Table 7.2 Functions of Republican websites

Group	Website of organisation with closest political links	Justification of political violence	Press releases	Full membership available/ advertised	Donations	Email newsletter	Members-only section
Continuity Army Council	Republican Sinn Fein, www.rsf.ie	Yes	Yes	Yes	No	Yes	No
Fianna na hEireann	Fianna na hEireann, http://fianna.netfirms.com/	No	Yes	Yes	No	No	No
Irish National Liberation Army	Irish Republican Socialist Movement, www.irsm.org/	Yes	Yes	Yes	Yes	Yes	No
Irish Republican Army	Sinn Fein, www.sinnfein.ie	Yes	Yes	Yes	Yes	Yes	No

Source: Author's research.

Table 7.3 Functions of Loyalist websites

Group	Website of organisation with closest political link	Justification of political violence	Press releases	Full membership available/advertised	Donations	Email newsletter	Members-only section
Loyalist Volunteer Force	Ulster Loyalist Information Service,[1] www.ulisnet.com	Yes	Yes	Yes	Yes	No	No
Orange Volunteers	Loyalist Voice, http://free.freespeech.org/ovs/	Yes	Yes	No	Yes	No	No
Red Hand Commandos	Red Hand Commandos, http://www.freewebs.com/red-hand/[2]	Yes	No	No	No	No	No
Ulster Defence Association/Ulster Freedom Fighters	Tullycarnet Ulster Political Research Group, http://www.tullycarnetuprg.ionichost.com/	No	Yes	Yes	No	No	No
Ulster Volunteer Force	Progressive Unionist Party, www.pup-ni.org.uk	No	Yes	Yes	No	No	No

Source: Author's research.

Notes:
1 Site no longer online.
2 Site states that it is merely for information purposes and does not support the views of the Red Hand Commandos.

not identify any current members of their organisation on their websites. Contact with these organisations is strictly limited to email correspondence with the webmaster. The Progressive Unionist Party is the exception, providing email addresses for both its leader David Ervine and its Chief Electoral Officer (www.pup-ni.org.uk, accessed 15 May 2004). Loyalist organisations do use the Internet to issue statements to the mass media. The Tullycarnet Ulster Political Research Group website issues press releases on grassroots issues, such as the redevelopment of a local park (www.tullycarnetuprg. ionichost.com, accessed 10 May 2004). The Orange Volunteers issue press releases via solidarity websites such as Loyalist Voice. The links provided by Loyalist sites provide the starkest contrast with their Republican counterparts. Republican websites provide links to groups engaged in struggles of 'national liberation', Irish diasporas as well as groups who share their Marxist principles. Diasporas in the United States provide crucial financial resources that sustain Republican organisations, so it is not surprising that Loyalist sites typically provide fewer links to diasporas or international solidarity organisations. The links provided on Loyalist sites are almost exclusively groups based in the United Kingdom. Loyalist Voice, for example, links 'exclusively' to websites such as the Yorkshire Loyalists and Cumbria Loyalists (http://free.freespeech.org/ovs/, accessed 10 May 2004). In sum, Loyalist organisations appear to use the Internet less effectively for organisational linkage.

Justification of violence

The Internet allows Republican organisations to expound their core tenets and ideologies. The conventional mass media do not provide the necessary 'space' in which these groups can provide a detailed justification for campaigns involving political violence. Republican organisations broadly seek a 32-county socialist Irish republic as the solution to the Troubles, i.e. the historic conflict over British versus Irish rule for Northern Ireland. Consequently, Republican websites rarely refer to the political entity of Northern Ireland. Rather, the Irish Republican Socialist Movement refers to Northern Ireland as a 'colonial statelet' or the 'occupied six counties', denying the legitimacy of its position within the United Kingdom.[11] Republican websites depict their 'military activities' as morally justified in the context of Unionist political discrimination and British military aggression against their communities. In their 'History of the Conflict' section, Sinn Fein justifies the Provisional Irish Republican Army offensive of 1969 as a legitimate response to the 'Battle of the Bogside' in Derry, unionist 'pogroms' in Belfast and the introduction of internment without trial.[12] The implication of this version of events in 1969 is clear. Republican organisations consider themselves participants in a 'just war' on behalf of the Irish working classes against the British occupation of Ireland. Groups such as Sinn Fein and Republican Sinn Fein depict violence as legitimate when used as a last resort.[13] Eulogies for

Republican terrorists killed during the Troubles permeate the websites of Republican organisations. Republicans use their Internet sites to provide their own history of the Troubles. They use their own frames to legitimise campaigns of political violence.

Loyalist groups also use the Internet to define their political ideologies. Loyalist organisations support the British presence in Northern Ireland and swear allegiance to the British monarchy. The term 'Northern Ireland' is employed at regular intervals on all of the Loyalist websites examined for this analysis. Loyalist organisations choose instead to attack Republicans and the government of the Republic of Ireland (or the 'imperialist government of Eire') on their websites (http://www.ulisnet.com/main.htm, accessed 2 March 2003). Loyalist political violence is justified on the Internet by solidarity sites such as 'Loyalist Voice'. The genesis of groups such as the Red Hand Commandos is attributed to Republican attacks on members of the Loyalist community (http://www.freewebs.com/red-hand/, accessed 16 May 2004). Loyalist terrorist activity is defined as reactive or defensive in nature. This is very similar to the justification of Provisional Irish Republican Army violence that features on the Sinn Fein website. Loyalist political violence is not discussed or justified on the 'official' Loyalist websites. The Progressive Unionist Party website does not provide a history of the Ulster Volunteer Force or Red Hand Commandos. The Progressive Unionist Party asserts that they only provide 'political analysis' to the leadership of the Ulster Volunteer Force or the Red Hand Commandos (www.pup-ni.org.uk, accessed 15 May 2004). The Tullycarnet Ulster Political Research Group similarly does not offer any comment on current Ulster Defence Association activity. This 'ideology-lite' website instead highlights Ulster Political Research Group activities in the Tullycarnet area, such as the organisation of discos for local teenagers (www.tullycarnetuprg.ionichost.com, accessed 10 May 2004). The website does not expound on the ideology of the organisation, nor define it as 'Loyalist'.

However, the assertions of these groups on their websites are negated by the recent Independent Monitoring Commission report into paramilitary activity. The International Monitoring Commission concluded that both the Ulster Political Research Group and the Progressive Unionist Party were directly linked to the proscribed Ulster Defence Association and Ulster Volunteer Force respectively.[14] These groups thus use their websites to deliberately blur the distinction between civil and 'uncivil' society. This is achieved not just by the rhetoric these groups employ, but also by the information they do not disclose on their websites. These groups do not use their websites to illuminate their links to political violence. They use their websites to portray themselves solely as community activists and political parties.

Fundraising and recruitment

Republican organisations use the Internet in a similar fashion to NGOs in their efforts to recruit members and raise funds. Membership of these organisations is open to applicants worldwide. Only Republican Sinn Fein stipulates that applicants must live in Ireland, Wales, Scotland or England (www.rsf.ie, accessed 18 May 2004). The procedure for joining each of these Republican organisations is identical. Online application forms are provided by each Republican organisation, to be submitted by the applicant along with a current telephone number and email address. This mirrors the online recruitment section of 'civil' groups such as the National Association for the Advancement of Colored People (www.naacp.org, accessed 2 March 2003). Potential recruits to Republican organisations are advised that they will be contacted by the organisation in due course. The Irish Republican Socialist Movement and Sinn Fein also solicit donations using an online application form. The Irish Republican Socialist Movement provides bank details for people who wish to contribute to their 'Fighting Fund'.[15] Republican groups are savvy in their utility of the Internet to aid recruitment and fundraising. These sites claim that they do not solicit resources for proscribed terrorist organisations; rather the 'Fighting Fund' is to sustain the Irish Republican Socialist Movement's *Starry Plough*. People visiting these sites are asked to join political parties such as Republican Sinn Fein. They are not invited to apply to become members of proscribed terrorist organisations such as the Continuity Irish Republican Army.

Loyalist websites lack the sophistication of their Republican counterparts. These websites do not provide online application forms on their websites. Solidarity sites such as the Ulster Loyalist Information Service solicit resources from visitors to their sites. The ULISNET site requests that members donate (amongst other items) bulletproof vests, computers and Christmas gifts. The website states that the bulletproof vests are for 'obvious uses'.[16] This explicit reference to paramilitarism is the exception rather than the rule for Loyalist websites. The official Loyalist websites do not solicit resources via their websites. However, the Progressive Unionist Party and Tullycarnet Ulster Political Research Group do advertise membership on their websites. It should be noted that they do not advertise membership of proscribed paramilitary groups. Like their Republican counterparts, these organisations use their websites to recruit members to political, rather than military, organisations. The Progressive Unionist Party invites potential members to phone or email the webmaster in order to get an application form.[17] This suggests that members are still recruited on the basis of face-to-face interviews rather than over a relatively anonymous web linkage. Loyalist organisations, despite their lack of technological sophistication, use the Internet in a similar fashion to NGOs. For example, GreenNet uses similar methods of recruitment on its websites as volunteers are asked to email or telephone GreenNet if they are interested in positions advertised on the web-site.[18] Both civil and uncivil society actors are likely to favour recruitment strategies that include face-to-face interviews.

Conclusions

Organisations with historic links to terrorism use the Internet in a similar fashion to NGOs. The Internet will facilitate increased organisational coherence and communication across national borders. This analysis shows that Northern Irish organisations with historic links to paramilitary groups use similar methods of recruitment and organisational linkage to established NGOs such as GreenNet. Loyalist and Republican groups use their websites to portray themselves as legitimate members of civil society. It is the covert nature of terrorist computer-mediated communication that distinguishes it from NGOs. Terrorists use information and communication technologies to plan and perpetrate atrocities. The scale of this covert communication is extremely hard to estimate. The threat of 'cyber-terrorism' is vastly exaggerated by nation-states as a means of justifying Internet restrictions. Cyberoptimists assert that the Internet will alter power relations in favour of marginalised groups. Yet empirical evidence suggests that it is simply too early to determine how the Internet will affect power relations. A 'cyber-sceptic' approach should be employed by nation-states, when assessing the risk posed by 'cyber-terrorism' or 'cybercortical' warfare. The Internet is simply not an appropriate vehicle for compelling millions to identify with the causation and effect of political violence. Republican and Loyalist groups are likely to continue to use 'big spectaculars' as a central part of their strategy. Psychological warfare, a necessary component of ethno-nationalist terror, is effectively conducted through manipulation of the television news flash and the front pages of newspapers. The Internet will supplement the existing relationship between these groups and the mass media. As with NGOs, organisations with historic links to terrorist groups use their websites to deliver messages to their members, supporters, the media and occasionally their opponents. These messages are only placed in the public domain when they are reported by the conventional mass media. While it is possible that the Internet could increase the longevity of such outsider groups as the Provisional IRA, by improving organisational coherence and the ability to commune covertly in cyberspace, the Internet cannot replicate the shared experience of the mass media. For terrorists, activities in the offline world are more likely to dictate their ability to survive or increase their political influence. Despite the government emphasis on cyber-terrorism, there is relatively little evidence of increased terrorist threat to citizens from the web pages of organisations linked to terrorism in Northern Ireland.

Notes

1 Human Rights Watch, 'Zimbabwe', http://www.hrw.org/reports/2002/zimbabwe/ (accessed 21 February 2003).
2 Euskal Herria Journal – Navarre: A Basque Journal, http://www.contrast.org/ mirrors/ehj/ (accessed 20 June 2004).

3 Ulster Loyalist Information Service, 'Projects', www.ulisnet.com/main.htm (accessed 2 March 2003). Please note this website is now offline.

4 'New Internet Terror Fear: Loyalists Are Using Web to Pick Targets', *Belfast Telegraph*, 15 March 2001.

5 Information Warfare Database, Terrorism Research Center, http://www.terrorism.com/iwdb/incidents.asp, (accessed 2 March 2003).

6 In 1999, a story emanating from a Hizbollah website claimed that a single coffin had been returned to Israel from Lebanon containing the body parts of several murdered Israeli marines. This caused a row between IDF officials and the families of the deceased.

7 Report issued by the Independent Monitoring Commission, 20 April 2004, available at http://www.news.bbc.co.uk/hol/shared/bsp/hi/pdfs/20_04_04_imcreport.pdf (accessed 22 April 2004); UK Terrorism Act 2000, www.homeoffice.gov.uk/terrorism/threat/groups/index.html (accessed 20 June 2004).

8 Websites were examined over a period of time from 2001 to 2004; these comments relate to how the websites appeared as of 2004.

9 Links in Solidarity, www.irsm.org/general/links (12 April 2004). Please note that Tupac Amaru is linked to the Peruvian terrorist organisation MRTA. Jaleo are a group of Andalusian Socialists.

10 Saoirse Online Newsroom, www.saoirse.rr.nu (accessed 14 April 2004); Electronic Starry Plough, www.irsm.org/irsp/starryplough (accessed 12 April 2004).

11 Irish Republican Socialist Committee, 'Thirty Years of Struggle', www.irsm.org/general/history/irsm20yr.htm (accessed 12 April 2004).

12 Sinn Fein, 'History of the Conflict 1968–1992', www.sinnfein.ie (accessed 15 May 2004).

13 'What is Irish Republicanism?', Ruairi O'Bradaigh, Republican Sinn Fein, www.rsf.ie (accessed 18 May 2004).

14 Report issued by the Independent Monitoring Commission, 20 April 2004, available at http://www.news.bbc.co.uk/hol/shared/bsp/hi/pdfs/20_04_04_imcreport.pdf (accessed 22 April 2004).

15 Electronic Starry Plough, http://irsm.org/irsp/starryplough/ (accessed 12 April 2004).

16 Ulster Loyalist Information Service, http://www.ulisnet.com/main.htm (accessed 2 March 2003). Please note this website is no longer available online.

17 Tullycarnet UPRG (accessed 10 May 2004).

18 GreenNet, 'Jobs and Volunteering', www.gn.apc.org/jobs.html (accessed 2 March 2003).

References

Barber, B. (1984) *Strong Democracy: Participatory Politics for a New Age*, London: University of California Press.

Conflict Archive on the Internet (CAIN) Loyalist and Republican Groups. Online. Available http://cain.ulst.ac.uk/issues/violence/paramilitary.htm (accessed 10 June 2004).

Council of Europe (1997) *Cultural Rights, Media and Minorities*, Strasbourg: Council of Europe Press.

Deibert, R.J. (2002) 'Dark Guests and Great Firewalls: The Internet and Chinese Security Policy', *Journal of Social Studies* 58, Spring: 143–159.

Denning, D. (2000) 'Cyberterrorism, Global Dialogue'. Online. Available http://www.cs.georgetown.edu/~denning/publications.html (accessed 10 March 2003).

Denning, D. (2001) 'Cyber Warriors: Rebels, Freedom Fighters and Terrorists Turn to Cyberspace', *Harvard International Review* 23 (2), Summer: 70–75.

Ferdinand, P. (ed.) (2000) *The Internet, Democracy, and Democratization*, London: Frank Cass.

Giddens, A. (1995) 'The New Context of Politics: New Thinking for New Times', *Democratic Dialogue*. Online. Available http://www.democraticdialogue.org/publications.htm (accessed 2 March 2003).

Hill, K.A. and Hughes, J.E. (1997) 'Computer-mediated Political Communication: The USENET and Political Communities', *Political Communication* 14: 3–27.

International Monitoring Commission (2004) *International Monitoring Commission Report*, 20 April. Online. Available http://www.news.bbc.co.uk/hol/shared/bsp/hi/pdfs/20_04_04_imcreport.pdf (accessed 22 April 2004).

International Policy Institute (2004) *Terrorist Group Profiles*. Online. Available www.ict.org.il/inter_ter/orgdat (accessed 10 June 2004).

Lekhi, R. (2000) 'The Politics of African America Online', in Ferdinand, P. (ed.), *The Internet, Democracy, and Democratization*, London: Frank Cass.

Locke, T. (1999) 'Participation, Inclusion, Exclusion and Netactivism: How the Internet Invents New Forms of Democratic Community', in Hague, B.N. and Loader, B.D. (eds), *Digital Democracy Discourse and Decision Making in the Information Age*, London: Routledge.

Manrique, C.G. (2002) 'The Internet and World Politics in an Age of Terror', Paper presented at the American Political Science Association annual meeting, Boston, MA.

Moore, R.K. (1999) 'Democracy and Cyberspace', in Hague, B.N. and Loader, B.D. (eds), *Digital Democracy Discourse and Decision Making in the Information Age*, London: Routledge.

Norris, P. (2001) *Digital Divide: Civic Engagement, Information Poverty, and the Internet Worldwide*, New York: Cambridge University Press.

Noveck, B.S. (1999) 'Paradoxical Partners: Electronic Communication and Electronic Democracy', in Hague, B.N. and Loader, B.D. (eds), *Digital Democracy Discourse and Decision Making in the Information Age*, London: Routledge.

Pew Internet and American Life Project (2001) 'How Americans Used the Internet after Terror Attack', 15 September, Washington, DC: Pew Internet and American Life Project. Online. Available www.pewinternet.org (accessed 27 September 2002).

Spears, R. and Lea, M. (1994) 'Panacea or Panopticon: The Hidden Power in Computer Mediated Communication (CMC)', *Communication Research* 21 (4): 427–459.

Tucker, D. (2001) 'What's New about the New Terrorism and How Dangerous Is It?', *Terrorism and Political Violence* 13, Autumn: 1–14.

Walzer, M. (1995) *Towards a Global Civil Society, International Political Currents*, Volume 1, Oxford: Berghahn Books.

Wilson, R. (1997) 'The Media and Intrastate Conflict in Northern Ireland', *Democratic Dialogue*, July. Online. Available http://www.democraticdialogue.org/publications.htm (accessed 2 March 2003).

Zanini, M and Edwards, J.A. (2001) 'The Networking of Terror in the Information Age', in Arquilla, J. and Ronfeldt, D., *Networks and Netwars: The Future of Terror, Crime, and Militancy*, Santa Monica, CA: Rand Corporation.

8 Virtual parties in a virtual world

The use of the Internet by Russian political parties

Luke March

This chapter focuses on the use of the Internet by political parties in contemporary Russia. As a transitional state with an embryonic party system, Russia offers an instructive study of factors influencing the adoption of information and communication technology (ICT) by political parties as well as the relationship among the Internet, politics and civil society. For example, Russia's Internet audience was still small in 2004, some 14.9 million total users, just 10 per cent of the population (Public Opinion Foundation, 2004). There remain significant obstacles to sustainable growth, such as the low level of average incomes, sharp regional economic divides and the parlous condition of the communications infrastructure. Nevertheless, the audience is growing rapidly, and may reach some 26 million by 2010 (Korotkov, 2002).

Moreover, Russian President Vladimir Putin has indicated that promoting both an information society and political parties are top-level priorities. The Russian government's 'Electronic Russia' programme introduced in 2001 promises ambitious levels of Internetisation of public infrastructure (Korotkov, 2002). Similarly, the 2001 law on political parties was intended to consolidate Russia's fluid party system, by filtering some 197 parties, 'movements' and 'blocs' into a half-dozen major parties and between 20 and 30 contenders for power (Sakwa, 2002). Nevertheless, both initiatives have incited controversy as evidence of Putin's 'managed democracy' – a manipulative attitude towards civil society that has threatened the meagre achievements of Russia's 'democratic transition'. For example, the Electronic Russia programme has been criticized for a top-down approach to information provision (Semenov, 2002). It has coincided with a marked increase in state control over offline electronic media and greater attempts to monitor Internet content. The party law promised rigorous new criteria for party registration (such as a minimum national membership of 10,000 and an audit of party documents) that might restrict strong party formation as much as promote it.

In such a context, does the Internet help Russian parties serve as useful pillars of civil society? This work focuses on party website content as evidence of how parties are using the Internet for internal and external development. It uses evidence from Russia's 1999 elections and a survey of party websites conducted before the 2003 elections.[1] The chapter does not specifically look at the audience reaction to these sites, but aims to place party Internet use in the context of the general development of the Russian Internet, and party use of the web elsewhere. The study concentrates on the following issues:

1   What are Russian parties doing online? Given the pace of change in both party and Internet growth in Russia, this provides an important benchmark against which to measure future development.
2   What explains differences in the uptake of ICTs by different Russian parties?
3   How does the use of the web by Russian parties differ from other countries, and how can it be explained?
4   What light does Russian party web strategy shed upon the relationship among the Internet, politics and civil society in Russia and elsewhere?

Certainly, we can identify *potential* for the Internet to improve civil society and party development in democratising states. However, the Russian case shows that this potential is under-utilised. Overall, the Internet has tended to amplify the existing deformations of the Russian party system, in which parties are vehicles for the needs of the elite, rather than an aggregation of the desires of the electorate. Although most parties now see ICTs as vital, in general their use of the Internet remains limited and superficial. Differences between the web strategies of individual parties show that party philosophy strongly influences the scope of their uptake of ICTs. Political context plays a significant role in further limiting the overall effectiveness of the party Internet. In particular, the Russian Internet's narrow physical reach hinders its role, while the vast political capital advantages possessed by offline elite political actors have begun to influence politics on the net.

Virtual party possibilities

Several authors have addressed the Internet's ability to enable party change in the following ways (e.g. Margolis *et al.*, 1997; Rash, 1997; Coleman, 1999; Roper, 1999; Gibson *et al.*, 2000). Externally, the Internet helps parties with information dissemination: they are able to archive great quantities of information on websites and aim at a direct connection with voters unhindered by mediating third parties. In political campaigning this direct connection may facilitate a partial 'levelling of the playing field' between competitors, since traditional concrete offline resources (principally financial, membership and staffing) may play second fiddle to technological expertise and an unmediated message in a virtual realm. The possibility of combining novel technology simultaneously (written, graphic, photographic, video and sound) offers a stylistic appeal that may attract newer and younger supporters, while the more sophisticated sites may increasingly target and narrowcast their sites to specific social or geographical groups. The interactive elements of new technologies such as email and chat rooms are the more novel and important functions, allowing greater direct dialogue between party and voters. Furthermore, online shops and membership appeals may help a party's financial base significantly. Finally, the ability to site-network – to link sites together with well-placed web links and place party links on other web resources – is also a major boost to publicity and visibility over large distances.

Such elements boost the electoral and financial possibilities of political parties and so can benefit them as organisations, but the use of ICTs *within* the party organisation is equally significant. Not only can websites be used as online libraries, but web networks and email link party structures and members together. This helps with intra-party education and communication, particularly with larger parties, as well as aiding greater organisational openness and efficiency. In turn, organisational culture and identity may be reinforced by participation and networking opportunities fostered by ICTs. Finally, increased internal cohesion may accelerate the party's response to its environment, particularly at election time, when parties may rely on 'region-wide mobilisation of an active party base' (Rommele, 2003: 10).

Digital barriers

Those whom Norris (2001) describes as 'cyberoptimists' promised that the Internet would become a New Athenian agora of unmediated communication. Yet, other studies of the party Internet have been more circumspect, showing this is a 'medium in search of a purpose' (Coleman, 2001b). Few politicians know how to use the Internet effectively. Many websites compound information overload with a stylistic dullness and lack of interactivity (Gibson *et al.*, 2000; Coleman, 2001b) or merely provide flashy fashion statements that are devoid of meaningful content. These are at best hi-tech brochures in new 'shop-windows', at worst mere 'visiting cards' that continue offline, top-down information strategies with little adaptation to new technologies (Lofgren, 2000).

The most sophisticated studies concede that the uptake of ICTs by parties will differ according to a number of factors, such as party size, resource endowment, parliamentary privileges, national context and political culture (Gibson and Ward, 1998; Norris, 2001; Gibson *et al.*, 2003). Political agency is important too: the ideological goals of parties are vital in understanding how they use ICTs. Whether left-wing or right-wing parties use the Internet more effectively appears to vary with country and context, but 'New Politics' parties and radical/extremist parties are the most enthusiastic (if not necessarily the most effective) web users (Gibson *et al.*, 2000). Rommele (2003) further adds that a party's goals *qua* organisation will influence its ICT strategy. Parties that are vote maximisers or office maximisers (the latter are smaller parties seeking participation in coalition government) will aim to attract all social groups rather than focusing on their membership cohort. Consequently, their ICT strategy will attempt to increase their exposure in the offline media as they seek to broadcast the maximum possible information to the electorate at large. The participatory potential of ICT is likely to be subordinated to shorter-term electoral aims, or even used purely symbolically. In contrast, parties stressing intra-party democracy will prioritise the bottom-up, using the participatory and networking potentials of new media. Finally, policy- or ideology-seeking parties will combine top-down and bottom-up strategies: top-down for 'getting out the message' and bottom-up for inculcating policy or ideological expertise within the membership. Hence, there appear to be a plethora of competing individual, organisational, ideological and contextual influences on the use of the Internet by political parties.

The Internet and parties in democratising states

There are several added ways in which parties might colonise the Internet in former one-party states. What Mair (1997: 192) calls the 'open structure of [party] competition' may give great scope for new political organisations to fill the vacuum. The relative absence of established challengers potentially gives great incentive for new political organisations to use the Internet in order to 'level the playing field'. Furthermore, new organisations may be less encumbered by a conservative attitude to the web (Ward, 2001). So, the Internet might play a direct role in the construction of new parties from scratch, avoiding 'the usual costs of regional headquarters and physical participation in the party organisation' (Rommele, 2003: 10). New parties might provide a competitive incentive to innovation in web strategies, while the sheer size of a country such as Russia would be an incentive to party building in itself.

Yet, when one looks at the majority of parties that have actually emerged in many post-communist states, which are dubbed 'modern cadre parties' or cartel parties (Olson, 1998), one might be far less sanguine about the Internet's potential. These parties tend to be 'internally-created' (Duverger, 1964), that is formed by elite groups within parliaments, heavily dependent on the state for resources and possessing top-down internal structures and relatively unimportant memberships. Indeed, Russia's 'parties' have been dubbed 'pseudo-parties' (Sakwa, 1993). They are personalised, ideologically incoherent and weakly institutionalised, with little stable connection to an electorate and among the least trusted of all social institutions. A significant reason is the electoral system and the lack of incentives for strong parties: parties participate in elections for a national parliament (the Duma) that has weak powers vis-à-vis the president. Furthermore, parliamentary parties have no right to form a government, and Russia's presidential elections are non-party. One product of this fluid, elite-dominated situation has been the 'party of power'. As Oversloot and Verheul (2000) note, this is less a formal political organisation than an alliance of elite interests that attempts to mobilise electoral, financial and media support around the prevailing authorities, forming and discarding political parties in the process. Such a 'party' is an indication that the open structure of party competition is not necessarily a level one.

Indeed, looking at post-communist party types from the perspective of their ICT uptake, the situation looks bleak. The prevalent cartel/cadre model is identified by Rommele (2003) with the vote maximisation goal and the propensity to top-down 'broadcasting' of the party message through the Internet. The more interactive models of the adaptation of information and computer technology appear to have a marginal role in post-communist society, given the relative absence of mass memberships and ideologically focused parties.

Moreover, Zasurskii (2001) has called the Russian political–media relationship 'mediatisation'. He posits that, in the absence of constraints usually provided by a strong civil society, political parties and legal system, the electronic media have played an enhanced and unchecked role in converting communication and marketing skills into political and financial capital and vice versa. The media not only created so-called 'broadcast parties' (Oates, 2002) based on image and media exposure rather than ideology or organisation, but even acted as a party substitute, used by politicians for 'ensuring support and a link with the electorate, mobilising resources and lobbying' (Zasurskii, 2001: 106). Where voters have lacked the ability to challenge top-down information flows, 'mediatisation' easily becomes manipulation, and even offline politics become 'virtual', where 'the public world of gesture and image making masks a reality of private intrigue and complicity' (Wilson, 2001: 2–3). Given this unpromising context, how have parties responded in terms of Internet use?

The 1999 elections and the Russian party Internet

The Duma elections of 1999, in which the majority of parties sported websites, can be seen as the first Russian Internet election. In the previous presidential elections in 1996, only the liberal Yabloko bloc had a website, and this was an experiment not used for explicit electoral purposes (Ivanov, 2002a). It is particularly important to consider the 1999 Duma elections, as power had not yet consolidated around Putin and the political fighting was some of the most ferocious of the post-Soviet era. The particular structure of parties and elections in Russia should be noted as well. In these elections for the Duma (the lower house of the parliament), half of the 450 seats were selected from parties that garnered more than 5 per cent in a national party-list contest and the other half were elected through the 225 single-member districts in Russia. The upper house of the parliament, the Federation Council, is no longer directly elected. Although Russian presidents have always expressed preference for particular (pro-Kremlin) political parties, neither Putin nor Yeltsin ever ran with a party affiliation. Thus, the link between real political power and party organisations is muted, although some parties (especially the Communists) have managed to use electoral strength as a bargaining chip toward power in opposition to the Kremlin.

The 1999 election revealed several specificities of the Russian web:

- *Inexperience and incompetence*: As elsewhere, Internet presence appeared to be used as a symbolic necessity without a clear strategic purpose, either to demonstrate modernity or simply through peer pressure. This was most graphically demonstrated by the Unity bloc's website (www.edinstvo.org), which came online only on 7 December 1999, 12 days before polling. Coalition blocs continued to maintain separate websites of their components. For instance, the Union of Right Forces maintained 11, while its official site (www.sps.ru) was only inaugurated in 2001.
- *Scandals and negative campaigning*: Mediatisation is no more marked than in the role of 'political technologists' (pejoratively the *PRchiki*), who perform political PR for hire. These so-called 'masters of the black arts of cynical image-making' (Wilson, 2001: 2–3) increasingly dabbled online in the late 1990s as financial crisis hit the offline media (Ivanov, 2002a). In 1999, the use of the Internet in so-called 'black PR' or *kompromat* (literally the abbreviation for 'compromising material' in Russian) created sensations. Among the most notorious was the mirror site of Moscow Mayor Yuri Luzhkov (www.lujkov.ru). This appeared during the mayoral and parliamentary elections of 1999 and duplicated his official site (www.luzhkov.ru) in style and structure (even copying his signature), but contained disparaging references to him. While such negative Internet campaigning occurs elsewhere, the novelty of the Internet as a medium and the lack of legal regulation were key factors in amplifying its effect. Even when the Moscow mayoralty pressured www.lujkov.ru to close down, it soon reappeared on a site sponsored by the most notorious *PRchiki* – Gleb Pavlovskii's Foundation of Effective Politics, which had rumoured Kremlin backing.[2] Among several projects attributable to Foundation for Effective Politics were www.elections.ru and www.vvp.ru ('Vote Vladimir Putin'), which flouted legislation by publishing election results during vote counting, against the ineffectual protests of the Central Election Commission and Procuracy.
- *PR and image*: The Internet was occasionally effectively used in image making. Boris Nemtsov was the first Russian 'Internet politician', the first leading figure (when First Deputy Prime Minister in 1998) to have his own websites (www.nemtsov.ru and www.boris.nemtsov.ru), to explain his political activities and promote interaction with the public. His virtual political movement ('Young Russia', www.rosmol.ru) maintained an energetic Internet presence, which actively recruited members and aimed to form a virtual liberal community (Smetanin, 2002a, 2002b). Sergei Kirienko, briefly Prime Minister in 1998, was more proactive still in exploiting the web to form his liberal 'New Force' movement (www.kirienko.ru) in December 1998 and his high Internet rating assisted his ultimately unsuccessful challenge against Luzhkov for the post of Moscow Mayor in late 1999.[3]

- *The Internet as force multiplier*: The Russian Internet was also able to play a greater political role than its physical reach indicated. Indeed, it was heavily used by the elite and 'opinion formers': in 2000, over 40 per cent of users were qualified specialists or managers using the web primarily for work purposes (Comcon Market Research Company, 2000). Journalists saw the Russian Internet as perhaps the only mass medium left uncensored (Ivanov, 2002b), both because of the difficulty of censoring it and because the government long underestimated the possibilities of online media (Belonuchkin and Mikhailovskaya, 2002). A weak tradition of investigative journalism in the traditional mass media gave an added reliance on the Internet as an information resource, with many sites (such as www.smi.ru, www.APN.ru and www.rumours.ru) created exclusively for that purpose (Ivanov, 2002a).

Arguably, this use of the Internet as an elite domain amplifies its offline political effect. Given its physical limits, the only way for the Russian Internet to maintain a wider political influence has been to be retranslated by the offline media (Belonuchkin and Mikhailovskaya, 2002). This allows it to frame the news agenda, and even to influence many who have no physical access to a computer. Indeed, TV news regularly cites purely online sources (Tropkina, 2000), while the most successful political use of the Internet in 1999 was as what Rash (1997: 80–81) calls a force multiplier, which 'makes your resources seem larger and more effective than they really are and in the process may give you greater capabilities'. The synchrony of online and offline campaigning can make news. Had Nemtsov and Kirienko not already possessed a high-profile offline image as 'young reformers', their virtual popularity might not have soared. But the Internet perpetuated their image as progressive and capable leaders, which partially compensated for their departure from the government in 1998 and gave them momentum into the election campaign, ultimately helping them win leading positions in the Union of Right Forces.

However, the mediation of online message through the offline media has an ambiguous effect. Potentially, the Internet gets wider social coverage and a more informed offline journalistic community can emerge, but the dubious independence of the Russian offline media means that the Internet's supposed undiluted communication is compromised. For example, the online *kompromat* against Luzhkov reinforced a vigorous negative offline campaign against him. Less publicly, Nemtsov and Kirienko's status as Internet pioneers was heavily mythologized. Both used a PR agency (the Kremlin-linked Foundation of Effective Politics) for technical support and site administration, and their movements were avidly followed by news services close to this agency (such as www.lenta.ru and www.strana.ru). Nemtsov could initially barely use a computer, while emails to his personal web address were answered by agency employees (Ivanov, 2002a).

- *The Internet as a party resource*: The Internet showed little effectiveness as a feature of party campaigning in 1999. Most obviously, there was little correlation between the election results and the political preferences of Internet users (see Table 8.1), and negligible evidence of any 'levelling the playing field'. In particular, the two election front-runners (the Communists and Unity) had minimal online support and their success was almost completely due to substantial offline resources. These were financial, administrative and media in the case of Unity (the dominant 'party of power'), while the Communists possessed the largest and most disciplined party organisation. However, the proactive use of Internet media by the Union of Right Forces was shared by its other leaders (Anatoli Chubais and Irina Khakamada) and may have contributed to the party's breakthrough as the leading party among Russian liberals. The ensuing 2000 presidential election campaign saw nearly all candidates use websites as a new (admittedly supplementary) information resource (Ivanov, 2002a).

Russian parties online: web wide waste?

But what of contemporary party use of the Internet? In order to address this question in detail, a website survey form designed by Gibson and Ward for analysing the functions, style and delivery of the online presence of parties was adopted (Gibson and Ward, 1998). The key advantages of this form over others (Norris, 2001; Bieber, 2000) are its detail, comprehensiveness and comparability. The indices are designed to shed light on the aims of a website (such as information gathering, targeting voters, resource generation, etc.) and its achievement of these aims (such as stylistic sophistication and ability to attract visitors as well as the ease of site navigability). This form claims to use a nuanced set of criteria that can analyse a variety of websites in different countries and contexts as well as to analyse change over time. For comparative analysis, the data collected for Russian parties have been set alongside data that Gibson and Ward collected for Australian, US and UK political parties, using identical indices. Russian parliamentary parties were initially

Table 8.1 Website influence on voting patterns, 1999 Russian Duma elections

Party	Support among Internet users %	Vote total %
Union of Right Forces	26.6	8.5
Yabloko	25.0	5.9
Fatherland–All Russia	21.3	13.3
Communists	8.8	24.3
Unity	5.3	23.3
Zhirinovsky Bloc/LDPR	3.4	6.0

Source: *Nezavisimaya gazeta*, 23 November 1999. Sample size of survey was 3,325 respondents.

analysed in November 2002; then a comprehensive analysis of the 50 parties that been registered under the 2001 law on political parties was conducted in early March 2003.

Non-parliamentary pretensions

Russian non-parliamentary parties have traditionally been seen as 'divan parties' (since the membership could easily fit on a couch) without social support or meaningful membership (Sakwa, 2002). Few even register on opinion polls. Their virtual presence also appears to reflect organisations that are cadre-party wannabes, with an ephemeral organisation and a bias towards top-down information provision. Their websites were often virtually invisible, being hard to find through the main Russian search engine, yandex.ru, and receiving no mention on Yahoo! or Google. While all six parliamentary parties have websites, only 23 of the 44 non-parliamentary parties had an active website. This is only slightly more than the 50 per cent noted by Semetko and Krasnoboka (2003) in January 2001. However, newer sites had gone online in 2002 and 2003 roughly when they were registered. A difference from Semetko and Krasnoboka's data was that dedicated party websites were now more frequent than those that were basically the party leader's personal site, such as 'Enterprise Development' (www.grachev.ru), which may indicate increasing party institutionalisation.

The scores of Russian non-parliamentary parties on the comparative indices (summarised in Appendix A, Table 8A.1) confirm their poor performance on most indicators, particularly relative to UK non-parliamentary parties, although the parties compare better to the lower scores of the Australian parties. Stylistically, there was little to compel the visitor (see the low 'glitz' scores in Appendix A, Table 8A.2). Indeed, the front page of the Russian United Industrial Party (www.ropp.ru) was the only one to use multimedia effects, with a series of moving images of various industrial employees at work, interspersed by the Russian flag – and even this had been replaced by the conventional style of a welcome statement and leader photo by March 2003. Instead, most websites were cluttered with text, broken web links and clumsy graphics, and generally style was unmatched by substance. Most gave prominence to official documents such as the programme and constitution (legal requirements in any case). Information provision scores (Appendix A, Table 8A.1) were weak, and, considering that such new parties desperately need to get recognition from the electorate, the absence of relevant and detailed information on personnel and policies was remarkable. The weak institutional structure of parties was shown by the relatively few emails or web links on the sites – the latter were predominately links to either web designers or web ratings sites in any case. More staggering, given these parties' ephemeral existence, was the resource generation average of 1.2 (Appendix A, Table 8A.1). This is where institutional constraints were obviously apparent: mistrust of the banking system and the relative absence of credit cards and online transactions in Russia mean far fewer possibilities for the online shops and donations prevalent in US and UK politics. Yet, that barely explains the usual absence of any reference to membership or the single email address provided for that purpose.

However, several sites surpassed the weaker parliamentary party sites on a number of indices. The nationalist 'Eurasia' party had a stylish and detailed information resource (www.evrazia.org) with multiple language pages, news, newsletters, books and links. The philosophical information site to which this site is linked (www.arcto.ru) was one of the most-visited political sites. The Social Democratic Party site (www.sdprussia.ru) was the only one to have a rudimentary members-only page and was one of the better sites in design and content, while the Russian Conservative Party of Entrepreneurs (www.rkpp.ru) had provision for online membership and even a basic online shop. The mean participation score of 3.1 was greater than for Australian non-parliamentary parties, with forums, bulletin boards and visitors books prevalent, and several parties had active forums and chat rooms. However, this was often illusory – many features were devoid of content except for queries about membership or complaints about the lack of website renewal.

The view that party philosophy and organisational goals have a significant role in ICT strategy received some substantiation. Eurasia's participative website and wide networking reflect its self-perception as the vanguard of a radical anti-liberal front and a conscious adoption of the Internet as a tool to create a 'virtual Eurasia' (Dugin, 2002). Liberal or pro-Western parties such as the Social Democrats tended to display higher participation and networking scores, but there were exceptions – for example, the Greens (www.greenparty.ru) were neither strong networkers nor grassroots democrats as they are in other countries. Overall, there was little evidence of 'levelling the playing field'. Indeed, the strongest sites are backed by an established offline presence. Eurasia's leader Aleksandr Dugin is a well-known publicist and well-connected political adviser, while the Social Democrats are supported by the Gorbachev Foundation think tank. Both parties ultimately withdrew from the election, leaving their net potential untested.

Parliamentary potential

The scores for the Russian parliamentary parties are shown in Appendix B, Tables 8B.1 and 8B.2. On average, these sites were significantly larger, more complex, more networked and more stylish than those of non-parliamentary challengers. There were, however, key inter-party differences. There were two clearly weaker party sites for the Liberal Democratic Party (www.ldpr.ru) and the People's Party of the Russian Federation (www.narod-party.ru), while United Russia's successor Unity (www.edinros.ru) was a middling site. There were stronger sites belonging to the Communists (www.kprf.ru), the Union of Right Forces (www.sps.ru) and Yabloko (www.yabloko.ru).

The parliamentary parties highlighted information provision still more than the non-parliamentary ones, but were little better at giving an online account of themselves. Although the average score of 7.1 (Appendix B, Table 8B.1) does not compare badly with Australian parties, this is still less than half of the potential score (16). Absent again was any coherent and concise statement of beliefs and values, apart from ubiquitous programme documents and statutes. Symbolically, no party had an explicit section on policies (separate from general programmatic claims). Similarly, explanations of organisational history and structure were missing. The only partial exceptions were the Communists and Yabloko. The latter was the party clearest about its political stance and structure. For example, the slogan 'for a free, democratic and strong Russia' was prominent in the home page header. Yabloko displayed detailed organisational history and (albeit dated) information about electoral campaigns, while having the most detailed policy proposals (with an alternative budget on the site's first page and policy proposals in its sections 'actual themes' and 'what's important'). United Russia and the Liberal Democratic Party listed nothing explicit at all in this area. Leadership profiles varied in quantity and quality. Yabloko was again most detailed, with many pages showing the biographies, legislative activity and publications of its leaders, while the People's Party and United Russia provided mere sentences. The Union of Right Forces had a surprising coyness about its liberal values, yet its cluttered home page with numerous press releases and photos gave the impression of high activity.

The Union of Right Forces and United Russia had separate parliamentary fraction websites (www.duma.sps.ru and www.duma.edin.ru). These fraction sites gave detailed information about parliamentary deputies and activity as well as reinforced the impression that these parties sought especially to highlight activity, efficiency and influence rather than values or purpose. This might reflect their recent provenance (both parties were created in 1999) and the demands of the overall political context. Given the migration of lobbying and resources towards 'power' in Russia and the Duma's weak prerogatives, it is hard for parties to demonstrate to the voter that they do *anything*. However, fulfilling this imperative appeared to be at the expense of immediately useful information: although the Duma parties' information strategy conveyed that they were busy, it was rarely clear what they were busy *with*.

Another key emphasis of ICT strategy was producing a party archive and online library for interested party members. The Communist and Yabloko websites, parties with a core membership and relatively long-standing organisational history (founded in 1993), clearly demonstrated this. Their information-rich sites (particularly Yabloko) provided older and wordier information than others. However, there was a risk of too much information. Home pages over 25 kilobytes in size are slower to load, a particular problem in countries without high-speed Internet access (Gibson and Ward, 2000). Most parliamentary party sites for which data were available far exceeded this (Appendix B, Table 8B.2), with the Union of Right Forces site glacially slow in loading.

Party longevity, however, was no assurance of website complexity. The Liberal Democratic Party is the oldest (founded in 1989) but also among the weakest in quality of information. In essence, the party site is the site of its leader Vladimir Zhirinovsky. Unlike many other party leaders, Zhirinovsky did not have his own web page. Yet, this was unnecessary as most site material on the party website was devoted to his views and sayings, and reference to other structures, especially regional organisations, and personnel (except Zhirinovsky's nephew, fraction head Igor Lebedev) was absent.

The resource generation scores of parliamentary parties (average 1.3) were barely stronger than those of non-parliamentary challengers although the quantity of (free) online books on websites such as the Liberal Democratic Party's indicated some attempt to substitute for party bookshops. The Union of Right Forces was most advanced, with a charity fund page containing details of how to donate to needy causes. Getting a nationwide membership is particularly important under the new law on parties, and the Internet could clearly help here, but parties were barely using it to attract members. United Russia and the Union of Right Forces had no references at all to membership, while others had online forms to download and post. The verbose conditions laid out were hardly an incentive – only the People's Party, with a question-and-answer section, explicitly set out why someone would *want* to join. The only real evidence of innovation was Yabloko's stipulation of virtual membership, allowing Russians abroad or where there was no local party organisation to become candidate members of the party and to participate in all online activities. However, during scoring for this study, the party's membership page was not fully functioning.

In theory, a large number of emails on a party site should indicate organisational openness, while many hypertext links on a site should indicate a more externally directed organisation that aims to forge reciprocal contacts (Gibson and Ward, 2000). If so, least open was the Liberal Democratic Party, with just one email link to its press service. Most open was the Union of Right Forces, perhaps because of its origins as a coalition of movements (including New Force and Young Russia) that was forged only after election. The utility of the Internet in party building was something of which parties appeared aware; indeed both the Union of Right Forces and the People's Party provided email contacts for most regional organisations. The openness of other parties was more ambiguous. United Russia scored surprisingly highly (with 86 email contacts on its site) for an organisation noted for hierarchical internal discipline. However, all email addresses were on the parliamentary fraction sites of Unity, Fatherland and Russian Regions, from which United Russia was constructed (there were none on the party site proper), and nearly all were addresses of Duma deputies rather than designated party functionaries. This indicates, perhaps, the ethereality of the Russian party structure outside its Duma base.

Yabloko was rather less open. Like the Liberal Democratic Party, this could reflect a small parliamentary fraction (with 13 and 17 deputies respectively, the smallest parties represented there). It also was a conscious choice not to provide emails when resource reasons made a response unlikely and offence might be caused.[4] The Communists' external networking (predominantly to partisan radical left sources in Russia and abroad) also would appear to be the conscious policy/ideological choice of a party that still possesses an internationalist self-image (March, 2003). However, as Gibson and Ward (2000) noted with Australian parties, the number of emails and links was often little more than symbolic. Indeed, the author emailed nine Russian blocs in September 2002 with a request for interview. Only two parties replied to this by email (Yabloko and Fatherland), while others preferred to conduct discussions by phone or fax. If the potential electorate had such an experience with email contacts, then their presence is merely token and misleading.

However, whereas Western parties have been particularly criticised for not using ICTs such as emails explicitly soliciting feedback, chat rooms and comment boards in a truly interactive way (Coleman, 2001a, 2001b), the participatory emphasis of Russian political parties on these measures outscores their Australian counterparts. However, the chat rooms and guest books of the People's Party and United Russia were empty, the Liberal Democrats did not have one, and the 'dialogue' in all contained servile praise of party leaders to outright abuse of forum participants or political opponents. Nevertheless, the Communists' dozen forums were becoming far more sophisticated and well attended, while the liberal parties possessed well-developed forums. The Union of Right Forces regularly loaded opinion pieces into its chat rooms for discussion, while Yabloko ran a series of well-attended chat rooms, some offering the possibility of chat with parliamentary deputies. However, it remains unclear whether, as in many Western parties, such interaction will be a passing phase, eventually deemed to make the party too vulnerable to criticism in full public view on the site.

One area in which Russian parliamentary parties appeared to equal parties in the United States and United Kingdom was active political campaigning (Appendix B, Table 8B.1), particularly given that at the time of analysis the next parliamentary elections were nine months away. However, an average score of 4 out of 13 is hardly impressive, and is also somewhat misleading – Russian sites were far less sophisticated at providing explicit rebuttals to or attacks on political opponents. No party could really claim explicit policy achievements, but several developed sustained negative coverage of their opponents. The Communists ran a series of political cartoons ridiculing the government, and the Union of Right Forces section 'Us and Them' disparaged United Russia and the Communists equally. Yet, only the Union of Right Forces used its site to organise practical campaigns, such as an online petition against the proposed reinstatement of the statue of a founding father of the notorious Soviet KGB in central Moscow in autumn 2002.

The Communists were the only party to use their website to distribute campaign material to supporters. Although several parties distributed email bulletins to project the party message beyond the site to interested subscribers, these tended to be content-heavy and unfocused. While most sites possessed 'cookies', which allow personalised information to be collected and sites targeted to voters, there was little evidence of any ability to personalise one's party site. Confirming a general tendency towards a fuzzy focus and a catch-all appeal, few parties had pages or sites dedicated to specific constituencies (with the exception of youth pages). At first glance an exception, United Russia's page of links to a wide range of social groups with whom it had signed a social contract (women, trade unions, the deaf, etc.) was uncannily reminiscent of the Soviet Communist Party's symbolic claims of unity with all social strata.

If the functions of parliamentary party websites were a mixed bag, delivery was equally so (Appendix B, Table 8B.2). Sites were based on text and photos, with little variety except in the logos. As in other country studies of political party activity on the web, they offered little to convert the unconverted. Only the Liberal Democratic Party used multimedia extensively, with download-able videos and songs about or by Zhirinovsky, and a photo book of his inimitable fancy dress style. While these indicated Zhirinovsky's peculiar form of populist charisma (what some might less charitably term megalo-mania), they hardly compensated for the site's many other weaknesses. Only Yabloko had an English-language page, and the absence of such for the Communists weakened their internationalist credentials.

In other aspects most websites were clearly set out and easy to navigate. Moreover, most were updated several times daily, although fresh news bulletins on the front pages often concealed obsolete materials and non-functioning pages several levels down, reinforcing the view that the overriding aim of these parties was to keep up an image of activity, particularly for the 'opinion formers'. The Yabloko webmaster confirmed that the party website's main functions were providing information to journalists and maintaining the party's steady Internet audience, rather than significantly extending the party's support base. This was an important aim but was seen as futile given the Internet's limited reach.[5]

Explaining the uptake of ICTs by Russian parties

Overall, both Russian parliamentary and non-parliamentary parties demon-strated specific features. They used the Internet significantly less effectively than Western counterparts across most measures. The most pronounced weak-nesses compared with parties in the United States or the United Kingdom were in resource generation, information provision and participation, while their relative strengths were in networking, navigability and openness.

Those weaknesses reflect the physical and technological limitations of the Russian Internet, particularly the lack of donation and transaction possi-bilities. Yet, this was not a case of technological diffusion driving change, or we might expect the Russian parties to be far further behind their Australian counterparts (where the Internet audience in 2000 was more than seven times larger than Russia's in 2003). Rather, the ICT choices of parties reflect other features of the party system. The generally top-down ICT strategy resembles that of the Italian parties, which are also predominately personalistic and cadre organisations orientated towards the state (Gibson *et al.*, 2000). Like Italian parties, Russian parties appear to have little incentive to form grass-roots structures and, like them, they have not demonstrated any sustained intent to use the net for membership recruitment. Similarly, their predominant information strategy has been broadcasting to the political elite. However, the relatively high networking and openness scores of Russian parties do indicate some attempt to spread their geographical reach and hence build party structures in a fluid party system, albeit not in a way that really engages a membership.

At the same time, it must be said that uptake of ICTs does differ from party to party. There is certainly evidence to support the 'normalisation' thesis that established resource-rich organisations would begin to dominate the web. As elsewhere, parliamentary parties in Russia were bigger and better online and offline than most challengers who could not rely on the legislature's profile and resources. Size was clearly not everything – Yabloko and Union of Right Forces, two of the smaller parliamentary fractions, were among those with the best sites. United Russia's site was relatively content-free despite it having the second-largest parliamentary fraction and national membership (350,000 claimed in March 2003). Offline resources are notoriously opaque and difficult to measure in Russia. However, they may play a role behind several of the better parliamentary websites. Certainly, the fact that United Russia and the People's Party were both parts of the 'party of power' in 2003 may explain why their sites were stylistically 'glitzy', but weaker in substance. Quite possibly they were less information-rich online simply because their adequate offline resources made this less essential.

An examination of the 2003 Internet audience (Table 8.2) provides indirect evidence of 'normalisation'. In terms of hits, smaller parties such as Union of Right Forces and Yabloko were just holding their own against the growing online visibility of the 'parties of power'. In particular, the gradual increase

Table 8.2 'Hits' on Russian party websites, 6 February to 7 March 2003

Party/website	Monthly hits	Total hits
Putin's (unofficial) www.putin.ru	309,968	2,353,580
Communists www.kprf.ru	160,482	704,587
Union of Right Forces www.sps.ru	57,850	928,187
United Russia www.edinros.ru	46,056	206,677
Yabloko www.yabloko.ru	17,406	926,723
Liberal Democratic Party www.ldpr.ru	—	441,488
People's Party www.narod-party.ru	8,243	56,371

Sources: Hits to the whole site from www.rambler.ru; the average of statistics at 7 March 2003 from www.rambler.ru, www.mail.ru, www.spylog.ru.

in United Russia's online audience since the re-launch of the site in June 2002 indicated that, if the 'party of power' had underestimated the virtual realm in 1999, then this was changing. Another sign that offline popularity provided the major impulse to online interest was the emergence in 2002 of a new, supposedly 'unofficial' Putin home page (www.putin.ru) that quickly out-flanked all political party websites in popularity. Visitors could read the president's speeches and activities in detail, post opinions, download pictures of him and even view Putin's current location via a flashing dot on a global map. While hardly revolutionary, this site displayed a level of interactivity and humour lacking from most party sites.

Institutional factors, resources and political context do not appear to determine party ICT uptake, but do provide the constraints and incentives to which individual parties' philosophy and organisational goals provide a variety of responses. For example, each party shared the overriding aims of information broadcasting, presenting an active image and attracting a regular audience that can be attributed to their weak parliamentary influence and media exposure. But Rommele's (2003) categorisation of party ICT strategies according to broad party goals is also partially substantiated. The general heavy emphasis on information provision, lack of focused appeals and 'all-action' permanent campaigning confirm the view that many Russian parties are predominately catch-all vote maximising parties aiming for media-oriented broadcasting and the voter rather than the member, with the cadre/cartel tendencies already noted.

An emphasis on the personality of the top leader is something Rommele also attributes to vote-maximising parties. Evidence for this is more ambiguous: Zhirinovsky's Liberal Democrats are by far the most personalised (as befits the centralised leadership of an extreme right party), United Russia and the People's Party the least. Again, offline resources are the probable explanation – their nominal leaders are less important than their access to 'Power', and indeed links to the presidency and other state institutions were prominently displayed on the home pages of both parties. Yet, several parties do lean more towards participative intra-party democracy and policy/ideological models, even if to a limited degree. Liberal parties see ICT participation as a good in itself, but also in the Russian context as a symbol of Westernisation and as an investment for the future. The self-perception of the Union of Right Forces as the most 'Internet-savvy' party is more than just a fashion statement. Its 'Internet-into-Schools' campaign, whereby each Duma deputy helped schools in his electoral district connect to the Internet, had reportedly wired up some 740 computers by 2001, and attracted both requests and donations to the party site (Morozov, 2001). Yabloko's more incremental and less showy use of its site to build up its own institutional culture and stable audience reflected a more intellectual and less business-orientated party than the Union of Right Forces.

As Eurasia showed, illiberal parties can also be web pioneers. The Communists reinforce this: to judge by their online presence, they were the least vote-maximising of the parliamentary parties, closest to an amalgam of intra-party democracy and policy/ideology-seeking models. They combined a bottom-up participatory emphasis and a top-down emphasis on ideological agitation, which replicates their offline party organisation (March, 2003). Of all parties, the Communists most explicitly emphasised the Internet as an electoral medium before the 2003 elections. Appeals to party members to 'log on' and receive their new emails @kprf.ru were frequent. The website was markedly improved in October 2002, particularly enhancing its interactive components. The party's ICT priorities were a logical extension of its strategic goals. Electorally, the Internet was seen as a way of breaking the 'information blockade' provided by the biased electronic media.[6] Organisationally, ICTs helped supporters in far-flung regional organisations access the party's statements and press. Ideologically, the Internet was an extremely important symbol for a party with an ageing electorate, as it demonstrated progressiveness, modernity and youthfulness. This aimed to project the party's anti-globalisation profile as well as its ability to use global technology to unseat global capitalism (March, 2003).

Ultimately, the 2003–04 elections did not demonstrate any great leap forward in use of the Internet by political parties. Despite an increase in the Internet audience since 1999, political activity remained low: only 1 per cent of Russian Internet users accessed political sites in 2002 (Ochvinnikov, 2002). Moreover, offline resources were of greater impact still than in 1999. United Russia's victory in the Duma race with 37 per cent of the vote owed little to ICTs and more to Putin's popularity, and an election in which governmental patronage cast doubt on the fairness of the vote (Petrov, 2003). Another winner of the election was the nationalist Motherland bloc (formed in September 2003). This party maintained a glitzy but information-thin site (www.nps-rodina.ru) that was favourably received by web users, but the party owed its success far more to Kremlin offline media support. The parties with the better sites (Yabloko, Union of Right Forces and the Communists) were the chief losers of the election. Neither of the liberal parties managed to surmount the 5 per cent barrier to gain entry to parliament, while the Communist's party-list vote was halved from the 1999 elections to 12.6 per cent. It seemed that ICTs could hardly compensate for the overwhelming popularity of the president and the lack of visibility of an opposition. This was confirmed by the 2004 presidential elections in which Putin took 71.3 per cent of the vote.

There was some innovative use of ICTs in the most recent round of Russian elections, largely in negative campaigning. The Union of Right Forces purchased a series of alarmist banners on Russian sites (for example the web portal mail.ru) implying that a Motherland victory would introduce fascism. In 2002, Viktor Pokhmelkin (Union of Right Forces) criticised Russian parties for a lack of foresight in their Internet policies (Vinogradov and Chudodeev, 2002). Most parties, he asserted, operate according to the short-term calculation that very few voters use the Internet, and that the younger electorate that does so is least likely to vote. This was confirmed in

2003, as observers noted that under-utilisation of the web compounded the offline problems of parties. Yabloko's use of the web was seen as passive, while the Union of Right Forces itself allegedly failed to emulate party leader Kirienko in 1999 and actively court Moscow's Internet audience. Ironically, this appeared to be because 'Internet politicians' such as Boris Nemtsov appeared not to understand the Internet's full potential and accorded it low priority.[7] Similarly, the *PRchiki* were much less active online in 2003. Absent the relatively free offline political competition, novelty value and astute political leadership of 1999, online political competition appeared to *decline* in 2003–04.

Conclusions

Party adoption of ICTs in Russia is still at a rudimentary stage. Whereas this survey indicates an increasing stirring of party online activity well in advance of the 2003–04 election round, the limited reach of the Russian web itself means that what Russian politicians, still less parties, do online will not be a decisive electoral or party-building factor for some time to come. However, the longer-term prospects for e-parties in democratising states such as Russia are arguably much brighter. While confirming a distinct lag in party ICT adoption compared with developed democracies, it is not a uniformly bleak picture. The Internet offers new party systems the possibility of greater organisational integrity, efficiency and visibility in relatively open electoral fields. In theory, this should help educate an inexperienced electorate and compensate for the deficiencies of the newly free electronic media. At the same time, it can provide the linkage between civil society and the state that is so tenuous in many embryonic democracies. In Russia, there was limited movement towards this, particularly from the younger, more liberal politicians who have dabbled in virtual party building, in those party forums that were well attended and in the increasing sophistication of party websites. Russian parties use their websites primarily for unfocused information broadcasting in a way more reminiscent of online broadsheet papers than structured political parties. Yet, in the context of non-free media, these might become alternative information portals for an information-starved electorate and thus contribute to the pluralisation of the media *in toto*, as the Communists clearly hoped.

Moreover, since in many established democracies the Internet is still a medium looking for a meaning, perhaps one could judge parties in 'transition' states less harshly. Where parties are new and themselves searching for a meaning, ICT adoption may be more experimental and far less of a conservative 'add-on' than in more established party systems. There is less a sense of party websites solely 'preaching to the converted' in societies in which the Internet is still a novelty, where the electorate is more fluid and when catch-all information provision can be seen as a good in itself. Nevertheless, the political use of the Internet appears very much defined by the interaction of structure and agency, rather than any mystical 'democratic' quality intrinsic to the technology itself. Indeed, transition states, particularly post-Soviet ones such as Russia, are not a level playing field from the outset, and structural, institutional and cultural factors play at least a contextual role. Such states often lack the resource abundance of entrenched democracies, with pernicious consequences for Internet access, and may still confront entrenched interests guarding their privileges. In Russia, parties contended with their lack of national governing role, and in practice, as the 1999 parliamentary election began to demonstrate, their Internet message is transmitted among electronic media, personnel and an electorate socialised in a less information-friendly milieu.

However, this research has shown that weaknesses in ICT use by Russian political parties are also attributable to their marked underestimation of the membership and grassroots organisational possibilities of the new media. This is potentially very serious in countries in which civil society has little ability to control the financial and patronage power of the state. The participatory potential of the Internet is one of few ways in which new forces might reclaim some parity with the existing major players. What is more, the muzzling of the offline electronic media in Putin's Russia limits the number of outlets through which Internet sites might be retranslated to reach a broader offline audience unless sanctioned by the authorities. Thereby even the limited political effect of the Russian Internet in December 1999 (when it was exploited and retranslated by political forces and media in a *relatively* pluralist and competitive election campaign) may be absent in future.

Finally, to judge by existing studies, once the major offline players turn their attention online, they can assert a similar, even if not identical, online dominance. United Russia's increasing virtual presence might not necessarily bring online the worst of the state's offline 'virtual politics', since its success owed so little to ICTs. The peripheral political influence of the Russian Internet to date means that it may yet remain a medium in which opposition political forces can operate unfettered. Unfortunately, it simultaneously deprives them of a compelling immediate reason for doing so.

Appendix A

Table 8A.1 Russian non-parliamentary party websites, 1 to 7 March 2003: content analysis of website functions

Explanation	Information provision	Resource generation	Openness	Participation	Networking	Campaigning
	Information about party organisation, values, leaders	Membership, donations and purchases online	Total email contacts on site	Feedback and interaction	Total links out of site	Recruiting votes through pulling in voters to party message or pushing party message to voter
Agrarian Party	5	0	1	4	0	0
Conservative Party of Russia	7	0	1	4	1	0
Conceptual Party 'Unity'	3	1	3	4	1	0
Democratic Party of Russia	6	1	64	4	2	0
Enterprise Development	5	1	1	1	2	1
Eurasian Party	5	1	1	2	1	0
Eurasia	9.5	0	49	8	5	2
Greens	5	0	3	3	1	3
Liberal Russia	5	0	3	7	4	1
National-Patriotic Forces of Russia	4.5	1	1	2	0	1
National-Patriotic Party of Russia	4	2		0	0	1
National-Republican Party of Russia	4.5	1	1	4	1	0
National-Superpower Party of Russia	4	0	22	2.5	4	0
Party of Russia's Rebirth	4	2	0	0	2	1
Republican Party of Russia	5	2	4	2	2	0
Russian Communist Workers' Party–Russian Party of Communists	6.5	4	4	3.5	7	3

continued

Table 8A.1 continued

Explanation	Information provision *Information about party organisation, values, leaders*	Resource generation *Membership, donations and purchases online*	Openness *Total email contacts on site*	Participation *Feedback and interaction*	Networking *Total links out of site*	Campaigning *Recruiting votes through pulling in voters to party message or pushing party message to voter*
Russian Conservative Party of Entrepreneurs	3	8	12	1	1	2
Russian Network Party of Support for Small and Medium Business	8	0	58	3	0	1
Russian Party of Life	5	0	3	7	1	2
Russian Party of Stability	5.5	0	2	3	0	0
Russian Party of Workers' Self-Management	4	1	1	2	1	0
Russian United Industrial Party	6.5	0	1	1	0	0
Social Democratic Party of Russia	7.5	4	39	4	2	2
Mean	5.3	1.2	12	3.1	1.65	0.9
Mean score Australian non-parliamentary parties 2000[1]	5.5 (out of 13)	2.4	—	0.75	—	0.75
Mean score UK non-parliamentary parties 2001[2]	9.5	7.2	—	9.0	5.5	2.6 (out of 9)
Score range	0–16	0–13	0–n	0–n	0–21	0–13

Sources: (1) Gibson and Ward (2002); (2) Gibson *et al.* (2003).

Table 8A.2 Russian non-parliamentary party websites, 1 to 7 March 2003: website style and delivery

Measure	Score range	Ag. Party	Con. Party	C.P. Unity	Dem. Party	Enter. Dev.	Eur. Party	Eurasia	Greens	Lib. Russia	Nat.-Pat. Forces	Nat.-Pat. Party	Nat.-Rep. Party	Nat.-Sup. Party	Russ. Rebirth
'Glitz index'	0–6														
Home page design		2	2	2	2	2	1.5	3	3	3	2	2	2	2	2
Multimedia used		0	0	0	0	0	0	0	0	0	0	0	0	0	0
Total score	0–5	2	2	2	2	2	1.5	3	3	3	2	2	2	2	2
Access in principle (foreign language translation, ability to download, etc.)		0	0	1	0	0	0	2	0	0	0	0	1	0	0
Kb home page	0–n	—	—	13	15	8.2	—	—	—	37	6.5	—	—	—	14.6
Navigability	0–6	2	1	2	6	2	2	9	1	4	1	2	2	2	2
Freshness	0–6	3	0	2	2	4	0	5	3	3	1	0	1	0	3

Measure	Score range	Rep. Party	Con. Workers Party	Cons. Party Entrep.	Net. Party	Party of Life	Part of Stability	Workers Self-manag.	Soc. Dem. Party	United Ind. Party	Mean	Mean score Australian non-parliamentary parties 2000	Mean score UK non-parliamentary parties 2001
'Glitz index'	0–6												
Homepage design		2	3	2	2	2	1	2	2	3			
Multimedia used		1	0	0	0	1	0	0	0	0			
Total score	0–5	3	3	2	2	3	1	2	2	3	2.15	1.75	3.2
Access in principle (foreign language translation, ability to download etc.)		0	2	1	1	2	0	1	0	1	0.5	0	0.3
Kb home page	0–n	—	—	—	1.5	—	0.6	—	—	—	12.8	5	5.8
Navigability	0–6	1.5	3	1	1	4	1	0	2	1	2.3	1.25	2.5
Freshness	0–6	3	4	0	3	6	1	1	1	5	2.4	0.75	4.8

Appendix B

Table 8B.1 Russian parliamentary party websites, 1 to 7 March 2003: content analysis of website functions

Explanation	Information provision	Resource generation	Openness	Participation	Networking	Campaigning
	Information about party organisation, values, leaders	Membership, donations and purchases online	Total email contacts on site	Feedback and interaction	Total links out of site	Recruiting votes through pulling in voters to party message or pushing party message to voter
United Russia	5	0	86	4.5	4	3.5
Communists	10	2	6	7	12	6
Liberal Democratic Party	8	2	1	0	2	2.5
People's Party	3.5	3	72	3	3	0.5
Union of Right Forces	7	1	117	5	8	6.5
Yabloko	9	0	20	6	9	5
Mean	7.1	1.3	50.3	4.25	6.3	4
Mean score Australian parliamentary parties 2000[1]	6.8 (out of 13)	3.0	—	3.0	—	2.8
Mean score UK/US parliamentary parties 2001[2]	11.6	6.6	—	7.7	5.5	4.2
Score range	0–16	0–13	0–n	0–n	0–21	0–13

Sources: (1) Gibson and Ward (2002); (2) Gibson *et al.* (2003).

Table 8B.2 Russian parliamentary party websites, 1 to 7 March 2003: website style and delivery

Measure	Score range	United Russia	Com. Party	Lib. Dem.	People's Party	Union of Right Forces	Yabloko	Mean score	Mean score Australian parliamentary parties 2000	Mean score UK/US parliamentary parties 2001
'Glitz index'	0–6									
Home page design		3	3	2	3	3	3			
Multimedia used		1	2	2	0	0	0			
Total score		4	5	4	3	3	3	3.7	2.3	4.4
Access in principle (foreign language translation, ability to download, etc.)	0–5	1	1	1	1	1	2	1.2	0.7	1.1
Kb home page	0–n	44	87	—	11	—	—	47.3	12.5	19 UK
Navigability	0–n	3	3	2	5	16	12	6.8	3.8	2.8
Freshness	0–6	6	6	4	5	6	6	5.5	3.3	5.6

Notes

1 The research for this chapter was funded by the generous support of the Carnegie Trust for the Universities of Scotland, which facilitated a research visit to Moscow in December 2003.
2 Luzhkov was one of Putin's most significant rivals for power in 1999. He has since joined forces with Putin.
3 Author's interview with chief editor of lenta.ru Anton Nosik, 10 December 2003.
4 Author's interview with member of Yabloko press service Evgeniya Dillendorf, 24 September 2002.
5 Author's interview with administrator of Yabloko website Vyacheslav Erokhin, 16 September 2002.
6 Author's conversation with Communist Party of the Russian Federation press secretary Andrei Filippov; interview with Communist Central Committee Secretary for Information Policy Oleg Kulikov, both September 2002.
7 Author's interview with chief editor of rambler.ru Ivan Zasurskii, 18 December 2003.

References

Belonuchkin, G. and Mikhailovskaya, E. (2002) 'Politicheskii segment rossiiskogo Interneta', in Semenov, I. (ed.), *Internet i Rossiiskoe obshchestvo*, 70–90, Moscow: Moscow Carnegie Center.

Bieber, C. (2000) 'Revitalising the Party System or *Zeitgeist*-online? Virtual Party Headquarters and Virtual Party Branches in Germany', *Democratization* 7 (1): 59–75.

Coleman, S. (1999) 'Can the New Media Invigorate Democracy?', *Political Quarterly* 70 (1): 16–22.

Coleman, S. (ed.) (2001a) *Elections in the Age of the Internet: Lessons from the United States*, London: Hansard Society.

Coleman, S. (2001b) 'Online Campaigning', *Parliamentary Affairs* 54: 679–688.

Comcon Market Research Company (2000) 'Internet-auditoriya Rossii: strikhi k portretu', Survey from Comcon Market Research Company. Online. Available http://www.comcon-2.ru/default.asp?artID=47 (accessed 20 May 2003).

Dugin, A. (2002) *Evraziiskii put' kak natsional'naya ideya*. Online. Available http://www.evrazia.org/modules.php?name=News&file=print&sid=860) (accessed 27 October 2004).

Duverger, M. (1964) *Political Parties: Their Organization and Activity in the Modern State*, London: Methuen.

Gibson, R.K. and Ward, S. (1998) 'U.K. Political Parties and the Internet: "Politics as Usual" in the New Media?', *Harvard International Journal of Press/Politics* 3: 14–38.

Gibson, R.K. and Ward, S. (2000) 'A Proposed Methodology for Studying the Function and Effectiveness of Party and Candidate Websites', *Social Science Computer Review* 18 (3): 301–319.

Gibson, R.K. and Ward, S. (2002) 'Virtual Campaigning: Australian Parties and the Impact of the Internet', *Australian Journal of Political Science* 37 (1): 99–129.

Gibson, R.K., Newell, J.L. and Ward, S.J. (2000) 'New Parties, New Media: Italian Party Politics and the Internet', *South European Society and Politics* 5 (1): 123–142.

Gibson, R.K., Margolis, M., Resnick, D. and Ward, S.J. (2003) 'Election Campaigning on the WWW in the USA and UK: A Comparative Analysis', *Party Politics* 1: 47–75.

Ivanov, D.I. (2002a) 'Ispol'zovanie Internet-tekhnologii sub"ektami rossiiskogo politicheskogo protsessa v kontse 1990-kh-2001 gg', Dissertation for Candidate degree, Russian State Humanitarian University.

Ivanov, D.I. (2002b) 'Rossiiskii Internet kak sredstvo politicheskii kommunikatsii', *Russkii zhurnal* (russ.ru), 13 March.

Korotkov, A. (2002) *E-Russia in 2002–2010*, Presentation on website of Russian Ministry for Telecommunications and Internetisation. Online. Available http://www.minsvyaz.ru.

Lofgren, K. (2000) 'Danish Political Parties and New Technology: Interactive Parties or New Shop Windows?', in Hoff, J., Horrocks, I. and Tops, P. (eds), *Democratic Governance and New Technology: Technologically Mediated Innovations in Political Practice in Western Europe*, London: Routledge.

Mair, P. (1997) *Party System Change: Approaches and Interpretations*, Oxford: Oxford University Press.

March, L. (2003) 'The Pragmatic Radicalism of Russia's Communists', in Urban, Joan Barth and Curry, Jane (eds), *The Left Transformed in Post-Communist Societies: The Cases of East-Central Europe, Russia, and Ukraine*, Lanham, MD: Rowman & Littlefield.

Margolis, M., Resnick, D. and Tu, Ch-T (1997) 'Campaigning on the Internet: Parties and Candidates on the World Wide Web in the 1996 Primary Season', *Harvard International Journal of Press/Politics* 4: 24–47.

Morozov, A. (2001) 'Deputaty v roli internet-missionerov', *Nezavisimaya gazeta* online version (www.ng.ru), 27 December.

Norris, P. (2001) *Digital Divide: Civic Engagement, Information Poverty and the Internet Worldwide*, Cambridge: Cambridge University Press.

Oates, S. (2002) 'Tuning Out Democracy: Television, Voters and Parties in Russia, 1993–2000', Paper presented at the European Consortium of Political Research, Turin, Italy.

Ochvinnikov, B.V. (2002) 'Virtual'nye nadezhdy: sostoyanie i perspektivy politicheskogo Runeta', *Polis* 1 (5).

Olson, D. (1998) 'Party Formation and Party System Consolidation in the New Democracies of Central Europe', *Political Studies* 46: 432–464.

Oversloot, H. and Verheul, R. (2000) 'The Party of Power in Russian Politics', *Acta Politica* 35: 123–145.

Petrov, N. (2003) 'United Russia: A Fast-build Party Structure for the Kremlin and the Governors'. Online. Available www.carnegie.ru/en/print/67787-print.htm (accessed 29 December 2003).

Public Opinion Foundation (2004) 'Oprosy "Internet v Rossii" ', Vol. 7, Spring. Online. Available http://www.fom.ru (accessed 16 August 2004).

Rash, Jr, W. (1997) *Politics on the Nets: Wiring the Political Process*, New York: W.H. Freeman.

Rommele, A. (2003) 'Political Parties, Party Communication and New Information and Communication Technologies', *Party Politics* 1: 7–20.

Roper, J. (1999) 'New Zealand Political Parties Online: The World Wide Web as a Tool for Democratization or for Political Marketing?', in Toulouse, C. and Luke, T.W. (eds), *The Politics of Cyberspace*, London: Routledge.

Sakwa, R. (1993) *Russian Politics and Society*, London: Routledge.

Sakwa, R. (2002) *Russian Politics and Society*, 3rd edn, London: Routledge.

Semenov, I. (ed.) (2002) *Internet i Rossiiskoe obshchestvo*, Moscow: Moscow Carnegie Center.

Semetko, H.A. and Krasnoboka, N. (2003) 'The Political Role of the Internet in Societies in Transition: Russia and Ukraine Compared', *Party Politics* 1: 77–104.

Smetanin, M. (2002a) 'Boris Nemtsov-pervyi politik v rossiiskom Internete', *Russkii zhurnal* (russ.ru), 20 March.

Smetanin, M. (2002b) 'Virtual'noe partstroitel'stvo', *Russkii zhurnal* (russ.ru), 28 March.

Tropkina, O. (2000) 'Internet kak instrument politiki', *Nezavisimaya gazeta* online version (www.ng.ru), 19 August.

Vinogradov, M. and Chudodeev, S. (2002) 'Partiinaya pautina', *Izvestiya* online version (www.izvestia.ru), 16 July.

Ward, S. (2001) 'Political Organisations and the Internet: Towards a Theoretical Framework for Analysis', Paper presented at the European Consortium of Political Research, Grenoble, France.

Wilson, A. (2001) 'Ukraine's New Virtual Politics', *East European Constitutional Review* 10: 2–3.

Zasurskii, I. (2001) *Rekonstruktsiya Rossii. Mass-mediya i politika v 90-e*, Moscow: Izdatel'stvo MGU.

9 Hard to connect

Transnational networks, non-governmental organisations and the Internet in Russia

Diana Schmidt

Throughout the last decades, transnational advocacy networks have mobilised around issues of global relevance, such as human rights, the environment or women's rights. Involving non-governmental organisations (NGOs) on both domestic and international levels, these networks have proven successful in making information on local malpractices available to the global public in an effort to socialise states and international organisations into the 'community of civilised nations' (Risse and Sikkink, 1999). During the 1990s, two fundamental transformations gave additional impetus to transnational advocacy networks: the emergence of NGOs throughout post-communist Eastern Europe and the global spread of Internet technologies. Democracy-promoting networks have been created across West–East dimensions, and various overlapping networks became active via the Internet, dedicated to serving the information needs of activists worldwide. In theory, the Internet fuels both network formation and advocacy success by facilitating cross-border information exchange among groups involved. However, two present trends in Russia are raising doubts about the advocacy potentialities of domestic groups, namely the re-centralisation of governance, including a clampdown on the media, and the almost exclusive dependency of Russian NGOs on foreign assistance. In this context, the propagation of Internet technologies across the country is raising hopes for a mutually reinforcing relationship between emerging advocacy and online activities. In practice, there are tendencies towards thickening both activist and cyber networking interdependently, although without the overly successful diffusion of advocacy ideas as conceptualised in the literature on transnational advocacy networks.

Research on new social movements shows that, in Western democracies, the media are more an important method for mobilisation and pressure than more conventional channels of participation (Dalton and Kuechler, 1990). Although civil society scholars frequently mention that the Internet too has entered into the repertoire of collective mobilisation (Keck and Sikkink, 1998a; Kopecký, 2003; Take, 2000), this medium remains a black box in the advocacy networks literature. Despite references to the possible role of the Internet as 'an alternative centre for political activities and for informal socialisation' (Kopecký, 2003: 14), its importance for the networking behaviour of NGOs within post-Soviet contexts remains under-researched. Induced by the systemic transformation in Eastern Europe, scholars have engaged in linking civil society and transformation studies (Cohen and Arato, 1997; Merkel, 2000). Emerging forms of Internet mobilisation have entered the study of new social movements (Castells, 1997: 63–83; Cleaver, 1998), even with a view to political protest in post-authoritarian regimes (Krasnoboka and Brants, 2002; Taubman, 1998). However, post-communist NGOs that become part of transnational networks but remain situated within authoritarian regimes are largely excluded from the literature on the Internet and civil society.

This chapter explores how the Internet may serve as an alternative centre for advocacy activities of NGOs in contemporary Russia and how its introduction affects, for better or worse, transnational network building around global issues reaching into a post-communist country.[1] The chapter examines implications for actors and interactions linking the domestic and international levels. It is argued that more attention needs to be paid to transformative operational contexts of local organisations. The theoretical ambition is to challenge general assumptions on domestic NGOs within these networks, as carriers of ideas and information as well as in their intermediary role between the domestic and international arenas. Empirically, the chapter seeks to underpin the plausibility of such propositions by reference to Russian NGOs and reinforcing relationships between the evolution of transnational advocacy, aid and online networks across West–East dimensions, where synergies also imply unintended consequences such as asymmetrical and clientelistic network formation.

Acknowledging that quantitative data do not reveal much about the quality of NGO interactions (Henderson, 2003: 118) – all the more since Russian NGO activity is hardly a subject of statistics (CCNS, 2003) – the chapter builds on qualitative research on the realities of NGO work and web-based communication. Primary data, gathered by the author through a series of interviews, participant observation at NGO gatherings and experience in e-correspondence with Russian organisations, were triangulated with findings from existing case studies. The analysis focuses on the period since Vladimir Putin assumed the presidency in 2000 and the introduction of a more authoritarian governance style. Entailed consequences for activist networks have been neglected in the scholarly literature on Russian civil society, which heavily focused on liberal-democratic transformation paths during the 1990s. As part of extensive field research, the author has conducted more than 50 semi-structured face-to-face interviews with academics, webmasters and heads of domestic as well as transnational NGOs carrying out their work on global issues such as the environment, human rights, freedom of information and anti-corruption in Irkutsk and Ulan Udé, Siberia (September 2001), St Petersburg (July 2003), and Moscow (February 2002; August, December 2003; August 2004). Additionally, 17 local Internet-using NGOs[2] in other than those Russian regions were interviewed by means of structured email questionnaires (February and March 2003).

The first section of this chapter reviews conventional arguments regarding the role of information as well as domestic NGOs within transnational advocacy networks. The discussion then takes this investigation forward to the role of the media, and Internet communication in particular. The second part of the chapter presents findings from the Russian case, with a view to the recent emergence of Internet facilities as well as NGOs within an operational context of authoritarian governance. Against this background, the third part of this chapter investigates how Russian NGOs actually use the Internet for advocacy and networking. Finally, the chapter discusses resulting mismatches between theoretical assumptions on the Internet uptake of advocacy organisations and the realities in the case of Russian NGOs.

Transnational advocacy networks: information flows, NGOs and the Internet

> With the development of the World Wide Web, any government must be prepared to battle with an army of Internet-based desktop publishers who can in a matter of minutes upload documents, photos, and even live interviews or videos to lobby for their causes or counter what they perceive to be official propaganda.
>
> (Passage from a handbook on post-Soviet NGOs, quoted in Ruffin
> *et al.*, 1999)

Transnational advocacy networks are commonly defined as 'networks including those relevant actors working internationally on an issue, who are bound together by shared values, a common discourse, and dense exchanges of information and services' (Keck and Sikkink, 1998a: 2). Available communication technologies determine the pace of these exchanges. Relevant actors are usually domestic NGOs, transnationally operating NGOs, intergovernmental institutions and national governments.[3] The networks are concerned mostly with 'public interest causes – the environment, human rights, women's issues, election monitoring, anti-corruption, and other "good things" ' (Carothers, 1999/2000), which often involve both sensitive issues and informational uncertainty (Keck and Sikkink, 1998a). Participating in domestic and international politics simultaneously, networks may challenge state actors through a 'boomerang' pattern of influence, a constellation in which domestic NGOs bypass their government and directly search out international allies to bring pressure on their states from outside and to provide access, leverage, information and money to struggling domestic groups (Keck and Sikkink, 1998a).

It is commonly argued in the transnational advocacy networks literature that information 'binds network members together and is essential for network effectiveness' (Keck and Sikkink, 1998b: 226). Information is thus crucial both as a cause of and as a consequence from the transnational networking behaviour. The central role of information in typical advocacy issues helps to explain the drive to create networks (Keck and Sikkink, 1998b: 228). As information in these issue areas is both essential and dispersed, advocacy groups need contact with like-minded groups at home and abroad in order to get access to information necessary to their work and wider mobilisation around their concerns. Most transnational actors cannot afford to maintain staff people in a variety of countries, and links with local organisations allow them to receive and monitor information at a low cost. Local groups, in turn, depend on international contacts to get their information out and get some protection in their work (Keck and Sikkink, 1998b: 228). Moreover, it is a common assumption that NGOs are pioneering the provision of information on domestic evidence to the international community. However, recent evidence from post-communist advocacy networks shows that both new ideas and NGOs, as institutions in general and carriers of ideas in particular, are in many cases introduced by Western actors into the domestic domain (Henderson, 2003; Mendelson and Glenn, 2002). It also becomes apparent that conventional scholarly approaches contain a bias against NGO–state relations, when assuming that governments 'want to remain in power, while domestic NGOs seek the most effective means to rally opposition' (Risse and Sikkink, 1999: 16). NGOs are normatively conceived as pro-democratic actors 'who want to tell the truth' (Risse, 2000: 203) – which is a misplaced conception common to most of the work on civil society (Kopecký, 2003).

Post-Soviet societies are undergoing transformations from systems characterised by information secrecy and state control of the media. Clearly, any endurance of these historical legacies matters to the study of the ability of transnational advocacy networks, whose 'main currency is information' (Keck and Sikkink, 1998b: 218), to reach into these countries. Two recent global advocacy issues, information society and anti-corruption, have triggered intensified attention to information as means and objective of networks and its role in the post-communist world. Activists argue that any coherent domestic approach towards these two issues must integrate the institutional pillars of independent media and civil society, complemented by practical access to information and freedom of speech (Transparency International, 2000, 2003; USAID, 1999; UNESCO, 2002–03). In transformation countries, however, not only the ability of advocacy networks to gather and spread information but also efforts to introduce corresponding legislation conforming to EU or other international standards have proven problematic. In Russia and other post-communist states, public access to much information is still broadly denied to citizens.

Networking through the media and the Internet

The literatures on both transnational advocacy networks and NGOs suggest that the media play an essential role in network information politics, and that network actors are making greater use of the innovations in the field of Internet communication technology. The goals of mobilisation and persuasion imply that networks strive to attract media attention in order to reach a broader audience and have maximum influence on ideas, values and political convictions of people all over the world. Scholars argue that communications among governments, transnational and domestic advocacy networks are carried out in a public discourse in front of the international community and domestic civil society groups (e.g. Risse and Ropp, 1999: 250). Frequently, activists 'cultivate a reputation for credibility with the press' (Keck and Sikkink, 1998b: 228), sympathetic journalists become part of the networks, or activities in the form of spectacular action or framing ensure media attention (Take, 2000: 202).

Regarding the global arena, campaigns through international mass media aim at making the public eyewitness to questionable local practices and may thus demonstrate the strength of action before formal policy networks are in a position even to decide on effective countermeasures (Take, 2000: 203). Regarding the domestic dimension, NGOs also provide information to and educate the population about particular threats, risks, or violations of international agreements through their governments, in order to put pressure on the latter. New threats are generally identified by scientists or epistemic communities. However, it is mostly the NGOs, with the help of the mass media, which ensure that such issues come to the public's attention. It should be noted that many information exchanges are informal, such as telephone, email and fax communications or the circulation of small newsletters, pamphlets and bulletins (Keck and Sikkink, 1998b: 226). Today, the Internet seems to offer a new hybrid communication forum, which overcomes the old limits of both meetings and newspapers by combining the opportunities of interactive communication and possibilities to regularly provide information to a large number of people. Experience from Third World countries has shown that fax communication and computer technologies indeed had enormous impact on moving information transnationally, whereas conventional mail services and media have been both precarious and controlled. Evolving webs of North–South exchanges meant that governments could no longer monopolise information flows as they did even a few years before. However, there is also evidence that these forms of networking give special advantages to organisations that have access to such technologies (Keck and Sikkink, 1998b: 227). It is a legitimate question whether corresponding effects can be expected in the course of intensifying West–East networking aided by information and communication technologies.

As the quotation on page 165 suggests, optimism is common with a view to the empowerment of advocacy groups by the Internet in Eastern Europe. Yet, in the literature on transnational advocacy networks, the role of the Internet for non-governmental actors remains largely neglected. Research on the involvement of post-communist NGOs tends to focus on classic issue networks devoted to the environment, human rights and women's issues. In practice, however, two more recent transnational advocacy networks that have emerged during the 1990s are particularly active in Eastern Europe. These networks focus on issues in which information plays a more central role and are defined as (1) the network around challenges posed by the global information society; and (2) the network for fighting corruption on a global scale. The former is paying particular attention to the role of civil society within the process of developing a global framework for a democratic and sustainable information society. It also is concerned with the corresponding governance system for the Internet as a 'global facility available to the public'.[4] Advocacy work of the latter is based on the assumption that increases in transparency will reduce the levels of corruption in any country (Eigen, 2003: 107).

It is often expressed that Internet media facilitate lateral communication and erode traditional boundaries, hierarchies and hegemonies. Only gradually have scholars called for a more critical approach towards a phenomenon that is 'misunderstood and hyperbolised' (Watson and Barber, 2000: 193). While it is still 'in search of a purpose' (Coleman, 2001: 679), political scientists today – like the early Futurists who believed that emerging technologies are by their very nature good and can be put to work to solve implacable social and political problems – tend to be 'oversanguine in viewing email and the Internet in the same light as Glenn Frank saw the radio – namely, as automatically supportive of a more robust public sphere' (Wilhelm, 2000: 3). Yet, new technologies require new sociological thinking. In the media landscape, the sudden prominence of ICTs is changing the concept and functioning of transnational advocacy networks and state–society relations by transforming the role various groups of actors play therein and the ways in which they interact: 'Actually, the idea that a technology orders society turns out to be false yet again. It is not in the nature of electricity to determine the social mode of its use; the same is true of computer technology' (Touraine, 1988: 107). As evidence from Russian NGOs shows, providing 'tools to groups does not mean that they use them in useful or expected ways' (Henderson, 2003: 154).

Internetisation and NGO formation in Russia

When studying ICT utilisation by advocacy groups in Russia, it is important to take into account two simultaneous processes that began in the 1990s: the propagation of Internet facilities outside of elite institutions and the emergence of a third sector represented by NGOs. Regarding Internet propagation, three interrelated factors have significantly inhibited web-based networking by Russian NGOs: (1) an inadequate and imbalanced structural basis, (2) limited capabilities of potential users, and (3) legislative and regulative problems.

In terms of structural problems, although the Russian telecommunication system has undergone significant improvements in the last decade, online activism remains based upon a technological infrastructure of sparsely laid analogue phone lines, which is still considered 'one of the worst in Eastern Europe' (CCNS, 2003) and 'cannot handle a fraction of the necessary dial-up traffic that a typical online community would demand' (IREX, 2002: no. 627: 3). Despite rapid developments, there was still an estimated three- to five-year lag by the start of the new millennium (Semenov, 2001: 12), a significant delay in a cyber-networking era. In addition to the 'digital divide' between Russia and the West, there are strong territorial and social ICT divides within the country. The majority of Internet servers and about 38 per cent of all Internet users are Moscow-based (Perfiliev, 2002: 31; Stafeev, 2002). Moscow and St Petersburg are leading in computerisation and electronic networking, in terms of innovation, investment, quality of service and quantity of both users and providers. The centralised informatisation is being projected on to the regional level, where the servers and web portals are established in the administrative centres, nonetheless lagging some years behind the capitals. The structure of advocacy networks, however, is such that, although offices of all Western donor and domestic network organisations are located in Moscow, the majority of projects are being realised in the regions where political will to experiment is higher and the danger of upsetting certain powerful elites lower than in the capital. Yet, prospects for computerisation in the regions are getting less promising with an increasingly centre-oriented fiscal policy by the Putin administration.

Estimates of Internet use in Russia vary enormously, from between 4 and 8 million users (IREX, 2001: 196; Stafeev, 2002) to a possible 12.8 million (Perfiliev, 2002: 21) online (i.e. from about 3 per cent to 9 per cent of the Russian population of roughly 144 million). The lower estimate seems more realistic in terms of regular use, since people mostly rely on low-quality or sporadic ICT access in Internet cafés or at their workplaces. With regard to social composition, Internet users are predominantly youths, students, people with higher education and/or higher income (IREX, 2001: 199; Stafeev, 2002). Increasing commercialisation and monopolisation of Internet provision also have affected the composition of the audience. During the early 1990s, although heavily dependent on foreign funding and the goodwill of municipal authorities, non-commercial academic computer networks and local pilot projects developed the initial basis of 'Runet'.[5] Meanwhile, the prevalence shifted to commercial networks (Perfiliev, 2002; Stafeev and Webb, 2003). In St Petersburg, for example, non-profit organisations represent only about 7 per cent of the local Internet audience (CCNS, 2003). The lack of a substantial middle class, usually providing significant innovative potential in Western democracies, further limits the possible role of the Internet for lobbying. In addition, Internet costs are prohibitive to the majority of citizens. Access to NGO online activities as well as provision of these services is thus reduced, as both recipients and information-providing NGOs strictly restrict their daily online time.

Apart from its structural basis, the process of bottom-up network building heavily depends on the capabilities of potential users, i.e. local knowledge and

expertise. International assistance, which aims at enhancing online representation of Russian organisations, often expects stable and long-term effects.
According to NGO representatives, however, one of the major problems of
their work is indeed the short-term character of ICT-oriented projects and
difficulty in establishing a permanent base of expertise in constructing and
maintaining Internet presence. Finally, there are significant regulative problems with freedom of speech and journalism in Russia, including poor legal
protection for journalists, laws designed at media control rather than free
speech, state subsidies that function as control levers as well as harassment
and even murder of journalists who tackle sensitive subjects such as human
rights abuses or government corruption. The Internet has not escaped these
problems. Indeed, during Putin's first presidential term, efforts to determine
Internet contents were noticeable through increasing presence of state-
controlled web media and a government strategy to influence Internet users
through commercial competition and regulation. During Putin's second
term, beginning in 2004, further law amendments are to be expected. While
members of the State Duma's committees still deny any initiatives around
draft bills to regulate both the Internet and transnational networking, there
are concerns that new legislation including greater regulation of the mass
media, the Internet and foreign funding of Russian NGOs will further restrict
the potential Internetisation of Russian NGOs.

If the Internet is a relatively new phenomenon in Russia, so are NGOs.
However, what does the presence of NGOs mean for democratisation in the
post-Soviet sphere? The propagation of the Internet was welcomed by activists with little means who were seeking new opportunities to access and shape
the information flows on their behalf. While there were arguably successes in
some countries (for example, see Chapter 10), civic virtual networking has
faltered in others, such as Russia (see Chapter 8; Lenhard, 2003). In Russia,
'email was a revolutionizing experience for many activists when they first
encountered it' (Henderson, 2003), yet high hopes that Internet propagation
would fuel active advocacy networking, and vice versa, have not materialised.
Although thousands of activist groups emerged in Russia, this civic sector
has remained 'fragmented, weak, and strapped for cash' (Powell, 2002) and
'poorly connected with the public' (Henderson, 2003: 54). While 'we tend to
equate organisational density with organisational intensity' (Kopecký, 2003:
7), evidence from Russian NGOs demonstrates that 'activities are important
. . . groups cannot have an impact unless they distribute information, have
meetings, or provide services' (Henderson, 2003: 118). Yet so far, apart from
supplies and technologies, competition for Western funding and fear from
governmental interference among domestic groups significantly affect the
quality of interactions. The analytical focus here is therefore less on recent
quantitative and qualitative changes within the NGO sector but rather on the
interactive networking behaviour of organisations through information and
communication technologies in the context of transnational activism and
domestic authoritarian governance.[6]

There is growing evidence that advocacy groups in several respects diverge from the expectations generated from both scholarly and donor perspectives. Conscious efforts to transfer Western democratic experience to the Russian civil society have not been without capacity effects. Interests of donors and transnationally active organisations have fostered civil society formation and shaped the agendas and organisational design of domestic NGOs. They have also imported Western-style communication networks, in terms of infrastructure and ideas of communication, coalition building, and activist strategies (Henderson, 2003: 153; Powell, 2002: 127). Yet initial expectations have often been misguided or even unrealistic, since they underestimated the significance of Russia's specific institutional and cultural context – the 'institutional software', as Dryzek and Holmes (2002: 4) call it (Eichwede, 2001; Henderson, 2003; Stafeev, 2003). In Western democracies, active NGO sectors as well as intra- and inter-sectoral networking structures have developed over much longer periods of time and within different systemic conditions. Building on these experiences, it has become common to argue that new forms of governance linking transnational and domestic arenas require the participation of NGOs whose particular strengths lie in shaping reform. Under this argument, NGOs would exert pressure on governments and foster the transfer of international principles to domestic arenas, especially in post-authoritarian countries. Moreover, domestic NGOs in these countries are considered effective partners by international donor agencies, and increasing proportions of foreign aid budgets are being channelled through these groups (Carroll, 1992; Powell, 2002).

Regarding Russian NGOs, however, it is a relatively new idea that collective action integrates governmental authorities and activists and takes into account legal and economic aspects. The situation is different in that NGOs have been quickly established, but interaction mechanisms according to Western patterns are only slowly evolving – if at all. Democratic theorists consider Russia as one of the post-communist countries in which no previously existing democratic traditions could be recovered to back up civil society formation (Diamond, 1998; Keane, 1998). Civil society scholars have come to argue that non-governmental organisations actually never had the assumed participatory character and were from the very beginning created as small professional, dependent groups (Henderson, 2003; Powell, 2002), and surveys reveal a persistent lack of civic engagement and trust in democratic institutions among Russian citizens.

It is often maintained that regime-critical, dissident initiatives devoted to civil rights and environmental issues have been the forerunners of informal groups and movements that emerged during the Perestroika period and initiated the formation of the contemporary third sector. Yet from a legal standpoint, the existence of NGOs has only been legitimised since 1990, under the Law for Social Organisations.[7] From an evolutionary perspective, the birth and survival of NGOs in their current form, especially those devoted to issues of global or policy relevance, have been significantly fuelled by Western promotion of democratisation and civil society principles – and corresponding financial assistance – rather than resulting from bottom-up civil society formation or activism (Henderson, 2002, 2003; Powell, 2002). Internally, the Russian NGO sector suffers from a lack of expertise and recognition, low income levels and high unemployment rates that affect people's incentive to do voluntary work in small organisations.

Provision of funding, equipment and training by Western allies has considerably increased organisational capacities of Russian NGOs. But in an environment that provides no alternative sources,[8] foreign aid contributes to the emergence of a vertical, institutionalised and isolated civic community rather than fostering horizontal networking and civil society building from below. The Western 'monetary engine behind Russian civic organisations' (Henderson, 2002: 146) provides incentives for NGOs to initiate short-term projects that match the agenda of sponsors and produce measurable results. Material needs incite many organisations to contend with each other, duplicate each other's projects, or hoard information rather than mobilising sustained collective action around advocacy causes. As interviews with representatives of local NGOs in Eastern Siberia revealed, they are often reluctant to cooperate with each other and justify their focus on joint projects with Western partners by a feeling of being in a remote, disadvantaged position compared to their counterparts around Moscow.

Given the enormous size of Russia, spatial patterns of distribution are relevant from a networking perspective. The most active NGOs concentrate in the central and north-western regions, including Moscow and St Petersburg, the Ural region and Western Siberia. One major problem is that exchange and networking efforts of local NGOs through publications and conferences seldom go beyond the same circle of NGOs. In addition, the proclaimed 'trickle-down' civic approach proves problematic, relying on the uneven dispersal of skills and resources through a few centralised NGOs and leaving thousands of groups isolated and unfunded (Henderson, 2003: 153). The complexity and fluidity of institutional and economic conditions in the context of on-going transformation and reformation also hampers third sector formation. One crucial aspect is the tax system, being notoriously non-transparent, frequently amended, devoid of exemptions for non-profit advocacy organisations, and even obliging foreign donors to pay income taxes.

Western analysts and practitioners alike often neglect domestic transformative contexts, within which NGOs operate as members of transnational networks. In addition to the multiple challenges of the post-communist transformation, Russian NGOs are confronted with a newly authoritarian regime, as scholars concur that democratic growth has stalled or slipped away completely in Russia. Russia provides a prominent example of transformation in which 'formal institutions of democracy often masked quite undemocratic practices' (Sakwa, 2001: 93). In practice, this has meant re-centralising governance, including a reduction in the freedom of expression and information.

In the media sphere, which directly affects the Internet, there has been tightening and arbitrary application of respective laws; monopolisation of the media market and media support institutions; selective licensing and inappropriate tax regulations; restricted access to public information; libel or persecution of journalists; self-censorship; and falling professional standards and increasing bribery (e.g. IREX, 2001; Kenneth, 2003; Price and Krug, 2000). The international community has directed public awareness to these conditions by calling on the Russian government to end practices that limit media freedom as well as honouring individuals and organisations that are opposing these trends from below.[9]

Under President Putin, state relations with NGOs took a new turn with the Civic Forum, which was initiated as an official meeting of authorities and selected NGO representatives in Moscow.[10] This caused major controversies among experts and Russian NGOs. Organisations with stronger links to the international community, and the latter itself, initially welcomed this step as a governmental commitment to democratic reform. Local organisations might have felt gratitude at this federal-level acknowledgement of their importance (Henderson, 2003), but this was outweighed by growing concern that governmental civil society building in a centralised fashion would aggravate existing structural dependencies. Some believe that the government was uncomfortable with the idea of an NGO sector supported externally by Western foundations and thus sought to foster a civil society more reliant on domestic sources of support (Osterman, 2002). After President Putin openly criticised aspects of Western funding in his latest address to the Federal Assembly (JRL, 2004), activists increasingly came to agree with early critics, who perceived the Civic Forum as 'expensive lip service to the concept of civil society' (Kostyukov, 2001) and a further step in efforts to co-opt the organisations and to silence opposition (Henderson, 2003: 58).

Russian NGOs in general are now perceived to constitute a potentially influential voice and are increasingly subjected to the governmental agenda. Primarily, this applies to organisations working on environmental, human rights, corruption and information matters, which frequently touch upon so-called strategic issues or state secrets. In these circumstances, the Internet again comes to the fore as an alternative sphere for NGOs to exchange information and participate in networking, assuming that the Russian government cannot impede the propagation of the Internet across the country. An international conference, 'Russia in the Internet Age: Balancing Freedom and Regulation', revealed fundamental disagreements about the role of the government regarding Internetisation and its obligation to make public information available.[11] Western participants suggested that governmental attempts to control the new medium are 'fundamentally undemocratic and can only hurt Russia's economy'. US governmental representatives emphasised the Internet's social and economic benefits as well as the importance to entrust assessment of regulatory needs to the private sector and NGOs. NGO representatives from the United States stressed that a policy that provides for limited freedom of information contradicts the objective of democratisation. Russian NGO representatives called for state measures and investment to create the infrastructure necessary to develop an Internet society. Russian authorities argued that the government has fundamental responsibility for security and therefore overwhelming rights to withhold state information and to access private information. They also emphasised state budget constraints and the significance of cultural and economic differences between the US and Russia. However, the Western participants stressed that the key would be 'inducing cultural change that embraces the Internet' (IREX, 2002: 3).

The Russian government publicly acknowledges the need to develop network society structures based on international principles, although in a rather non-committal way. With initiatives such as the federal ten-year target programme 'Electronic Russia' (2002),[12] 'the Russian government took on a responsibility for leading the information technology revolution in Russia' (Semenov, 2001). Yet, an effective national strategy remains absent. Prepared programmes remain purely declarative and lack specification through corresponding short-term and regional programmes (Stafeev, 2003). In view of national plans being incoherent and in contradiction to governmental practice, both international and domestic NGOS emphasise the principal role of professional media associations and independent NGOs for the development of information infrastructures and the formation of a public sphere (IREX, 2001; UNESCO, 2002–03; CCNS, 2003; Kenneth, 2003). Yet within the context of on-going transformation and centralisation, can civil society actors actually use new Internet information and networking possibilities for advocacy purposes?

Making use of ICTs

Russia harbours innumerable places where no Internet reaches citizens outside the centres or off the main telecommunication lines, and local NGOs are often operating in an 'information vacuum' (CCNS, 2003), making international collaboration enormously difficult. Even where access to the Internet is technically possible, NGOs are confronted with hindrances in terms of finances, computer equipment, affordable providers, personnel and Internet acceptance. Most NGOs agree that it is essential to use ICTs, not only for advocating particular causes but also for improving the quality of life of the broader population (Stafeev, 2002). Yet, as one NGO concludes from its analytical and practical efforts in community networking, not all socially active people understand the benefits from virtual networking and civic groups often cannot imagine how the web could open windows of opportunities for them. It is not only Internet illiteracy but also, and more importantly, the mindset of local NGO leaders that is holding back online networking.

Organisations that are actively employing Internet facilities seem to quickly develop this understanding and emphasise numerous advantages of the new medium. Unanimously, interviewees cite speed, the wide reach of information exchange, the operative nature of the Internet and access to international news as particular benefits.[13] Advocacy organisations make use of ICTs, not so much for finding new partners but rather for broadcasting announcements through web portals and by distributing more specific messages through email lists (circular or individual mails to people with whom contacts are already established). Organisations that maintain their own web pages primarily use them for self-portrayal and providing links to other web pages, mostly within the advocacy community, e.g. to other Russian and foreign NGOs, news sites or sponsors. None of the interviewed organisations provided links to either governmental or business portals. Organisations that are actively publishing articles welcome that they can simply make those articles available online, instead of having to rely on print versions in local or national magazines.

The enthusiasm of cyberactive advocacy NGOs is often reflected in their agendas. Even single-issue organisations, devoted to particular societal or environmental concerns, additionally aim at improving information, education, discussion and involving the population in decision-making processes. One of the most cyberactive NGOs is the Moscow chapter of Transparency International, not least because this NGO puts particular emphasis on the development of information laws and Internet propagation in its effort to oblige authorities to make internal information accessible. However, according to representatives of this NGO, meetings are still important for the purpose of networking, since anti-corruption work is done by all kinds of NGOs and mostly not visible from the organisation's name or topical focus. While official meetings at international conferences take place only once or twice a year, the Internet is needed as a tool for communication during the times in between.

In the literature it is often maintained that ICTs have the advantage of making existing practices of communication and information gathering cheaper, faster and steadier, as well as encouraging information usage on a larger scale and in more detail. Furthermore, with political information gathered for one purpose becoming available for other purposes, the information infrastructure of a political system would rapidly grow (Agre, 2002: 322). This is different regarding the networking of Russian NGOs, since there are no existing practices in this sense. Entrenched social practices of informal and personal communication linger. At the same time, it is rather novel that activists become able to gather and disseminate previously unavailable information on political issues through ICTs. Additionally, there are new opportunities to initiate contact with foreign actors and to exchange electronic messages that would otherwise have spread much more slowly, or would not have left the country at all. But the full potential offered by Internet technologies is not being tapped, with lack of traditions and experience in developing and managing virtual networks beyond the local community as well as prevalent reluctance to share information, especially on politically sensitive issues, impeding a flourishing information infrastructure.

The main advantage of ICTs thus consists in facilitating the formation of transnational networks that grant domestic groups access to the international community. As costs are crucial, small travel budgets often constitute a bigger hurdle than Internet expenses to participation in international dialogue around advocacy issues. Virtual portals, conferences and email lists enable NGOs to compete with the comparatively big travel budgets of governments and corporations. In addition, Russian NGOs may gain instantaneous advice or support on specific questions and access to funding bodies. However, transnational online communication develops in an imbalanced fashion, with interested foreigners remaining largely unsuccessful in getting reliable information about or access to domestic groups via the Internet. As for the domestic level, it also remains uncertain whether information exchange in a virtual sphere may open exchange, or even interaction, among different societal sectors. Opinions and practices of the interviewees are divergent in this respect. Some Russian NGOs are never contacted by and never try to get into contact with authorities via email; others have email contact with local municipals on an irregular basis. Similar patterns apply to communication with business companies. Email communication with private persons is different in the sense that NGOs very often receive emails with questions or complaints. The critical aspect here is the audience, with senders being predominantly urban and younger citizens from both Russia and foreign countries.

Finally, the use of ICTs can neither avoid nor solve problems related to state control and information secrecy. Yet analysis of governmental interference of Internet communication is difficult, since authorities and experts refuse to comment on related questions. The current legislation obliges all Russian providers to link their devices to the Federal Security Bureau (FSB) and authorises the latter to access all Internet transmissions. However, in interviews with NGOs it was noticeable that only those organisations that actively use ICTs are actually aware of this circumstance, whereas others consider the tapping of telephone communications much more problematic.[14] Furthermore, activists complain about the tradition of authorities to conceal information and their ability to make any documents that could inform about the behaviour of authorities and ministries disappear indefinitely into filing cabinets. Gathering and exchanging publicly relevant information in general has become challenging not only for journalists, but for civil activists as well. There are an increasing number of cases in which NGOs, especially those with transnational links, are harassed and their computer equipment confiscated by dubious special forces.

Transnational advocacy and cyber networking with Russian NGOs

At the global level, the evolution of transnational networking implies three distinct processes in the spheres of advocacy, aid and Internetisation.

However, evidence from post-Soviet countries indicates that these three modes of transnational networking have simultaneously started to reach into domestic levels during the 1990s and are thus more intertwined than elsewhere. The collapse of communism marked the onset of interactions among transnational human rights or environmental advocacy networks and domestic groups. At the same time, local NGOs in developing and transformation countries gained the unwarranted reputation of being effective partners for international donor agencies and were increasingly used for channelling foreign aid. In response, local organisations were often created in order to apply for the increasing private and public funding available for non-governmental activities in Eastern Europe. Russia has received the largest share of Western democratisation assistance that has gone to this region, much of it devoted to civil society formation and various advocacy fields as part of good governance building. The simultaneously evolving Internet infrastructure allowed international allies and local groups to communicate with a view to transferring information and services. Internet utilisation and transnational networking with local NGOs are mutually reinforcing processes.

There have been some positive synergies among advocacy networks, aid networks and online networks operating across West–East dimensions. However, there is indication that there are unintended consequences when network categories overlap within a domestic context, in which both NGOs and Internet facilities are sparsely distributed and face the dual challenge of a highly centralised governance system and low participation of the wider population in advocacy around global issues. Typically, in societies with an insufficient online population and infrastructure, civic groups have minimal incentive to develop web portals, and intensive Internet use in developed regions aggravates the 'digital divide' between developed and undeveloped areas (Norris, 2001). Yet limited success in reaching the wider public through online activities is not solely related to infrastructure constraints. As interviews and recent studies (e.g. Henderson, 2003) confirm, Russian NGOs that had received grants tend to associate with other funded groups; in turn, groups out of the purview of Western assistance tend to associate within their circles. As the effects of aid are often contained within the very circles to which it is distributed, transnational networking becomes insular rather than involving new groups.

Although NGO representatives initially were 'joyful, even ecstatic about the bridges email could cross' (Henderson, 2003: 106), there is a large divide separating connected from unconnected groups (CCNS, 2003), which mirrors the divide between funded and non-funded groups in terms of organisational infrastructure. There is convincing evidence that funding guarantees access to technology and improves the networking and communication abilities of Russian NGOs, whereas non-funded groups 'often struggled to afford envelopes and paper to take care of daily business' (Henderson, 2003: 133). Unconnected groups, in turn, are often unable to establish contacts and access information needed to get organisational assistance and funding from abroad. While in-groups of transnationally connected NGOs are solidifying, unequal access to Internet communication may in turn intensify previously existing, and currently reinforced, disparities between Russian organisations in centre and peripheral regions as well as among local organisations.

As for advocacy and online networks across West–East dimensions, asymmetrical transnational relations between NGOs involved are problems similar to what Henderson (2003: 155–166) terms the unintended consequences of foreign 'supply-driven civic development', 'principled clientelism' and 'guardian civil societies'. In such cases, domestic NGOs hardly correspond to the concept generated by the literature on transnational advocacy networks, as they serve neither as oppositional pressure groups nor as carriers of advocacy issues into wider publics. Rather, their relations with foreign allies largely determine their organisational capacities and topical agendas. Moreover, as they face multiple problems related to e-communication that are different from Western experiences, international and domestic groups tend to divert advocacy attention to the topic of informatisation as such.

In sum, transnational aid, activist and ICT networks *in combination* made substantial impact on transnational NGO interconnectedness. However, findings from Russian NGOs challenge optimistic assumptions that the Internet facilitates lateral communication among local groups and erodes traditional boundaries, hierarchies and hegemonies within domestic governance systems. Moreover, while Internet utilisation clearly supports transnational networking, it is unlikely that the provision of new communication technologies alone would have fostered networking among Russian organisations. As Dahl (1998: 157) argues from the prescriptive view of democratic theory, introduced ideas are of little use for democratisation unless they are strongly supported by citizens and leaders. This line of thought can be resumed with a view to the introduction of networking ideas and networking practices in Russia: the Western language of advocacy, civil society and democracy is meaningfully introduced only when understood and spoken by both the population and the government. As long as new technologies, information and institutions are disregarded by citizens and controlled by the political leadership, the recent presence of ICTs and NGOs cannot be a sufficient condition for sustaining network pressure around particular issues. Furthermore, the domestic situation of traditional media as well as the ability of advocacy groups to keep close links with journals and newspapers is of greater relevance than commonly assumed from a cyberoptimistic perspective.

In order to gain a better understanding of networking mechanisms in the Russian case, more research needs to be conducted on how domestic advocacy NGOs are positioned between the authoritarian state and transnational, pro-democratic networks. Regarding the advocacy literature in general, attention must be paid to asymmetrical relations across West–East dimensions as well as within highly centralised countries. With a view to domestic NGOs as agents within these network structures, on the one hand,

and within authoritarian governance structures on the other, further empirical insights are needed into the particular role of Internet facilities to overcome or reinforce dependencies involved.

Notes

1 For insightful and helpful comments on earlier versions of the chapter, thanks to colleagues in Cologne, Belfast and Russia and to the participants of the 2003 European Consortium for Political Research workshop on The Changing Media and Civil Society in Edinburgh, Scotland. This chapter also benefits from valuable insights gained through discussions at conferences and personal conversation with Russian researchers and practitioners. The financial contributions of the Queen's University Belfast, through a Support Programme for University Research scholarship and a Queen's Alumni Fund Travel Scholarship are gratefully acknowledged.
2 Representing a respondent turnout of only 12 per cent, this survey may itself demonstrate the limited efficacy of purposeful online communication.
3 The term NGOs is used here to include organisations such as interest groups, advocacy groups and citzens' associations operating in the third sector between the state and the market, their main functions, goals and resources thus being non-governmental and non-profit-making.
4 See information on the negotiations around the World Summit on the Information Society at: www.wsis-cs.org.
5 The term Runet refers to domains in Russian language and is commonly used for distinction from the notion of Russian Internet contained by territorial boundaries. It comprises three categories of sites: academic, commercial and political. The 'history' of the latter only dates back to 1994 (Belonuchkin and Mikhaylovskaya, 2002: 69).
6 On modifications in organisational density and working priorities, see CCNS (2003); Webb and Stafeev (2003) on the changing scope and composition of the NGO sector during the 1990s; or Henderson (2003: 151) on changing donor preferences since 2000.
7 The Federal Law for Social Organisations (passed in October 1990) has been, and is being, continually amended and renamed.
8 If there have been hopes for increasing support from the Russian business community, these have ceased since the Yukos scandal, as corporations are now avoiding involvement in any funding of civil society formation.
9 For example, the Organisation for Security and Cooperation in Europe (OSCE) and the Council of Europe have asked Russian authorities to bring the Russian criminal code into line with European press freedom standards. The 2003 OSCE Prize for Journalism and Democracy went to Anna Politkovskaya, reporter of the *Novaya Gazeta*, who has been persecuted for chronicling charges of military abuse in Chechnya. In a more antagonistic way, the international media watchdog Reporters Sans Frontières has set up a gallery of 'predators of press freedom' headed by Vladimir Putin (http://www.rsf.fr/article.php3?id_article=1075).
10 The gathering took place in November 2001 and was organised via a German–Russian intiative. For details, see www.petersburger-dialog.de.
11 The conference took place in Moscow in February 2002 (cf. IREX, 2002: 3, 6).
12 For the full text of the programme, see: http://www.e-rus.ru/eng/erus.shtml?id=19.
13 Author's research.
14 Author's interviews.

References

Agre, P.E. (2002) 'Real-time Politics: The Internet and the Political Process', *Information Society* 18: 311–331.

Belonuchkin, G. and Mikhaylovskaya, E. (2002) 'Political Segment of Russian Internet: Development and Prospects', *Internet i rossiiskoe obshchestvo*, Moscow: Carnegie Moscow Centre. Online. Available http://pubs.carnegie.ru/books/2002/08is.

Carothers, T. (1999/2000) 'Civil Society', *Foreign Policy* 117, Winter: 18–29.

Carroll, T.F. (1992) *Intermediary NGOs: The Supporting Link in Grassroots Development*, West Hartford, CT: Kumarian Press.

Castells, M. (1997) *The Power of Identity: The Information Age – Economy, Society and Culture*, Vol. II, Oxford: Blackwell.

Centre of Community Networking and Information Policy Studies (CCNS) (2003) *ICTs in Russian Civil Society Sector Organisations/Analytical Review*, St Petersburg, Russia: Centre of Community Networking and Information Policy Studies. Online. Available http://www.communities.org.ru/papers/01/ictsinnp.rtf (accessed 25 February 2003).

Cleaver, H. (1998) 'The Zapatistas and the Electronic Fabric of Struggle', in Holloway, J. and Pelaez, E. (eds), *Zapatista! Reinventing Revolution in Mexico*, London: Pluto Press.

Cohen, J.L. and Arato, A. (1997) *Civil Society and Political Theory*, 4th edn, Cambridge, MA: MIT Press.

Coleman, S. (2001) 'Online Campaigning', *Parliamentary Affairs* 54: 679–688.

Dahl, R.A. (1998) *On Democracy*, New Haven, CT: Yale University Press.

Dalton, R.J. and Kuechler, M. (eds) (1990) *Challenging the Political Order: New Social and Political Movements in Western Democracies*, Cambridge: Polity.

Diamond, L. (1998) *Political Culture and Democratic Consolidation*, Centro de Estudios Avanzados en Ciencias Sociales: Estudios Working Papers, Vol. 118.

Dryzek, J.S. and Holmes, L. (2002) *Post-Communist Democratisation: Political Discourses across Thirteen Countries*, Cambridge: Cambridge University Press.

Eichwede, W. (2001) 'Von außen gesehen: Russische Entwicklungen, westliche Perzeptionen', in Höhmann, H.-H. and Schröder, H.-H. (eds), *Russland unter neuer Führung. Politik, Wirtschaft und Gesellschaft am Beginn des 21.Jahrhunderts*, Bonn: Bundeszentrale für politische Bildung.

Eigen, P. (2003) *Das Netz der Korruption. Wie eine weltweite Bewegung gegen Bestechung kämpft*, Frankfurt and New York: Campus Verlag.

Henderson, S.L. (2002) 'Selling Civil Society: Western Aid and the Nongovernmental Organization Sector in Russia', *Comparative Political Studies* 35 (2): 139–167.

Henderson, S.L. (2003) *Building Democracy in Contemporary Russia: Western Support for Grassroots Organisations*, Ithaca, NY and London: Cornell University Press.

IREX (2001) 'Media Sustainability Index. Russia', in I.M. International Research and Exchange Board (ed.), pp. 191–204. Online. Available http://www.irex.org/pubs/msi_2001/20-Russia.pdf.

IREX (2002) *Russia in the Internet Age: Balancing Freedom and Regulation*, IREX policy paper, Washington, DC: Independent Media International Research and Exchange Board. Online. Available http://www.irex.org/pubs/policy/index.asp 001.

JRL (2004) 'Address to the Federal Assembly of the Russian Federation. President Vladimir Putin', no. 10, JRL (Johnson's Russia List), 8225, 26 May. Online. Available www.cdi.org.

Keane, J. (1998) *Civil Society: Old Images, New Visions*, Cambridge: Cambridge University Press.

Keck, M.E. and Sikkink, K. (1998a) *Activists beyond Borders: Advocacy Networks in International Politics*, Ithaca, NY and London: Cornell University Press.

Keck, M.E. and Sikkink, K. (1998b) 'Transnational Advocacy Networks in the Movement Society', in Meyer, D S. and Tarrow, S. (eds), *The Social Movement Society: Contentious Politics for a New Century*, Lanham, MD: Rowman & Littlefield.

Kenneth, C. (2003) 'Experts Decry Lack of Press Freedom: Mass Media as an Instrument of Democracy and Government and Private Corporations' Media Policies in Russia', Study conducted by the Russian Union of Journalists, Moscow-based International Press Club, Journalism Department of Moscow State University, the Gorbachev Fund and the Universities of Calgary and Mount Ellison, reported in Canada's *JRL, The Russia Journal*. Online. Available www.cdi.org/russia/johnson/7033-15.cfm.

Kopecký, P. (2003) 'Civil Society, Uncivil Society and Contentious Politics in Post-Communist Europe', in Kopecký, P. and Mudde, C. (eds), *Uncivil Society? Contentious Politics in Post-Communist Europe*, London: Routledge.

Kostyukov, A. (2001) 'Civil Society Lines Up for Display to the President: An interview with Yabloko Leader Grigory Yavlinsky', *Obshchaya Gazeta*, 22–28 November.

Krasnoboka, N. and Brants, K. (2002) 'Old and New Media, Old and New Politics?', Paper prepared for the workshop 'Political Communication, the Mass Media and the Consolidation of Democracy', European Consortium of Research, Turin, Italy.

Lenhard, M. (2003) 'Netzwerkerinnen in Russland. Die digitale Vernetzung der Frauenbewegung', in Schetsche, M. and Lehmann, K. (eds), *Netzwerker-Pespektiven*, Rogensburg: Roderer.

Mendelson, S.E. and Glenn, J.K. (eds) (2002) *The Power and Limits of NGOs: A Critical Look at Building Democracy in Eastern Europe and Eurasia*, New York: Columbia University Press.

Merkel, W. (ed.) (2000) *Systemwechsel 5: Zivilgesellschaft und Transformation*, Opladen: Leske & Budrich.

Norris, P. (2001) *Digital Divide: Civic Engagement, Information Poverty and the Internet Worldwide*, Cambridge: Cambridge University Press.

Osterman, G. (2002) 'Grazhdanskii Forum v Otsenkach Pressy'. Online. Available http://www.smi.ru/01/11/22/43205.html.

Perfiliev, Y. (2002) 'The Territorial Organisation of Russia's Cyberspace', *Internet i rossiiskoe obshchestvo*, Moscow: Carnegie Moscow Centre. Online. Available http://pubs.carnegie.ru/books/2002/08is.

Powell, L. (2002) 'Western and Russian Environmental NGOs: A Greener Russia?', in Mendelson, S.E. and Glenn, J.K. (eds), *The Power and Limits of NGOs: A Critical Look at Building Democracy in Eastern Europe and Eurasia*, New York: Columbia University Press.

Price, M.E. and Krug, P. (2000) *The Enabling Environment for Free and Independent Media*, Oxford. Online. Available www.medialaw.ru/e_pages/publications/ee/index.html.

Risse, T. (2000) 'The Power of Norms versus the Norms of Power: Transnational Civil Society and Human Rights', in Florini, A.M. (ed.), *The Third Force: The*

Rise of Transnational Civil Society, Washington, DC: Carnegie Endowment for International Peace.

Risse, T. and Ropp, S.C. (1999) 'International Human Rights Norms and Domestic Change: Conclusions', in Risse, T., Ropp, S.C. and Sikkink, K. (eds), *The Power of Human Rights: International Norms and Domestic Change*, Cambridge: Cambridge University Press.

Risse, T. and Sikkink, K. (1999) 'The Socialization of International Human Rights Norms into Domestic Practices: Introduction', in Risse, T., Ropp, S.C. and Sikkink, K. (eds), *The Power of Human Rights: International Norms and Domestic Change*, Cambridge: Cambridge University Press.

Ruffin, M.H., Deutschler, A., Logan, C. and Upjohn, R. (1999) *The Post-Soviet Handbook: A Guide to Grassroots Organisations and Internet Resources*, Seattle, WA: University of Washington Press.

Sakwa, R. (2001) 'Parties and Organised Interests', in White, S., Pravda, A. and Gitelman, Z. (eds), *Developments in Russian Politics*, Vol. 5, Basingstoke: Palgrave.

Semenov, I. (2001) 'The Information Revolution in Electronic Russia', *Carnegie Briefing Papers* 3 (7), Moscow: Carnegie Moscow Centre. Online. Available http://pubs.carnegie.ru/english/briefings/2001/issue01–07.asp.

Stafeev, S. (2002) 'IT News in Russia: Community Networking in Post-Soviet Russia', *Community Technology Review*, Fall–Winter. Online. Available www.comtechreview.org.

Stafeev, S. (2003) 'Russian e-policy: A Civil Society View', Centre of Community Networking and Information Policy Studies, unpublished document.

Stafeev, S. and Webb, S. (2003) 'Community Informatics in Russia: Needing to Make a Leap', in Marshall, S., Taylor, W. and Yu, X. (eds), *Closing the Digital Divide: Transforming Regional Economics and Communities with Information Technology*, Westport, CT: Praeger.

Take, I. (2000) 'The Better Half of World Society', in Albert, M., Brock, L. and Wolf, K.D. (eds), *Civilizing World Politics: Society and Community beyond the State*, Lanham, MD: Rowman & Littlefield.

Taubman, J. (1998) 'A Not-So World Wide Web: The Internet, China, and the Challenges to Nondemocratic Rule', *Political Communication* 15: 255–272.

Touraine, A. (1988) *Return of the Actor: Social Theory in Postindustrial Society*, Minneapolis, MN: University of Minnesota Press.

Transparency International (2000) 'The National Integrity System', Ch. 4 in Transparency International (ed.), *TI Source Book 2000*, Berlin: Transparency International.

Transparency International (ed.) (2003) *Global Corruption Report 2003. Special Focus: Access to Information*, Berlin: Transparency International. Online. Available http://www.globalcorruptionreport.org/gcr2003.html.

UNESCO (2002–03) *Krupnaia Programma V. Kommunikatsiia i informatsiia* [Large-scale Programme V. Communication and Information], Moscow. Online. Available http://www.unesco.ru/programs/communications/31c-5rus_prog5.pdf.

USAID (1999) *From Transition to Partnership: A Strategic Framework for USAID Programs in Europe and Eurasia*, United States Agency for International Development, Bureau for Europe and Eurasia. Online. Available http://www1.worldbank.org/wbiep/decentralization/ciesin/PDABS123.pdf.

Watson, P. and Barber, B.R. (2000) *The Struggle for Democracy*, Toronto, Ontario: Key Porter Books.

Wilhelm, A.G. (2000) *Democracy in the Digital Age*, London: Routledge.

10 Murder, journalism and the web

How the Gongadze case launched the Internet news era in Ukraine

Natalya Krasnoboka and Holli A. Semetko

> It is horrible to admit, but only through acquaintance with the [Georgiy] Gongadze case, have millions of inhabitants of our country heard the word 'Internet' for the first time.
>
> (The online paper *Ukrainska Pravda*, November 2000, after its founder Gongadze was abducted and killed)

The current stage of the political Internet's development in Ukraine is a truly remarkable example of the diversity of options this medium offers for democratic transformations. Challenging most of the current practices and uses of the medium elsewhere, the development of the Ukrainian Internet provided support for some of the earliest optimistic predictions of this new technology's implications for democracy. The Internet in Ukraine sets a political agenda for the Ukrainian parliament, president and other mass media by running its own criminal, journalistic, legal and political investigations as well as by accusing top-level officials of illegalities and providing evidence to back up these accusations. The Internet in Ukraine appeals to international organisations and experts; serves as a watchdog in national elections; monitors the national media; and highlights plagiarism in the media. This new medium also has a literary side, making the whole country laugh – and sometimes cry – at its jokes, stories and poems. It has shocked the nation with the taped revelations from the President's cabinet. Is this a miracle of democracy? No, it is just that an appropriate combination of necessary conditions appeared almost simultaneously in Ukraine.

This chapter examines those conditions through the lens of the protests surrounding the disappearance and presidential scandal connected to the murder of opposition Internet journalist Georgiy Gongadze in 2000. This chapter identifies the similarities and differences between the ways in which the different news media – newspapers, television and the Internet – covered these critical protest events in Ukraine. This chapter argues that the particular elements of the Gongadze case and the lack of coverage of the public protest in the traditional mass media opened up the opportunity for the

Internet in Ukraine to develop as an authoritative alternative source of information.[1]

Contentious politics and the mass media

Before turning to the specifics of the Gongadze case, the Internet and the Ukrainian media, it is important to consider the general role of the media in covering 'contentious' politics, i.e. the politics of strikes and demonstrations rather than that of voting or campaigning. Access to the mass media is key for political participation, yet actors in contentious political action often have little access to the traditional mass media. Sidney Tarrow (1998) found that, while the media can 'build connective structures' among large numbers of people to deal with issues, at the same time participants of contentious politics often have to 'compete with the media, which transmit messages that movements must attempt to shape and influence' (Tarrow, 1998: 22). Thus, media play the outstanding role in spreading information about contention and allowing uninvolved citizens to take their own positions in the conflict between protestors and the powerful. By doing this, media also frame contention, very often in a way unaccepted by protestors. Michael Lipsky (1968: 1151) made another direct point on this issue: 'If protest tactics are not considered significant by the media, or if newspapers and television reporters or editors decide to overlook protest tactics, protest organizations will not succeed.'

Empirical studies conducted in the area of media and contentious politics only confirm the ambiguity of media coverage. Different research groups working on various historical periods and countries have registered certain selection and description biases in the media approach to the study of contention (Danzger, 1975; Snyder and Kelly, 1977; Berk, 1983; Kielbowitz and Scherer, 1986; Gamson *et al.*, 1992; Small, 1994; McCarthy *et al.*, 1996; Mueller, 1997). According to most of their findings, only larger and more violent protests are covered. Additionally, an act of contention needs to fit the on-going media cycle of attention and not contradict corporate and other sponsored interests of media organisations. Empirical evidence suggests that acts of contention often become a challenge for media institutions, questioning their limits of objectivity and unbiased behaviour. Coverage of contention by the media is also a challenge to researchers, particularly those who support a democratic model of media behaviour and believe in the potential objectivity of media reporting.

The appearance of the Internet has provoked many optimistic discussions about its possible political uses. It would appear that potential actors of contention should broadly benefit from options provided by this new medium of communication. The Internet has been seen as an alternative, cheap and fast creator of a different reality, a reality that could be constructed by protesters themselves and not mediated or distorted by other institutions such as the traditional mass media. At the same time, the marginal nature of the

Internet as a mass medium would tend to limit a monopoly of powerful political and economic interests behind it. Finally, the very definitions of contention and the Internet include many common features, such as network, interaction and broad access.

Recent anti-globalist and environmentalist actions have shown examples of Internet use for the purposes of contention (Cilser, 1999; Ostry, 2000; Hammond and Lash, 2000). Research done in authoritarian and transitional societies also confirms the use of the Internet by groups of protestors, who in this way spread their own information and vision of political reality (Kalathil and Boas, 2001; Taubman, 1998; Rodan, 1998; Ott and Rosser, 2000). However, evidence of Internet use for the purposes of contentious action is much broader than the current research is able to grasp. So-called transitional societies (in which political conditions for expression of alternative voices and positions are less strict than in authoritarian regimes) are particularly useful in presenting examples of the intensive and systematic use of the Internet for purposes of political and social contention (Semetko and Krasnoboka, 2003; Krasnoboka and Brants, 2002). The local character of these uses together with the lack of scientific investigation and the current pessimistic mood concerning the abilities of the Internet to affect political participation in general transforms these into non-events for the rest of the world. However, this chapter presents compelling evidence that the Internet can become an important tool of political activism and contention under certain political conditions and contexts.

Ukraine as a case study in comparative traditional and online media

The on-going political crisis in Ukraine began in late November 2000, had passed through several stages and had re-ignited in late 2004 over the disputed 2004 presidential election results. National and foreign experts considered the 2000–01 crisis to be the biggest since Ukraine obtained its independence in August 1991. The duration, intensity, spread and number of social groups represented in this crisis were far greater than in 1990, a protest that mainly involved students from Kyiv universities and resulted in the resignation of the prime minister. This chapter will take a detailed look at the first wave of mass protest demonstrations in 2000–01 as a part of the broader political crisis. These mass protests took place from 15 December 2000 to 15 March 2001, with the largest and most violent demonstration taking place on 9 March 2001.

The student protest of 1990 in the twilight of the Soviet state came as a big surprise for many, even more so because of its peaceful nature and the fact that many of the demands of the protestors were met. People expected violence, police involvement and punishment of students. The absence of all this became clear evidence of new times and democracy. Ten years and two months later people went on the streets again, this time not only students and not only in the capital city of Kyiv.[2] The disappearance and subsequent discovery of the corpse of Internet journalist Georgiy Gongadze became the impetus for public attention on the problem of free speech and the nature of the journalistic profession in Ukraine by 2000. The situation was even more deeply dramatised when the leader of the Socialist party, Olexandr Moroz, publicly accused the top officials, including President Leonid Kuchma, of organising Gongadze's kidnapping and murder. The issue then received national and international attention, although there were unclear and slow reactions from the country's officials to Moroz's accusations.

Two weeks after the accusations by Moroz, the first large-scale demonstration took place in Kyiv on 15 December. The conflict then developed quickly to involve new civil and political groups and covered all the regions of the country of 48 million people. Tent villages became a common symbol of the protest and emerged in all the major cities of Ukraine. On 21 December 2000, the protest leader of the new Ukraine Without Kuchma movement in the parliament demanded the resignation of powerful state ministers as well as the launching of impeachment proceedings against President Kuchma. In January 2001, protest actions spread across the country, coming back to the capital in February 2001 as several groups of protestors from the regions marched on Kyiv. Each weekend in February saw new action by Ukraine Without Kuchma. By that time, separate opposition groups had united in the Forum of National Salvation. On 1 March 2001, police in Kyiv used force for the first time and dismantled protestors' tents. On a national holiday honouring a poet on 9 March 2001, the political opposition in parliament and protestors together tried to prevent President Kuchma from laying flowers near the monument to the poet. Clashes with the police resulted in violence. It continued through the day with police beating protestors, including members of parliament. In addition, police threw into prison dozens of young people (some of them innocent bystanders or journalists reporting on the protest). During this stage of the crisis, the demands of the protestors and the political opposition concerning the resignation of powerful ministers were met.[3]

Media coverage of the Gongadze protest

According to official statistics, there are 744 television and radio companies in Ukraine.[4] Most of these companies are local or cable and satellite. However, according to the Human Rights Watch report (2003), 63 per cent of these companies either do not broadcast or are barely solvent. Three main national channels jointly cover around 85 per cent of the country's territory. The first national channel, called UT-1, is state owned and covers 98 per cent of the country. Two other channels – UT-2 with 95 per cent coverage and Inter with 62 per cent coverage – are privately owned and affiliated with the Social Democratic Party (United), a powerful group in the presidential circle. There are around 2,600 newspapers published in the country,[5] including many local or regional newspapers as well as newspapers devoted to hobbies and advertisement. All newspapers in Ukraine have relatively low circulation due to financial constraints on the side of both producers and the consumers. There are also many newspapers founded or supported by political parties. At the national level, there are about 10 to 15 popular newspapers. Most of them are oppositional papers; however, only two national dailies, *Den'* and *Facty* (Day and Facts), have the biggest circulation and accessibility throughout the country. There are approximately 1,000 news websites on the Ukrainian Internet. This number includes online papers and information portals as well as online versions of offline media.[6] It is difficult to identify the exact number of online papers, but use of various search engines showed around 40 websites of online papers in 2001–02 (Krasnoboka, 2002). However, as in the case of traditional newspapers, about 10 to 15 of the online papers are markedly more popular in the country, with *Ukrainska Pravda* (Ukrainian Truth) and *Korespondent* (Correspondent) maintaining their lead. There are on average 7,000 to 10,000 daily visits to the websites of *Korespondent* and *Ukrainska Pravda*.[7] However, the status of online papers is not yet legally defined, meaning that they are not officially recognised as the mass media.

How both the traditional media and the Internet[8] covered this crisis became an intense subject for debate in Ukraine. On the one hand, the position that the majority of traditional media outlets took in this crisis confirmed existing doubts about the level of democratisation and freedom of speech in the post-Soviet communication and information space. It appeared as if television and the press had returned to Soviet times, in which the state and the Communist Party strictly controlled news construction. While there was some coverage and discussion of contentious events in the Soviet Union in samizdat literature[9] (Downing, 1996, 2001) and word of mouth (Bauer and Gleicher, 1953), this would only construct a weak parallel reality when compared with the monolithic power of the Soviet mass media. While the Soviet media enjoyed considerable freedom in the late Soviet period as the power of the Communist Party eroded, overtones of Soviet habits of control and self-censorship were still apparent. For example, Ukrainian Soviet television markedly failed to report on the full extent of the student protests and hunger strikes in 1990, just months before the collapse of the Soviet Union in 1991. The main state television channel showed peaceful groups of people crossing a major square with no tents, no protestors and no police even as the demonstrations expanded.

The 2000–01 political crisis became the first test for the national media under different political conditions. The on-going political crisis had become a new challenge for the Ukrainian media. However, many recent developments inside and around media in the country produced major doubts about the ability of media to take an independent position. Despite the switch from Soviet to Ukrainian rule, the main mass media remain under the control of national authorities (Brants and Krasnoboka, 2001; Krasnoboka and Brants, 2002). These controls include state ownership of certain national outlets; the financial weakness of the majority of media outlets that leaves them dependent on state subsidies; a technical dependency on state facilities such as printing houses and the postal system; the state-organised distribution of media licences; and a wide range of possibilities for lawsuits against journalists. This media environment has reinforced Soviet practices of censorship by editors, media owners and authorities as well as self-censorship by journalists themselves.

Content analysis has found that these elements of state control in the Ukrainian media system have had a serious impact on news selection and presentation, leading to the emergence of the new state logic in Ukrainian media (Krasnoboka and Brants, 2002). This trend has been confirmed by media monitoring by both the European Institute for Media (Düsseldorf, Germany) and the National Democratic Institute (Washington, DC) during the 1998–99 elections in Ukraine. In their turn, the Freedom House organisation has registered a rapid decline in media freedom in Ukraine in past years[10] and the Committee to Protect Journalists named President Kuchma as one of the ten worst enemies of the press in the year 1999 and again in 2001 (CPJ, *Enemies of the Press List*, 1999, 2001). Kuchma's re-election as president in November 1999 and the creation of a pro-presidential majority in parliament have only made matters worse for media freedom in Ukraine. Journalists disloyal to the presidential regime have been dismissed, threatened with physical violence or had economic and legal sanctions imposed against them. In 2000–01, four journalists were killed in the country and six more attacked (CPJ, *Attacks on the Press*, 2000, 2001). In cases when the entire journalistic team was disloyal to national or local authorities, sanctions were imposed against the outlets (e.g. nationwide newspaper *Silski Visti* and several regional newspapers).

These were the conditions under which journalist Georgiy Gongadze launched the first online paper in the country, called *Ukrainska Pravda* or Ukrainian Truth. It should be noted that the Ukrainian Internet had been characterised by a relatively low level of development and quality, although political parties starting using the Internet in a basic fashion in the 1997–98 elections (De Landtsheer *et al.*, 2001). National newspapers in Ukraine went online at about the same time as political parties. However, their online format did not differ from their offline versions. Typically, the printed version of the text was posted online a day after the print issue. Local newspapers and television channels are still under-represented on the Internet (Krasnoboka, 2002). Yet the nature, content and political importance of the Ukrainian Internet started changing rapidly when Gongadze launched *Ukrainska Pravda* as an exclusively online paper in April 2000. President Kuchma and his closest allies became a target of extremely critical stories, with accusations of corruption and political persecution. Ironically, however, the online paper became much more widely known after the September 2000 disappearance of its creator. His subsequent murder and the serious political scandal that followed turned public attention to the Internet.[11] It also stimulated the evolution of online journalism in Ukraine (Krasnoboka, 2002).

Although Gongadze's *Ukrainska Pravda* was the only online newspaper in April 2000, a few months later the online media became serious competitors with the traditional media in Ukraine. Their number increased significantly to more than 40 original online media by mid-2001. Most significantly, these online publications were distinctly more confrontational of the established power bases in the country, giving more attention to oppositional and independent news and showing similarities with the samizdat literature of the Soviet era (Krasnoboka and Brants, 2002). Original online papers are the Internet news media that do not have any offline version. In contrast to the Western notion of well-developed, web-only publications, there are many online papers in Ukraine that exist on the personal funds of journalists or activists or – more recently – on grants from international non-governmental organisations. Their rapid development and compatible role in the media environment in Ukraine are worthy of special attention (Semetko and Krasnoboka, 2003; Krasnoboka, 2002).

Gongadze, who had considerable experience in traditional journalism, launched his online paper after authorities shut down his analytical programmes on television and radio. He was confrontational with Ukrainian authorities at a time when most journalists were toeing the political line. Five months after the launch of his online paper, he disappeared and his beheaded corpse was found in a shallow grave near Kyiv almost two months later. The first news about his disappearance was widely reported in the Ukrainian media, including on national television. The story became considerably more controversial when Ukrainian Socialist leader Moroz accused President Kuchma in a parliamentary session of being involved with the organisation of Gongadze's disappearance. Moroz produced a tape, allegedly of Kuchma and his associates discussing how to get rid of Gongadze. Mass demonstrations ensued.

According to Ukrainian observers, the first day of the scandal immediately produced a distinct demarcation between the online and the traditional media. The majority of the national media failed to adequately cover the story of Kuchma's purported involvement in the disappearance, which included the evidence of the tape recording. According to data from opinion polls, Ukrainians were not satisfied with the completeness and objectivity of the media coverage of the political crisis (Korespondent.net, 24 February 2001). Out of the 89 per cent of citizens who had heard something about the tape scandal, 61 per cent expressed disappointment with its coverage by the national media. At the same time, online media demonstrated a radically different approach. Their coverage of Gongadze's disappearance, murder and all further developments did not decrease or change in direction. On the contrary, from September to December 2000 several new websites appeared and some of them immediately opened discussion forums about Gongadze. News about Gongadze's fate presented by the Internet sites created an engaged audience that closely followed all developments. Any new information was immediately picked up by the Internet audience and often transmitted to a larger circle of people via telecommunications and personal contacts.

The coverage of the events of 28 November 2000 showed the unusual power and speed of the Internet in covering contentious events. Within half an hour of his speech in parliament, the accusations made by Moroz were posted on the Internet. Immediately after his accusations, Moroz played the tape that was allegedly the voice of the President and other officials discussing options for Gongadze's elimination. Almost simultaneously those tapes were available on the Internet in Ukrainian, Russian and English transcriptions via the website of the Dutch national newspaper *De Volkskrant*.[12] In addition, the online media set up hour-by-hour reporting from street protests; presented videos in which the security officer Mykola Melnychenko claimed to have taped the President; and broadcast interviews with Moroz and other public figures on the issue. An open letter from Ukrainian students, intelligentsia and members of the Ukrainian diaspora calling for President Kuchma's resignation was published and signed online. The crisis spurred all the participants in the opposition, new and old, either to launch new websites or to increase the use of their existing ones. One special website was created to coordinate future actions of opposition while another was begun to discuss on-going events, tactics and strategy of the protest surrounding Gongadze's disappearance.[13] The leading journalist of the largest national newspaper *Den'* resigned in protest over the biased approach of her newspaper and created a website devoted to media developments in the country. In addition, the member of parliament who had been investigating the disappearance of Gongadze created a website to collect information about corruption and investigations against top officials.

As the crisis developed, the Ukrainian Internet experienced a tremendous increase in the number of visitors to political websites and forums. On 7 December 2000, Gongadze's online paper registered its first million visitors, this in a country in which officially less than 1 per cent of the population – which would come to about 400,000 people – had access to the Internet at that time. The marked contrast between the coverage of the Gongadze crisis in the traditional and online media created two distinctive realities of the crisis. In turn, it also created two distinctive publics. The first public, which was the smallest, received news as well as a broad range of primary information from the Internet. The second, and far larger, audience received its news from newspapers and television. What sort of information and analysis of the crisis did people receive from traditional media and the Internet? How much did it differ? How much information was reported and how much was left behind and by whom? How different were the two realities created by traditional media and the Internet?

The Internet clearly offers an easier path for those involved in contentious politics. As Tarrow (1998) points out, groups involved in contentious politics are often cut 'off from the regular resources which are important for collective action' and forced to use 'innovations at their margins' (p. 2), i.e.

low-entry, low-cost and relatively weakly regulated resources such as the Internet. The new media in Ukraine (Internet sites and media launched with the help of foreign capital) have experienced fewer difficulties with the state control in Ukraine than traditional media. In addition, the online media in Ukraine have shown themselves more ready to support opposition politicians and present a broader range of information and analysis (Krasnoboka and Brants, 2002). Thus, it would be expected that the Internet sites would offer a different dimension of contentious politics. However, how different and in what way? The Gongadze case provides an excellent opportunity to measure these differences and attempt to build theories about how and why these differences matter in a relatively closed media system. The following questions should be considered:

1 Are the traditional national media more likely to be loyal to the president?
2 Are national media less likely to give protestors a chance to speak and clarify their positions?
3 Do national media report only those protest events that correspond with their own interests? By the same token, do they avoid reporting events that would possibly negatively affect their political or corporate interests?

In order to explore these questions, a project analysed three Ukrainian media outlets: the national daily newspaper *Den'*, the national commercial television channel 1+1 and the news website Korespondent. All three outlets are privately owned. The newspaper *Den'* is closely affiliated with the then-head of the Council on National Security and Defence Evhen Marchyuk. The television channel 1+1 is affiliated with another powerful group in the presidential circle – the Social Democratic Party (United) and its head Victor Medvedchyuk. The online paper *Korespondent* is funded by the Ukrainian–international publishing group that has several other publications in the country, including the popular English-language weekly *Kyiv Post*. All three are the most popular outlets of their type in the country. Another similarity among these outlets is their relatively unbiased character. For example, the television channel 1+1 is, as a rule, less concerned with the position of the president in its reports than the state-owned prime national channel. In addition, the online paper *Korespondent* is less radical in its coverage of the protest than Gongadze's own online *Ukrainska Pravda*. In its turn, the newspaper *Den'* – one of the two biggest national dailies – seems to be less biased and less close to the president than the newspaper *Facty* (affiliated with the name of the president's son-in-law).

Researchers coded all articles or broadcast stories in which the reference and focus on the mass demonstrations and protest actions of the Ukraine Without Kuchma movement were in the headline as well as in the leading paragraph of news stories. The period covered is from 15 December 2000 (the day of the first mass demonstration in Kyiv) to 15 March 2001 (a week after the biggest and most violent demonstration of the first wave of the political crisis).[14] Newspaper articles, television news stories and the Internet articles have been chosen as units of analysis. The project analysed 294 news stories that were focused on mass demonstrations and protest actions, including 49 articles in *Den'*, 161 news broadcasts on 1+1 and 84 articles on the *Korespondent* website. The project tracked the following characteristics of the stories:

- The number of stories per day published by each outlet.
- Protest details, including time, place, size, number of protestors, goals, evolution of the protest and history of the event. The analysis also looked at whether the protestors were given a chance to speak for themselves.
- Content details, including the main subjects, actors, narratives, references, quotes, overall tone and any evidence of disdain towards the subject matter. Each story was coded for a maximum of three subjects and three actors. Overall tone of positive, mixed, neutral or negative was important in particular in terms of tracking loyalty to the president. Negative coverage of the protest, as well as disdain on the part of journalists towards the protest, was considered to represent loyalty to the president. Coders also considered whether there was any appearance of disdain in the story, defined as a spoken or written effort by journalists to reveal the reality behind some actors and their actions, to uncover some hidden goals and meanings. We consider disdain to see how it may be used to express loyalty or disloyalty to the president.
- The final aspect of the research explored the possible connections between protest coverage and corporate media interests. This will be discussed in a qualitative way.

Results

On average, *Den'* published two articles daily, the television channel 2.4 news stories per day and the Internet news site 2.2 articles per day on the crisis. Coverage increased in all outlets in March 2001, when the largest protest events took place. Overall, the television channel had the highest number of items devoted to the protest. The television channel covered the protest in the most regular manner and competed with the Internet in the number of news stories during the high points of protest activity. The newspaper had the lowest number of articles devoted to the Ukraine Without Kuchma movement and it did not cover the protest peaks as regularly as did television and the Internet.[15] These findings are displayed in Figures 10.1 and 10.2. The Internet site was more precise about details of protests than either the television channel or the central newspaper. While all three mostly reported events taking place in Kyiv, both 1+1 and *Den'* did not always give the location of the protests (the television channel in 12 per cent of the reports and *Den'* in

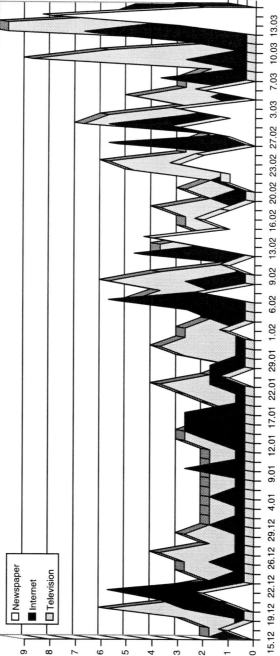

Figure 10.1 Number of news stories about mass protests per day (15 December 2000 to 15 March 2001).

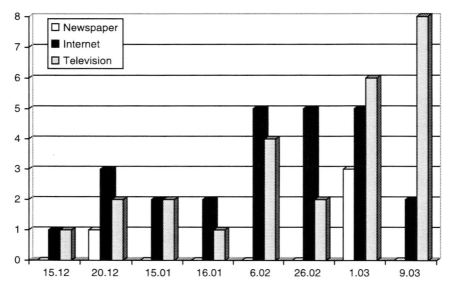

Figure 10.2 Number of news stories during the days of the largest protests
(15 December 2000 to 15 March 2001).

51 per cent of the articles). On the other hand, only two of the 84 articles on
the Internet failed to give the location of the protest. In addition, the Internet
was much more likely to give an estimate of the number of protestors than
the other two forms of media (see Figure 10.3).

The project also attempted to identify primary narratives through which
the protest news was presented. A very large number of television and Internet news stories were presented in terms of the sanctions or accusations
expressed on both sides as well as in terms of the protest's evolution. Both
traditional outlets stressed the unpopularity of the protest, although the
newspaper was more likely to do this than television. The newspaper also
framed its reports in terms of sensationalism, absurdity and the political
profit to be gained by some politicians in the protests. There was also
discussion of the protest in terms of destabilisation, possible conspiracy and
provocation behind the protest. The newspaper and the Internet site often
presented their news through the prism of a pre-revolutionary situation
emerging in the country, with attention to possible violence and forced reso-
lutions. The television channel and the Internet site presented many protest
issues in terms of conflict, scandal and tension (see Table 10.1).

All three media outlets discussed the issue of the Ukraine Without
Kuchma protest as well as the emergence of a tent village in the central
square of Kyiv, with the newspaper paying great attention to this topic. The
Internet site focused more on the goals, demands and actions of the protestors than the other two media sources. The three media outlets all reported

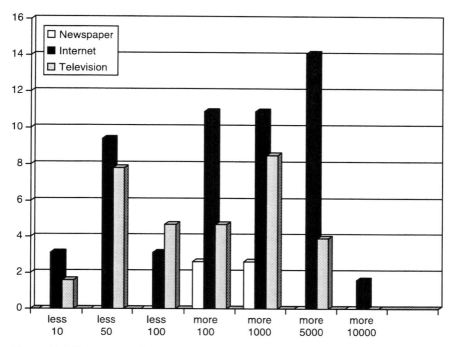

Figure 10.3 Percentage of news stories that mention the size of protests (15 December 2000 to 15 March 2001).

Table 10.1 Primary narratives

Narratives	Newspaper %	Television %	Internet %
Sanctions/accusations/judicial matters	0	29.2	32.1
Evolution of the protest	0	27.3	26.2
Unpopularity of the protest	24.5	5.0	0
Sensationalism/absurdity/political profit	16.3	1.2	1.2
Pre-revolutionary situation/ violence/ force	12.2	2.5	8.3
Conflict/tension/scandal	2.0	9.9	7.1
Destabilisation/conspiracy/ provocation	8.2	1.9	4.8
Dialogue between political forces	6.1	3.7	0
Investigative	6.1	0.6	3.6
Tensions/disagreements between protestors	0	5.0	1.2
Other	24.6	13.7	15.5

Total number of newspaper narratives = 49.
Total number of TV narratives = 161.
Total number of Internet narratives = 84.

on the dismantling of a tent village and clashes with police, but the Internet site paid more attention to the threats to protestors and their arrests (see Table 10.2). The spread of the protest across the country and the demonstrations organised by the Ukraine Without Kuchma movement attracted significant attention from the television channel and the Internet site. *Den'* did not report on the spread of the protest at all. In addition, while 1+1 and *Korespondent* covered the resignation of the power ministers and the possible impeachment of Kuchma, the *Den'* newspaper gave poor coverage to these issues. In terms of the coverage of actors, participants in the Ukraine Without Kuchma movement and those in other political opposition groups were the most prominent two categories of actors in all outlets (see Table 10.3).

Table 10.2 Main subjects reported

Subject	Newspaper %	Television %	Internet %
Ukraine Without Kuchma/ tent village	38.8	18.0	10.7
Goals, actions, demands of protestors	8.2	8.1	14.3
Dismantling of a tent village/ clashes with police	8.2	13.0	7.1
Threats/arrests	4.1	12.4	17.9
Resignation of the power ministers/ impeachment	2.0	5.6	7.1
Political institutions (tensions/dialogue)	6.1	3.7	3.6
Picket/protest	2.0	9.9	7.1
Spread of the protest over the country	0	9.3	11.9
Other	28.6	16.1	19.0

Total number of newspaper subjects = 49.
Total number of TV subjects = 161.
Total number of Internet subjects = 84.

Table 10.3 Main actors

Actor	Newspaper %	Television %	Internet %
Ukraine Without Kuchma	26.5	37.9	29.8
Opposition	16.3	11.2	10.7
Police/security service	6.1	6.2	10.7
President	4.1	5.0	7.1
Official representative/authority	14.3	4.3	2.4
Judiciary/prosecution	0	4.3	7.1
Other	32.7	31.1	32.1

Total number of newspaper actors = 49.
Total number of TV actors = 161.
Total number of Internet actors = 84.

While the police and security service were the third-most-prominent actors for the Internet site and the television channel, official representatives and authorities were the third-most-popular group in the coverage by *Den'*. President Kuchma, unsurprisingly, was among the most prominent individual actors for all three outlets. The television channel and the Internet site also stressed the role of judiciary and prosecution in their stories of the protest, but the newspaper did not mention them.

The Internet was quite distinctive from the other two media in the attention it paid to the goals of the protest and its history. All of the Internet articles reported the goals of the protest, compared with 84 per cent of the television news stories and only 51 per cent of the newspaper stories. Even more strikingly, 73 per cent of stories on the Internet referred to the history of the protest, compared with only 23 per cent of the television reports and just 16 per cent of the newspaper stories. In addition, the overall tone of the newspaper's articles about the protests was either critical or negative (53 per cent) or mixed (33 per cent). Both the television channel and the Internet news site preferred a neutral tone of reporting (79 per cent for the television channel and 77 per cent for the Internet site). The television station had mixed coverage in 16 per cent of its stories, compared with 9 per cent of the Internet stories. The newspaper was also much more likely to express disdain towards the protestors (nine times), the opposition (nine times) and Moroz himself (three times). The television channel expressed disdain towards protestors only twice and once towards the opposition. The Internet news site did not express disdain at all.

Finally, the project examined whether protestors were given opportunities to voice their demands and elucidate their positions by looking at the references to actors and quotes from actors across the three media. It transpired that all of the media outlets did not seem keen to quote actors in their stories. Quotes were entirely absent in 63 per cent of the newspaper articles, 66 per cent of the television news stories and 54 per cent of the Internet news stories. When political actors were quoted, the leaders of the protestors were the most often quoted by the television channel and the Internet news site. In the newspaper, political experts had the highest number of quotes – while the leaders of protestors were not quoted at all.

Analysis

Previous analyses of press coverage in Russia suggested that newspapers have been much less conservative than television during the last years of Soviet rule and the first years of independence (Mickiewicz, 1997; Voltmer, 2000). However, it would appear that the Ukrainian newspaper *Den'* is the most conservative news outlet out of the three analysed in this report. The content analysis shows a clear pattern of biased reporting. *Den'* had the lowest number of articles devoted to the coverage of the protest among the three media outlets coded for this project. There was little in the way of locations, numbers of protestors, goals of the protest or the history of the events.

In addition, a qualitative review shows that *Den*'s predominantly analytical articles were presented in the context of the unpopularity of the protest among larger groups of the population; sensationalism; the absurdity of protestors' accusations and demands; the political profitability of actions; the possibility of their violent and forced resolution; and the conspiracy and provocation behind them. The negative tone of the articles alongside the expressions of disdain toward protestors and opposition actors reiterated the pro-presidential position of the newspaper. Based on the content analysis, it is clear that the *Den'* newspaper chose a highly biased type of coverage for the Gongadze protests, failing to clarify, analyse or explain the reasons, developments and insights of the protest. Journalists at this newspaper were prone to extremely critical evaluations of protestors and opposition.

What are the political and corporate links of *Den'* that would suggest a top-down interest in this particular political line at the paper? As noted above, *Den'*, one of the two biggest and most popular national dailies in the country, is closely connected with the head of the Council on National Security and Defence, Marchyuk, and his wife is the editor in chief of the paper. There is compelling evidence that would link Marchyuk to a pro-Kuchma line. Although protestors did not call for his resignation during these protests, Marchyuk belonged to the same group of 'power' ministers who were the major targets of serious political and criminal accusations. Secondly, Marchyuk himself was directly accused of hiding evidence connected with the tragic death of a popular national politician. Finally, he had been named by his enemies as one of the masterminds behind the tape scandal, which shook the President's trust in him. Media observers had noted that *Den'* was faithful to Marchyuk's interests in general, as well as in terms of the Gongadze protests.

While the coverage in the newspaper was distinctly biased against the protests, the differences were not so immediately clear between the 1+1 television channel and the online paper. Both outlets devoted considerable time and space to reporting on the protest. Major subjects, actors and narratives of the coverage were very similar as well. In addition to being mentioned in stories, protestors and opposition leaders were given a number of chances to speak out. The tone of the coverage was predominantly neutral in both outlets. In quantitative terms, the television channel paid more attention to the protest than the news site, as there were twice as many news items on the protest reported by the television outlet. Significant differences between the two outlets are apparent when there is a further examination of the actual content of the reports on the size of the Gongadze demonstrations, the goals of the protestors and previous developments within the protest. In nearly 70 per cent of the stories, the television channel did not report the number of protestors, whereas the online paper reported protestor numbers in just over half (53 per cent) of its articles. All of the Internet articles indicated the goals of the protestors, while only 84 per cent of the television stories did so. Moreover, 73 per cent of the Internet news linked a reported event with previous developments, while the television channel made these links in just under a quarter (23 per cent) of its news items. Taking these observations together, it is clear that, although the television channel devoted a lot of time and space to the coverage of the conflict, the Internet did a better job of presenting the protests clearly, placing them within the general political developments in the country as well as stressing their seriousness and importance.

These suggestions are confirmed by a qualitative comparison of news texts in these outlets. For example, the announcement of the president's meeting with the leaders of protestors became one of the first news stories presented very differently by television news and the Internet news site.

TV channel 1+1:

> Participants in yesterday's protest action in Kyiv could not start the hunger strike as they threatened to do so if the president did not meet them. Such conversation has taken place today. The president listened to the complaints concerning authorities' actions in the investigation of the case of the disappeared journalist Georgiy Gongadze as well as to the demands to dismiss power ministers.
>
> (20 December 2000)

Online paper *Korespondent*:

> We remind you that during the meeting with the participants of the protest action who have built up a tent village on the Independence Square, President Kuchma has agreed to dismiss power ministers if the prime minister signs the appropriate document. Kuchma has met with protestors after their demands have been supported by nearly 5,000 participants of the demonstration who later have marched through the central street of Kyiv towards the parliament.
>
> (20 December 2000)

Reports on protest developments in the regions also showed the different emphasis on the television channel and the online paper. Television discussed the legal aspects in the regions and the decline in protest activities in the regions. The Internet questioned the nature of police and court repression against the protesters as well as stressed that, despite tremendous pressure from local authorities to stop the regional protests, new waves of protest events continued across the country. When the protests returned to Kyiv on 6 February 2001, there were violent clashes on the main city square. The television channel reported the view from the square, showing youngsters from two radical groups under black flags fighting with each other and other protestors. The online paper aired the suspicion of some protestors that the fight had been organised by policemen disguised as protestors. The online paper also highlighted the presence of two buses of special police troops who showed their weapons through bus windows to protestors.

On that day, one of the television reports on 1+1 concluded on the following note:

> The words of [famous Ukrainian poet Taras] Shevchenko, who questions whether Ukraine can ever be a peaceful heaven, have been proven. The absence of any social upheavals during last ten years has resulted in a worldwide syndrome to burn something. Now Ukraine has joined the cycle of countries where such forms of protest are regular. Today the picture of the president has been burned. Simultaneously people have been warming up. The action will go on but it is useless to hope for satisfaction of the radical demands. Moderate participants of the action have started conversations about a dialogue between the authorities and the opposition.

While the television trivialised the national significance of the protest, an Internet report on Korespondent.net the next day underlined the political meaning of the burning in effigy of the President:

> Starting around 4 p.m., a demonstration unimaginable in its numbers during the past four years has ended with the burning of an effigy of president Leonid Kuchma. After that, the meeting was over. 'People, tell everyone that our boss burned very well' said the co-ordinator of the action, Yury Lutsenko, giving farewell words to passers-by. While the effigy was burning, hundreds of people lit leaflets with the pictures of the current president and chanted: 'Boss, burn, burn brightly!' In his concluding speech before the burning of the effigy, Lutsenko said that the action would last until the moment when authorities dismissed power ministers and members of the parliament started the procedure of presidential impeachment.
>
> (7 February 2001)

In addition, the presence of Gongadze's mother at the meeting and her speech were particularly stressed by the website.

As noted above, most of the Internet articles finished with a summary of previous protest developments or history of the protest that stressed its breadth and political importance. On the other hand, only on very few occasions did the television channel 1+1 discuss previous developments or the history of the protest. In the majority of the television news stories, the link between protest actions, the disappearance of Gongadze and the publication of audiotapes by Moroz was not established. Moreover, protest actions themselves were not properly linked and not presented in order. The television channel also did not present much about the staged events of the opposition (such as a mock trial of Kuchma) or show the slogans and caricatures of the protestors. From the qualitative assessment, it is clear that the coverage of the 2000–01 protest by the television channel was far more extensive than could be imagined during Soviet times and was both broader and more neutral than that on other Ukrainian national television channels or in *Den'*. However, compared with the Internet, television coverage of the protests was still incomplete and fragmented. The commercial television channel 1+1 did report on the events, but failed to present the broader picture in terms of the reasons behind the protest, its development into a widespread political movement or the demands of the protestors.

What about the political and commercial concerns of the 1+1 station in terms of the protest coverage? Before and during the crisis, the channel experienced serious tensions with the head of the Ukrainian security service, whose resignation was demanded by protestors. Moreover, Social Democratic Party leader Medvedchuk, a known political supporter of the 1+1 channel, clearly benefited from the development of the protest and its demands. As a leader of one of the most powerful groups in the presidential circle, he would only welcome attacks on other powerful groups represented by the accused power ministers. On the other hand, certain loyalty and certain limits of coverage had to be set up for the television channel due to the direct involvement of President Kuchma in the crisis and the danger to the media outlet's future if the president were directly attacked. These tensions reveal the particular problems of the pressure on media outlets in the post-Soviet environment. While freedom of speech has been at least partially introduced in the country, there are significant constraints on media outlets. While it is difficult to draw the exact line between political influence and editorial decisions, it is clear that 1+1 television downplayed elements of the protest that fundamentally challenged the Kuchma regime.

Among the three outlets analysed for this chapter, the protest coverage by the online paper was both the most detailed and the most favourable to the protestors. It was certainly not the type of radical coverage that could be found on other Internet sites. However, its moderate nature allowed readers to follow events and to see them in their evolution and connectivity. More importantly, the website coverage stressed the exceptional nature of the Gongadze protests and the seriousness of the demands of the protestors. It is difficult to say that the Internet coverage was unbiased towards the national authorities. However, the comparison of this website with other news sites makes it the most neutral and unbiased among them. By contrast, protest coverage presented by the national daily newspaper brought back the atmosphere of Soviet times and tended to portray the opposition as a minority group of dispossessed dissidents.

By registering significant differences in the protest coverage between more traditional and online media, we should also take into account that these groups of outlets function not only under different organisational constraints, but varying technical constraints as well. This fact is most visible in the case of Ukrainian newspapers that are not published on Monday (for example) and for this reason can react to a given event the next day at the best. Television stories in their turn are supposed to be relatively brief, which does not allow this outlet to discuss at length any particular event. In this respect, the Internet is free from these constraints of both time and space. It can react to events as they are unfolding and discuss them at any length, including feedbacks from readers and even the direct participants in the events. However, by admitting technical limitations of traditional media we do not see them as having a crucial effect on the content of their coverage. Even a short TV report as well as a newspaper article published the next day can contain totally different information if not restricted by organisational policy and political factors.

Finally, it is important to stress once again that this project examined the most neutral among the three types of media outlets in the country. This means that some other national newspapers and television channels can be located farther on the political right in their support of the presidential forces and in their stigma of opposition, whereas the vast majority of the online papers can be located further on the political left in their support of the protest and in their stigmatisation of presidential forces.

Conclusions

The role of the Internet in Ukraine's social movement has become a remarkable example of the use of new technologies for contentious politics. Cut off from the regular resources that are important for collective action, members of the movement could only use the 'innovations at their margins' mentioned by Tarrow (1998: 2). The Internet, available to only 2 per cent of Ukrainians in 2000, had become the only reliable and permanent connection with the voice of the opposition. Television is the only source of information accessible to almost 90 per cent of the population. However, or for this reason, on many occasions television is the most controlled medium in the country. At the same time, the Internet is still a black hole for the country's officials. Not expecting any danger from this new technology, mainly known in the country as a tool for entertainment and pornography, the authorities did not try to exert control over it. Not seeing the potential danger coming from the Internet as a medium, as a public place and as a newsroom, the authorities failed to produce a special policy in the case of possible involvement of the Internet in contention. As the result of this omission, those in Ukraine who have access to the Internet, as well as Ukrainians abroad and those in the international community, were informed about the first signs of contention surrounding Gongadze's disappearance almost immediately. Aside from its direct involvement in the protest and the close coverage of events, the Internet has been fulfilling still another function: it has become a 'counter-reporter' of events for the traditional media. It has set up a rather high level of minimal protest coverage that the traditional media cannot ignore if they still try to proclaim their devotion to the principles of objectivity. The traditional media were obliged to report due to all the reasons mentioned above. Now that the

Internet had been established as an important, alternative media source, it became an important outlet for opposition parties and candidates in the 2002 Ukrainian elections as well (Krasnoboka and Semetko, 2003). In addition, the Internet continues to be a refuge for Ukrainian journalists who choose to break away from biased or controlled media outlets, as many of them have gone online. Without the Internet as a new place of refuge, many of these journalists might never have openly expressed their criticisms.

The Gongadze case was the story of a single journalist who disappeared in Ukraine. He is one of a long list of journalists that have disappeared, were murdered or (supposedly) committed suicide in independent Ukraine. His case could have passed unnoticed and never been revealed. This did not happen, however, due to the emergence of the Internet. Gongadze was murdered for his professional activity as an oppositional journalist, but also as the first online journalist. The widespread national and international attention as well as the condemnation that his murder has received has shown the power, importance and reliability of online journalism and of the Internet as an alternative source of information. Now it is possible only to speculate on how many other lives (particularly of those involved in the tape scandal and protest actions) the Internet has helped to save through publication of alleged tapes, press releases, contacts with the international community and, even more critically, providing immediate alternative information about events in the country. In Ukraine, the Internet has served as a key information and political tool in the hands of Ukrainian political and civil opposition.

How does the case presented in this chapter fit a broader picture of Internet use? Was it just a one-time event in a particular country? Or does it tell us something about the power of the Internet compared to more traditional media? We recognise that there are many voices for cyberpessimism around the globe as the use of the Internet in many parts of the world has failed to establish or even reinforce democratic practices. We believe, however, that the Internet potential can still meet early optimistic predictions of its implications for democracy worldwide. Yet, for the Internet to be able to do so, certain general conditions should be met. Our case study shows that such conditions can include a general situation of contention in the country; the lack of its coverage in traditional media; and the availability of strong oppositional groups and voices (both political and civil) that can explore the potential of the Internet.

Notes

1 The authors would like to thank the co-editor of this book, Sarah Oates, and participants of the European Consortium for Political Research workshop for valuable comments.
2 There have been many small-scale economic and social protests and demonstrations taking place throughout Ukraine, but none had as strong an impact on society as the Gongadze protests.

3 Minister of Interior, who is responsible for police, as well as the head of the National Security Service and the General Prosecutor.
4 National Council of Ukraine on Television and Radio Broadcasting, 2002: http://www.comin.gov.ua.
5 State Committee on Information, 2002, consulted on http://www.telekritika.com.ua.
6 Consulted on http://www.topping.com.ua.
7 Consulted on http://www.topping.com.ua.
8 While using the term 'Internet' throughout the text, this chapter focuses predominantly on news websites as one of the segments of political and news Internet in the country.
9 Samizdat, an abbreviation for the Russian phrase 'self-publication', generally took the form of home-made leaflets or pamphlets and was virtually the only printed opposition to the Soviet regime within the boundaries of the USSR.
10 In its rating of press freedom in the world Ukraine moved from the first category of 'partly free' countries with a score of 39 in 1996 to the second category of partly free countries with a score of 60 in 2002. In 2004, Ukraine's rating is 68, which brings the country to the category of not-free countries.
11 The online population in Ukraine has increased over 75 per cent (from 400,000 users in the middle of 2000 up to 700,000 users at the beginning of 2001). Data on the Internet access and use in the country presented in this chapter were consulted in the following sources: http://www.nua.ie, http://www.pravda.com.ua, http://www.korespondent.net, http://ain.com.ua, http://www.worldbank.org and http://www.osce.org.
12 Within several days the *De Volkskrant* website (http://www.volkskrant.nl) registered around a million hits to its website from all over the world. Around 300,000 were from Ukraine.
13 E.g. http://www.maidan.org.ua; http://www.samvydav.net; http://www.gongadze.com.ua.
14 Texts of television news stories have been taken from the archive of the channel's website http://www.1plus1.net. This archive does not provide the original order of news stories in the news programme but reports all major news stories throughout a day. Thus, there can be several news items devoted to the protest within one day. Texts of newspaper news have been taken from the website of the newspaper, which is identical to its offline version and preserves a similar design and news order.
15 There is a possible technical explanation. This newspaper is published five times a week (Tuesday to Saturday) while many protest actions occurred on weekends. However, the overall coverage of the protest by the newspaper leads us to suggest that even if immediate coverage had been technically possible it would not have resulted in a different approach to the coverage.

References

Bauer, R. and Gleicher, D. (1953) 'Word of Mouth: Communication in the Soviet Union', *Public Opinion Quarterly* 17: 297–310.
Berk, R. (1983) 'An Introduction to Sample Selection Bias in Sociological Data', *American Sociological Review* 48: 386–398.
Brants, K. and Krasnoboka, N. (2001) 'Between Soundbites and Bullets: The Challenges and Frustrations of Comparing Old and New Democracies', in Zassoursky, Y. and Vartanova, E. (eds), *Media for the Open Society: West–East and North–South Interface*, Moscow: Faculty of Journalism/IKAR Publisher.
Cilser, S. (1999) 'Showdown in Seattle: Turtles, Teamsters and Tear Gas', *First Mon-*

day 4 (12). Online. Available http://www.firstmonday.dk/issues/issue4_12cisler/index.html.

Committee to Protect Journalists (CPJ) (1999, 2001) *CPJ Enemies of the Press List*. Online. Available http://www.cpj.org.

CPJ (2000) *Attacks on the Press: Annual Report, Country Summary*. Online. Available http://www.cpj.org/attacks00/europe00/Ukraine.html.

CPJ (2001) Attacks on the Press: Annual Report, Country Summary. Online. Available http://www.cpj.org/attacks01/europe01/Ukraine.html.

Danzger, M. (1975) 'Validating Conflict Data', *American Sociological Review* 40: 570–584.

De Landtsheer, C., Krasnoboka, N. and Neuner, C. (2001) 'User Friendliness of Political Web Sites in Eastern and Western European Countries', Paper presented at the annual conference of the International Communication Association, Washington, D.C.

Downing, J. (1996) *Internationalizing Media Theory: Transition, Power, Culture*, London: Sage.

Downing, J. (2001) 'Samizdat in the Former Soviet Bloc', in Downing, J., *Radical Media: Rebellious Communication and Social Movements*, London: Sage.

European Institute for Media (1999) *Monitoring the Media Coverage of the Presidential Elections in Ukraine. Final Report*, Düsseldorf: European Institute for Media.

Freedom House (2002) *Nations in Transit*. Online. Available http://www.freedomhouse.org.

Gamson, W., Croteau, D., Hoynes, W. and Sasson, Th. (1992) 'Media Images and the Social Construction of Reality', *Annual Review of Sociology* 18: 373–393.

Hammond, A. and Lash, J. (2000) 'Cyber-Activism: The Rise of Civil Accountability and Its Consequences for Governance', *Information Impacts Magazine*, May. Online. Available http://www.cisp.org/imp/may_2000/05_00hammond.htm.

Human Rights Watch (2003) 'Negotiating the News: Informal State Censorship of Ukrainian Television'. Online. Available http://www.hrw.org.

Kalathil, Sh. and Boas, T. (2001) 'The Internet and State Control in Authoritarian Regimes: China, Cuba, and the Counterrevolution', *First Monday* 6 (8). Online. Available http://firstmonday.org.

Kielbowitz, R. and Scherer, C. (1986) 'The Role of the Press in the Dynamics of Social Movements, Research in Social Movements', *Conflict and Change* 9: 71–96.

Korespondent.net, 24 February 2001. Online. Available http://www.korespondent.net.

Krasnoboka, N. (2002) 'Online Journalism Goes Underground. Internet Underground: Phenomenon of Online Media in the Former Soviet Union Republics', *Gazette (International Journal for Communication Studies)* 64 (5): 479–500.

Krasnoboka, N. and Brants, K. (2002) 'Old and New Media, Old and New Politics?', Paper presented at the European Consortium of Political Research Joint Workshop Sessions on Political Communication, the Mass Media, and the Consolidation of Democracy, Turin, Italy.

Krasnoboka, N. and Semetko, H. (2003) 'Political Bias in the Soviet Style? Television in Ukraine's 2002 Parliamentary Election', Paper presented at the International Communication Association meeting, San Diego, CA.

Lipsky, M. (1968) 'Protest as a Political Resource', *American Political Science Review*, 62: 1144–1158.

McCarthy, J., McPhail, C. and Smith, J. (1996) 'Images of Protest: Dimensions of Selection Bias in Media Coverage of Washington Demonstrations, 1982 and 1991', *American Sociological Review* 61 (3): 478–499.

Mickiewicz, E. (1997) *Changing Channels: Television and the Struggle for Power in Russia*, Oxford and New York: Oxford University Press.

Mueller, C. (1997) 'International Press Coverage of East German Protest Events, 1989', *American Sociological Review* 62: 820–832.

National Council of Ukraine on Television and Radio Broadcasting (2002) Statistical data. Online. Available http://www.comin.gov.ua.

National Democratic Institute (1999) *Ukrainian Election Report*. Online. Available http://www.ndi.org.

Ostry, S. (2000) 'Making Sense of It All: A Postmortem on the Meaning of Seattle', in Porter, R. and Sauve, P. (eds), *Seattle, the WTO, and the Future of the Multilateral Trading System*, Cambridge, MA: John F. Kennedy School of Government, Harvard University.

Ott, D. and Rosser, M. (2000) 'The Electronic Republic? The Role of the Internet in Promoting Democracy in Africa', *Democratization* 7 (1): 137–155.

Rodan, G. (1998) 'The Internet and Political Control in Singapore', *Political Science Quarterly* 113 (1): 63–89.

Semetko, H.A. and Krasnoboka, N. (2003) 'The Political Role of the Internet in Societies in Transition: Russia and Ukraine Compared', *Party Politics* 1: 77–104.

Small, M. (1994) *Covering Dissent*, New Brunswick, NJ: Rutgers University Press.

Snyder, D. and Kelly, W. (1977) 'Conflict Intensity, Media Sensitivity and the Validity of Newspaper Data', *American Sociological Review* 42: 105–123.

State Committee on Information (2002) Statistical data. Online. Available http://www.telekritika.com.ua.

Tarrow, S. (1998) *Power in Movement: Social Movements and Contentious Politics*, Cambridge: Cambridge University Press.

Taubman, J. (1998) 'A Not-So World Wide Web: The Internet, China, and the Challenges to Nondemocratic Rule', *Political Communication* 15: 255–272.

Voltmer, K. (2000) 'Constructing Political Reality in Russia', *European Journal of Communication* 15 (4): 469–500.

11 Pathologies of the virtual public sphere

Heinz Brandenburg

This chapter discusses the theoretical debates surrounding the democratising potential of cyberspace. Proponents of deliberative democracy did not go on a search to discover an effective and inclusive forum of public deliberation on a mass scale and come across the Internet. Rather early cyber-enthusiasts quickly embraced the notion of the public sphere and the theory of deliberative democracy developed by Jürgen Habermas and claimed that the Internet provides just that – a virtual public sphere. This discussion goes beyond evaluating the generic potential and actual patterns of use of the Internet for public deliberation. It focuses on whether the virtual public sphere is self-evolving or instead needs to be engineered. An 'Atlantic divide' is emerging over this question. Policy makers and academics in Europe, and particularly the United Kingdom, propose putting the web to use by administrating public debate forums through government action. In the United States, a concept of decentralised self-management is advocated.

Habermas and the rediscovery of participatory democracy

For most of the second half of the twentieth century – in the aftermath of Schumpeter (1950) and Downs (1957) – normative democratic theory had been on the defensive. It resurfaced in the 1990s with theoretical debates surrounding the notion of deliberative democracy. This trend towards conceptualising democracy again in more substantive and participatory terms owes much to the first English publication in 1989 of Jürgen Habermas's *The Structural Transformation of the Public Sphere*.[1] According to Elster (1992: 1), theorists of deliberative democracy derived at least one of their key assumptions from Habermas, namely 'the idea that democracy evolves around the transformation rather than simply the aggregation of preferences'. Endogeneity of preferences, i.e. the evolution of individual opinions through dialogue, is a core element in any definition of deliberative democracy: 'authenticity of deliberation requires that communication must induce reflection upon preferences in non-coercive fashion' (Dryzek, 2000: 162). Deliberation is, at least nominally, a key element in representative democracies. Legislators are not bound by their mandate and consistently have, in all Western parliamentary systems, rejected the notion of prospective control by their constituents, most famously so Edmund Burke in 1774:

> Your representative owes you only not his industry, but his judgment; and he betrays instead of serving you, if he sacrifices it to your opinion. . . . Parliament is not a *congress* of ambassadors from different and hostile interests; which interests each must maintain, as an agent and advocate, against other agents and advocates, but parliament is a *deliberative* assembly of *one* nation, with one interest, that of the whole; where, not local purposes, not local prejudices ought to guide, but the general good, resulting from the general reason of the whole.
>
> (quoted in Elster, 1992: 3)

Deliberative democracy as a normative theory departs from the liberal, representative model by expanding deliberation beyond the realms of political institutions such as parliament.

Even though voting has been demoted somewhat as an act of political participation in deliberative models, most deliberative theorists would still acknowledge that the essential principle that defines a political system as democratic is the aggregation of preferences. But whereas social choice theorists are predominantly concerned with the democratic deficiency that derives from the contingency of aggregation upon the method employed, deliberative democratic theorists focus instead on the potential deficiency of the preferences that are aggregated. Individual preferences are deemed insufficient if they are formed in isolation. Elster (1992) refers to the French delegate to the Assemblée Constituante of 1789, Sieyes, as a proponent of this view:

> In a democracy (a pejorative term at the time), he said, people form their opinions at home and then bring them to the voting booth. If no majority emerges, they go back home to reconsider their views, once again isolated from one another. This procedure for forming a common will, he claimed, is absurd because it lacks the element of deliberation and discussion.
>
> (Elster, 1998: 3)

Dryzek even argues that at least some of the disequilibrium conditions identified by social choice critiques could be overcome through deliberation, since dialogue may help to disentangle the multiple dimensions of choice – the multidimensionality of a choice context being the necessary condition for the occurrence of vote cycles (Dryzek, 2000: 41). Deliberation is argued to improve collective decision-making processes, by (a) producing more enlightened preferences and (b) arbitrating between elite decision making and public opinion, thereby creating legitimacy through publicity in the Kantian meaning of the term.

Habermas exemplified his normative concept of a public sphere with reference to what he labelled the 'bourgeois public sphere' that materialised at the end of the Enlightenment period, before and briefly after the French Revolution to varying degrees in Britain, France and Germany. He argues that only in the late eighteenth century did public discussion of political matters come into fashion, partly driven by the emergence of publicity of political processes, i.e. newspapers being entitled to print records of parliamentary sessions. With the demise of the principle of government secrecy, politics entered the public realm and was reflected in tearooms, clubs and other places of free, bourgeois association. This nascent public sphere remained exclusionary, with entry being reserved to those who owned private property. One might argue that political debates and forums therein remained somewhat fragmented. Habermas suggests that here public opinion formed, received distribution via the emergent press and was hence fed back to the political decision makers who up until then had been in a position to ignore the sentiments of the larger populace.

The transformation of the public sphere that Habermas goes on to describe is indeed an erosion of the public sphere as a realm of free, discursive opinion formation. Habermas, like so many others, blames the mass media and their increasing commercialisation for the continuous erosion and effective demise of deliberative elements in Western political systems. He argues that even political debate has been perverted into a media spectacle that no longer involves the public but instead is displayed in front of their eyes for mere consumption instead of active and engaged participation. With regard to public opinion, he argues that 'the contents of opinion' are effectively 'managed by the culture industry' (1989: 246). Public opinion as we know it is either a fabrication or at best the aggregation of isolated individual opinions that have not been tested and challenged and are not formed in a meaningful manner.

> The communicative network of a public made up of rationally debating private citizens has collapsed; the public opinion once emergent from it has partly decomposed into the informal opinions of private citizens without a public and partly become concentrated into formal opinions of publicistically effective institutions.
>
> (Habermas, 1989: 247)

The web as public sphere

From the outset, ARPANET,[2] which laid the technological foundation for the evolution of the Internet, was conceptualised as a time-sharing function that would not only enable many-to-many communication, but also allow users to make 'nontrivial' use of the medium. The Internet moved from a simple sender–receiver model of communication towards one of active participation, cooperation and a free exchange of ideas that culminates in consensual agreement, which is of course the essential definition of deliberation:

> A communications engineer thinks of communicating as transferring information from one point to another in codes and signals. But to communicate is more than to send and to receive. [. . .] We believe that communicators have to do something nontrivial with the information they send and receive. And we believe that we are entering a technological age in which we will be able to interact with the richness of living information – not merely in the passive way that we have become accustomed to using books and libraries, but as active participants in an ongoing process, bringing something to it through our interaction with it, and not simply receiving something from it by our connection to it. [. . .] Any communication between people about the same thing is a common revelatory experience about informational models of that thing.
>
> (Licklider and Taylor, 1990: 21f.)

Early enthusiasts of the developing Internet have pointed out that the value of web technology for society lies not just in its capacity to distribute infinite amounts of information, but also in its potential to facilitate interpersonal communication. The infamous J.P. Barlow,[3] who is reputed to have been the first to apply the science fiction concept of 'cyberspace' to the emerging Internet, makes the following point:

> The global supply of words, numbers, statistics, projections, analyses, and gossip . . . what I call the DataCloud . . . expands with thermonuclear vigour and all the Virtual Reality we can manufacture isn't going to stop that. But it may go a long way toward giving us means to communicate which are based on shared experience rather than what we can squeeze through this semi-permeable alphanumeric membrane. If it won't contain the DataCloud, it might at least provide some navigational aids through it.
>
> (Barlow, undated)

In his *A Declaration of the Independence of Cyberspace* (1996), Barlow describes the communicative processes on the web as 'global conveyance of thought'. We do indeed find, particularly in the theoretical and prescriptive output of his former collaborators at the Berkman Center for Internet and Society at Harvard Law School, a more scholarly reflection of this overly optimistic view on the emancipative and deliberative potential of web technology. Hauben (1999), for example, concludes from empirical research into Usenet groups and other forms of what she labels deliberation on the web, that:

> [. . .] it is through the free wheeling and rambling discussion that the online medium makes possible, that one can more thoughtfully consider diverse views. The Internet helps to remove the constraints to communication, to make it possible to explore what the underlying dispute or

agreement is, and then to determine the new view that will resolve the issue in contention.

[. . .] This helps to generate the diversity of the variety of viewpoints that one has to consider to analyze a question or problem. In this process the wide ranging discussion made possible by the Internet is not limited to two communicators, but can include a large and almost unlimited number.

(Hauben, 1999)

In general, wherever consistently positive accounts of the public sphere character of cyberspace are given from a scholarly perspective, the individuals and institutions behind that research and theory tend to be actively involved in the promotion and development of deliberative forums on the web or initiatives towards e-democracy or cyber-democracy. In the US, this takes the form of civic, i.e. private, non-profit, projects and initiatives, for example the Center for Democracy and Technology, which allocates funds from a wide range of organizations and corporations, and 'works to promote democratic values and constitutional liberties in the digital age'.[4] The tendency in Europe is instead towards joint ventures between public and academic institutions in an at least partly top-down effort to facilitate public deliberation and government access online, such as the Oxford Internet Institute or Media@lse.

We find that cyber-enthusiasm is much more uninhibited in the US discourse than it appears to be in the European setting. Thornton (2002: 5, 7) gives an account of how quickly the notion of the 'information superhighway' was embraced by economic elites as well as political elites from across the political spectrum. Former US Vice President and 2000 Democratic presidential candidate Al Gore envisaged how 'these highways . . . will allow us to share information, to connect, and to communicate as a global community'. US Congressional leader Newt Gingrich and his advisers hailed the Internet as a liberating force from an economic point of view, claiming that 'in cyberspace . . . market after market is being transformed by technological progress from a "natural monopoly" to one in which competition is the rule'.

Engineering a public sphere on the web

In Europe, for example in the United Kingdom, we find not only a more cautious reception to the new media and their democratising and liberalizing potential but also a different focus of prescriptive research in conjunction with non-profit and public institutions. The focus in US cyber-democracy projects is largely on preserving freedom of speech and the absence of outside regulation, while the European focus is much more on access, mobilisation and integration. This is exemplified in the various joint initiatives involving the Oxford Internet Institute at the University of Oxford; Media@lse, the media and communications programme at the London School of Economics and Political Science; The Hansard Society for Parliamentary Government; Citizens Online, a not-for-profit organisation; and the Institute for Public Policy Research (IPPR), a left-centre think tank. The agenda of these institutional networks points towards engineering 'a civic commons' (Blumler and Coleman, 2001), i.e. creating a viable Internet-based communicative network that effectively enables public deliberation and links it directly with government institutions in order to make the workings of government more transparent and more responsive to the outcomes of public deliberations.

The argument behind these initiatives, most poignantly outlined by Blumler and Coleman (2001), builds on a mass-media critique very much like that of Habermas. Mass media, through commercialisation, are increasingly incapable of providing balanced information and of engaging citizens sufficiently in the political realm. In conjunction with widespread cynicism about politics and increasing frustration about the ineffectiveness of voting as political participation, the assessment of the current state of British and other Western democracies is grim. An effective reinstatement of a functioning public sphere is heralded as a possible remedy. The Internet is seen to 'have a potential to improve public communications and enrich democracy', but it is argued that 'that potential is vulnerable, however, mainly because an infrastructure for its proper realisation is lacking' (Blumler and Coleman, 2001: 5). Because of increasing commercialisation of the Internet and inequality of access, the medium is not understood as a democratising force. Instead of considering cyberspace to constitute a viable public sphere in itself, these initiatives allege that a public sphere, a 'civic commons in cyberspace', can and ought to be engineered. While Blumler and Coleman acknowledge that various 'exercises of online consultation, promoting informed deliberation on public policy issues, have been piloted', they conclude that these initiatives have been too fragmented in nature. They claim that, only 'with suitable policies and institutional support, some of the emancipatory potential of the new media could be realised' (Blumler and Coleman, 2001: 5).

Perhaps because of the academic background of many of its founders and early users, the Internet is a highly self-reflective medium. Keyword searches on a portal such as Yahoo generate listings of as many as 30,900 sites containing 'E-Democracy', 2,390 containing 'Cyberdemocracy' and a total of 60,300 containing the exact phrase 'public sphere'.[5] Debates about the democratising potential, the meaning of public sphere and its potential or factual realisation of the virtual kind are by no means restricted to scholarly debate but feature heavily on discussion boards and within newsgroups.

Although the initial phase of uninhibited cyber-enthusiasm may be over, replaced by more cautious theoretical approaches and increasing tendencies towards 'technorealism' amongst users,[6] there do not appear to be any voices seriously questioning the democratising *potential* of web technology. Debates rather unfold around the question of how to realise that potential.

Alleged potential of computer-mediated communication

What, then, does this potential consist of? First, there is the technological potential. Bill Gates has put it this way: Internet technology 'is going to give us all access to seemingly unlimited information, anytime and any place we care to use it' (Gates, 1995: 184). Fernback and Thompson (1995) raise some valid concerns about the rationale behind the design of both hard- and software and the consequences thereof. Their point is that efficiency rather than concern with the needs of users, together with the cartel conditions under which both soft- and hardware design and distribution proceed, has at times resulted in subobtimal solutions from the user's point of view:

> For example, more comprehensible computer interfaces than DOS (for IBM standard personal computers) or UNIX were imaginable. The historical development of DOS, UNIX . . . serve to illustrate why, for a variety of reasons (the justifications for which a technologically compliant public had no arguments), an arcane disk operating system was implemented that effectively excluded many people from understanding microcomputers.
>
> (Fernback and Thompson, 1995: 13)

Computer as well as web use is, to a non-trivial extent, a question of skills and experience. The medium requires far greater adaptation than is the case for any of the traditional media.

The tenth Graphic, Visualization and Usability Center www-survey (http://www.gvu.gatech.edu/user_surveys/survey-1998-10/) shows that forms of net use that are associated with interactivity, community building or the virtual public sphere idea are practised more as the skill and experience level of the user increases. Years of net access and self-assessed expertise are not only correlated with one another, but also significantly and linearly correlated with the intensity of social Internet use and satisfaction therewith.

As the user adapts to the technology, he or she becomes increasingly drawn into its patterns of social use. It is less likely that users acquire the technology initially for information-gathering or deliberative uses. In that sense, technology can independently affect patterns of behaviour. This could of course be interpreted as evidence for the hypothesis that web technology is a democratising force – that is in case the emerging patterns of computer-mediated communication (CMC) can be judged to foster the substance of democracy.

Another aspect of technological potential is referenced by the Swiss media sociologist Hans Geser who argues that digitalisation allows for the deconstruction of textual, audio and visual information into identical units (BITS) that form the basis for a comprehensive integration of diverse forms of communication (such as private correspondence, group discourses, book publications and official announcements) which up until now were processed through separated media worlds (Geser, 1996: 2–3). He suggests that digitalised computer networks constitute a 'super-medium' in embryonic form. We can already grasp the capacity of the medium without the medium itself having evolved so far as to fully realise its potential. Web technology has the potential to overcome the historical (vertical and horizontal) segmentation of elements of the political and public sphere. According to Geser, vertical segmentation occurs when increasing organisation in civil society coincides with increasing segregation from the political centre (the formal institutions), while horizontal segmentation consists of localisation of and detachment between publics. Although segmentation into narrow interest groups and private associations is likely (or indeed already is occurring with the spread of the medium), technically all forms of organisation, from decentralised communication between citizens (horizontally) to government–citizen interaction (vertically), share a common space in which they are unavoidably networked. Geser posits that, in the computer networks, 'a horizontally and vertically differentiated but at least potentially all-encompassing public sphere constitutes itself' (Geser, 1996: 19, author's translation).

Conventional cyber-scepticism argues that the medium may be potentially all-encompassing, but in effect proves to be socially exclusive. Critics such as Schement (1996, 1999) and Golding (2000) suggest that both the context in which the new media were introduced (during a period of economic stagnation) and the requirement of on-going expenditures for equipment, software and content (in contrast to the one-time buys that characterise traditional media, such as TV and radio) produce a social divide into information-rich and information-poor. This refers not only to a social problem within Western societies, but additionally to the inequality of access among countries dubbed the 'global digital divide' (DiMaggio *et al.*, 2001: 312).

An educated guess as to how many people are online worldwide suggests a total of 605.6 million users as of September 2002.[7] Of these, 62 per cent are to be found in Europe, the US and Canada combined, with only 1.04 per cent located in Africa. Average penetration of new media and web access reaches above 30 per cent in Western societies, with the Nordic countries leading the way. Both Iceland and Sweden are estimated already to have in excess of two-thirds of their population connected since September 2002. In sharp contrast, average penetration lingers around 0.25 per cent in sub-Saharan Africa.

The social or global digital divide reduces the debate about the virtual public sphere to a policy question of removing barriers of access as long as we accept the notion that 'citizenship depends on the free flow of information and access to the means of communication in a democracy' (Wilhelm, 2000: 40). There have been attempts, most notably in Britain, to bridge the digital divide by generating mass access to new media in places such as libraries. However, Wilhelm raises the additional question of whether 'sporadic, ad hoc access to the Internet at a library or school is sufficient to develop quality skills required to participate fully in the life of the community'.

Beyond access: patterns of 'deliberation' on the web

A more substantial research question arises once we look beyond the issue of access. The question of access is about allowing the technology to fulfil its alleged potential for democratising society, building communities and constructing a public sphere. As noted earlier, there appears to be an Atlantic divide with regard to the question of whether the Internet is already or will inevitably come to constitute a viable public sphere. The position of cyber-enthusiastic citizens as well as academics and cyber-literate politicians in the US appears to be that the Internet can self-manage in the absence of any form of government intervention, censorship and legislation. In contrast, the dominant position amongst scholars and policy makers in mainland Europe as well as in the United Kingdom is that we need constitutional engineering beyond giving mere access to people, namely the proactive creation of constitutive elements of a virtual public sphere, funded and partially initiated by public institutions.

Both positions, however, borrow from Habermas in defining how this public sphere should look. Utopian expectation on the libertarian side finds an almost identical reflection in terms of normative positions and prescriptive guidelines on the engineering side. Coleman and Gøtze (2001), for example, outline the benchmarks for the design of a viable public sphere, which gives a mirror image of how Rheingold (1994) and others have envisioned how the virtual public sphere would look if allowed to blossom freely:

> Methods of public engagement can be described as deliberative when they encourage citizens to scrutinise, discuss and weigh up competing values and policy options. Such methods encourage preference formation rather than simple preference assertion. Public deliberation at its best is characterised by:
> * Access to balanced information . . .
> * An open agenda . . .
> * Time to consider issues expansively . . .
> * Freedom from manipulation or coercion . . .
> * A rule-based framework for discussion . . .
> * Participation by an inclusive sample of citizens . . .
> * Scope for free interaction between participants . . .
> * Recognition of differences between participants, but rejection of status-based prejudice.
>
> (Coleman and Gøtze, 2001: 6)

This catalogue of requirements for citizen deliberation amounts to a more elaborate rephrasing of Habermas's 'ideal speech situation'.

With regard to Coleman and Gøtze's first point, the Internet does make *more* information *more* accessible. However, precisely because it is a medium of use and not of consumption, will the provision of the individual with information remain at best uncertain, if not systematically insufficient? The experimental studies conducted by Tewksbury and Althaus (2000) compared the knowledge of current affairs resulting from use of a news website with the knowledge level resulting from newspaper reading (using *The New York Times* and its website as sources for one week of news exposure). The subjects of their experiments who read the paper turned out to be able to recall more of the important news events of that week (468) and also were able to recall more news story details (471). In contrast, they found that Internet users made intensive use of the less restrictive format that the news website offers by reducing the time afforded to current affairs reading, and instead ventured into the entertainment sections of the site (467). The printed newspaper format facilitates orientation by the use of headlines and story placement, which have few equivalents in the web format. One might argue that newspaper readers, like television viewers, are patronised, insofar as a set of priorities and a consumption structure is forced upon them. Yet this measure of pre-selection (gatekeeping beyond the initial entry of events or stories into the news mix) appears to have benefits for the reader that elude the more active, yet unguided web user. Even if one were to argue that prioritisation by the news media is unlikely to be entirely unbiased, the study hints at the possibility that web users tend to instead minimise and randomise their news exposure rather than accomplishing the gatekeeping themselves and hence circumventing the media.

The fact that the Internet as a medium of information retrieval increases choice by no means guarantees an improved information infrastructure for citizens in terms of amount or balance of information. This is part of the rationale behind initiatives to engineer a deliberative environment on the web instead of simply assuming that the Internet provides one. The problem remains that providing access does not guarantee use.

Comprehensiveness and balance of information qualify as preconditions for effective deliberation. However, the remaining items on Coleman and Gøtze's catalogue deal with external and internal norms for interaction. This reflects on the problem that the 'ideal speech situation' suggested by Habermas is a normative principle, which requires the guarantee of certain contextual conditions. It requires openness, inclusiveness and non-coercion both externally and internally. Web-based civic movements in the US focus largely on non-intervention from outside, in order to guarantee free flow of information and discussion within the web. They give limited attention to the question of how to accomplish an ideal speech situation within web communities. Evidence from various Usenet and other newsgroup analyses indicates that neither openness nor reciprocity appears to be characteristic of online debates. Both Wilhelm (2000) and Dahlberg (2001) found that online political discussion tends to be monological rather than dialogical in nature. The vast majority of postings provide rather than seek information. Few instances remain of responses to postings from other members, and overall 'many online fora experience a lack of respectful listening to others and minimal commitment to working with differences' (Dahlberg, 2001: 17).

Wilhelm (2000: 99) used his content analysis of Usenet postings to measure the degree of homogeneity of newsgroups. He found strong evidence for Huckfeldt and Sprague's (1995: 53) hypothesis, which posits that:

> groups that are evenly divided in opinion, or approximately so, must be rare. Asymmetry in the distribution of beliefs within groups is likely to be prevalent, particularly since it is known that individuals tend to seek out politically like-minded individuals.

According to Sunstein (2001a), the Internet may not only be insufficient as a means to bolster democracy, but can indeed even have detrimental consequences for the evolution of public opinion insofar as it facilitates and encourages segmentation into small and narrowly issue-based communities, which results in what he labels 'group polarization':

> With respect to the Internet and new communications technologies, the implication is that groups of like-minded people, engaged in discussion with one another, will end up thinking the same thing that they thought before – but in more extreme form.
>
> (Sunstein, 2001a: 65)

Examples presented as evidence to the contrary tend to be derived from academic discussion boards. An example is the case of philosophy students on Jürgen Habermas's listserv who are discussing with ideal deliberative discipline, reciprocity and mutual respect the question of why Professor Habermas himself is not present on his own listserv, whether there is a general tendency for high-status academics to excuse themselves from deliberative forums on the web, and whether this may result from disdain or simply insufficient familiarity with the medium (Perzynski, 1999). Such an illustration is not indicative of the nature of citizen discourse on the web, although an additional point can be made that citizen deliberation on the web shares some similarities with Habermas's ideal type of the bourgeois public sphere of the late eighteenth century, insofar as the preconditions of access and leisure for effective inclusion into the structure of online communities result in predominantly 'little more than a middle-class residents association in cyberspace' (McClellan, 1994: 10).

Unlimited filtering: in defence of traditional mass media

Ultimately, the Internet is a mass medium, but with an increasing tendency towards *customisation*, which refers to the control and activeness of the user. According to Sunstein (2001b: 1), a scholar who is a contributor to scholarly debates about both deliberative democracy and the democratising potential of web technology, the 'apparent utopian dream ... of complete individuation' has as its primary consequence that 'people can decide, in advance and with perfect accuracy, what they will and will not encounter'. In that sense, the customised mass medium encourages selectiveness and escapism, insulation and rational ignorance, rather than enhancing citizenship and integrating communities. What are labelled communities on the web instead take the form of ad hoc associations with fewer obligations than exist in physically convening communities. Sunstein goes on to argue that unlimited filtering, which is the quintessential practice of Internet use, significantly decreases the likelihood of chance encounters with information and dissenting opinions. In his view, against all predominant criticism, the mass media serve an important cause as 'general interest intermediaries' (2001b: 2) who help to confront the individual with information and opinions that he would not have chosen to be confronted with. By encapsulating into narrowly defined interest groups and customising the information flow, the user potentially disconnects from the larger society, moving towards either individuation or intensified small-group association.

Discussion

The on-going debate about revitalising democracy through online citizen deliberation suffers from a number of deficiencies, inconsistencies and false assumptions. First, the almost uncritically accepted assumption that deliberation and the existence of a functioning public sphere are necessary and sufficient conditions for the existence of 'true' democracy is entirely unwarranted. Both Habermas and the protagonists of deliberative democracy argue this point on a normative level. Admittedly, widespread cynicism about – and disapproval of – political elites has given them fuel in their normative debate with elitist or minimalist democrats. It should be noted, however, that public discontent with political elites and representative systems in general does not amount to a widespread demand for inclusion in a deliberative system that affords active participation and high information levels. Apathy is not necessarily indicative of a deep-seated but frustrated wish for participation. Schumpeter's account of democratic practice is still a valid analysis of the state of affairs. It is also not necessarily elitist, but rather a justification of representative systems. And just as representation is an approximation of democracy, so is deliberation. Even Habermas acknowledges that inclusive and exhaustive debate amongst entire societies is not achievable, but should instead be approximated by pluralistic discourse that might leave a large number of citizens without explicit voice. This leaves us with the question of which might be the more viable and just approximation of self-government: the representative option, the deliberative option or a combination of the two. Proponents of the virtual public sphere are consistently avoiding an assessment of the credentials of deliberation and instead take for granted that a Habermasian public sphere needs to be revived.

Second, the public sphere(s) that the online world is generating tend(s) to be asymmetrical with regard to access, use, group polarisation, individual filtering and observable patterns of online engagement that appear to systematically fall short of the ideal speech condition. The technology may be regarded as a useful tool for organisational and social purposes – it may even have strong subversive potential – but will of itself not alter the nature of the established Eurocentric and non-participatory model of representative democracy. The IT revolution may well be said to have generated a communication environment that replicates on a much larger scale that which existed during what Habermas has described as the bourgeois public sphere. Then, there were decentralised print media that were part of civil society's communication infrastructure and not yet the commercialised mass media that they were later to become. Deliberation took place within civil society, was distributed and publicised through the print media. The print media, in turn, fed information and opinions, hence reinforcing deliberation. Such an infrastructure can be generated (or is indeed being generated as we speak) through IT. What the infrastructure lacks, however, is the social homogeneity, inclusiveness and symmetry of the using public, which the exclusive nature of the bourgeois public sphere 200 years ago ensured. The modern public, even if linked through web technology, remains segmented rather than pluralistic. Online deliberation is a cacophony of detached dialogues, if not monologues, that are not intertwined and that are not leading towards establishing a societal consensus on values and ends as much as means. Thus, it fails to meet what Habermas defined as the ideal ratio of a functioning public sphere.

Third, the lesson that 'public sphere engineers' in the United Kingdom and elsewhere have learnt from their analysis of the insufficiency of Internet technology – namely to create an online commons instead of leaving the evolving online world to itself – is again problematic. It is problematic primarily because it proactively removes the boundary between civil society and state that Habermas propagates as necessary for the public sphere to generate a meaningful and autonomous public voice. The core elements of an engineered online public sphere are as follows: (1) state funding; (2) moderation of public debates through the provision of online zones of constructive debate; (3) the introduction of a gatekeeping function that seeks to continuously summarise the proceedings in the virtual public sphere; (4) the active involvement of political elites with the debating publics (Blumler and Coleman, 2001: 16–21). This violates the principle of civic self-organisation and the idea that civil society, facilitated by a communicative infrastructure (which ceased to exist in the age of mass media and ultimately undermined the bourgeois public sphere), generates in bottom-up fashion a coherent and constructive dialogue that reaches political elites without being sanctioned by them. Furthermore, an engineered public sphere (or online commons) needs to be populated. This requires providing information, proactively educating people in the use of communication and, finally, moderating their discursive exchanges. Ultimately, a functioning public sphere that constructively and exhaustively debates the means and ends of politics either presupposes the non-existence of any anthropological assumptions of rational choice (such as free-riding) or calls for the eradication of these assumed notions. And we are indeed left with the problem that public cynicism about politics and distrust in elites and representative structures is primarily just that: a non-constructive frustration with existing structures. Cynicism cannot be taken as an indicator of frustrated willingness to participate. The core requirement for a functioning public sphere is citizenship. That means that, in order to effectively engineer an online public sphere, one also has to effectively engineer an online public.

Notes

1   The German original, *Strukturwandel der Oeffentlichkeit*, was first published as early as 1962.
2   Initial research on an integrated time-sharing function between desktop computers was funded by the Advanced Research Projects Agency (ARPA) from 1962 onwards.
3   According to his home page, J.P. Barlow 'is a retired Wyoming cattle rancher, a former lyricist for the Grateful Dead, and co-founder of the Electronic Frontier Foundation. Since May of 1998, he has been a Fellow at Harvard Law School's Berkman Center for Internet and Society, following a term as a Fellow with the Institute of Politics at Harvard's John F. Kennedy School of Government' (http://www.eff.org/~barlow/).
4   http://www.cdt.org/mission
5   With this advanced search option, one excludes references to sites that may include the individual words 'public' and 'sphere' at some point but not necessarily in combination with one another.
6   See, for example, http://www.technorealism.org/, which promotes a non-utopian approach, yet ultimately links a critical approach to the use of technology with the normative virtue of involved citizenship. In the same vein, the Berkman Center for Internet and Society at Harvard Law School hosted a conference on technorealism as early as 1998.
7   See http://www.nua.ie/surveys/how_many_online/index.html.

References

Barlow, J.P. (1996) *A Declaration of the Independence of Cyberspace*, Davos. Online. Available http://www.eff.org/~barlow/Declaration-Final.html.
Barlow, J.P. (undated) *Being in Nothingness: Virtual Reality and the Pioneers of Cyberspace*. Online. Available http://www.eff.org/Publications/John_Perry_Barlow/HTML/being_in_nothingness.html.
Blumler, J.G. and Coleman, S. (2001) *Realizing Democracy Online: A Civic Commons in Cyberspace*, IPPR/Citizens Online Research Publication No. 2. Online. Available http://www.citizensonline.org.uk/pdf/realising.pdf.
Coleman, S. and Gøtze, J. (2001) *Bowling Together: Online Public Engagement in Policy Deliberation*, London: Hansard Society.
Dahlberg, L. (2001) 'Computer-Mediated Communication and the Public Sphere: A Critical Analysis', *Journal of Computer-mediated Communication* 7 (1). Online. Available http://www.ascusc.org/jcmc/vol7/issue1/dahlberg.html.

DiMaggio, P., Hargittai, E., Neuman, W.R. and Robinson, J.P. (2001) 'Social Implications of the Internet', *Annual Review of Sociology* 27: 307–336.

Downs, A. (1957) *An Economic Theory of Democracy*, New York: Harper and Row.

Dryzek, J.S. (2000) *Deliberative Democracy and Beyond: Liberals, Critics, Contestations*, Oxford: Oxford University Press.

Elster, J. (1992) 'Introduction', in Elster, J. (ed.), *Deliberative Democracy*, Cambridge: Cambridge University Press.

Fernback, J. and Thompson, B. (1995) 'Virtual Communities: Abort, Retry, Failure?' Online. Available http://www.well.com/user/hlr/texts/VCcivil.html, Update on 'Computer-Mediated Communication and the American Collectivity: The Dimensions of Community within Cyberspace', Paper presented at the annual convention of the International Communication Association, Albuquerque, NM, May 1995.

Gates, B. (1995) *The Road Ahead*, New York: Viking Books.

Geser, H. (1996) *Auf dem Weg zur 'Cyberdemocracy'? Auswirkungen der Computernetze auf die oeffentliche politische Kommunikation*. Online Publications: 'Towards Cybersociety and "Vireal" Social Relations'. Available http://socio.ch/intcom/ t_hgeser00.htm.

Golding, P. (2000) 'Forthcoming Features: Information and Communications Technologies and the Sociology of the Future', *Sociology – Journal of the British Sociological Association* 34 (1): 165–184.

Habermas, J. (1989) *The Structural Transformation of the Public Sphere*, Cambridge, MA: Polity Press.

Hauben, R. (1999) 'The Internet: A New Communication Paradigm', in *Representation in Cyberspace Study*, Berkman Center for Internet and Society at Harvard Law School. Online. Available http://cyber.harvard.edu/rcs/hauben.html.

Huckfeldt, R.R. and Sprague, J.D. (1995) *Citizens, Politics, and Social Communication: Information and Influence in an Election Campaign*, Cambridge and New York: Cambridge University Press.

Licklider, J.C.R. and Taylor, R.W. (1990 [1968]) 'The Computer as a Communication Device', in *In Memoriam J.C.R. Licklider*, Palo Alto, CA: Systems Research Center (reprinted from *Science and Technology*, April 1968).

McClellan, J. (1994) 'Netsurfers', *Observer*, 13 February.

Perzynski, A. (1999) *Habermas and the Internet*. Online. Available http://socwww. cwru.edu/~atp5/habermas.html.

Rheingold, H. (1994) *The Virtual Community*, London: Secker & Warburg. Online. Available http://www.well.com/user/hlr/vcbook/.

Schement, J. (1996) *Beyond Universal Service: Characteristics of Americans without Telephones, 1980–1993*, Community Policy Working. Paper No. 1, Washington, DC: Benton Foundation.

Schement, J. (1999) 'Of Gaps by which Democracy We Measure', unpublished manuscript.

Schumpeter, J. (1950) *Capitalism, Socialism, and Democracy*, 3rd edn, New York: Harper and Row.

Sunstein, C. (2001a) *Republic.com*, Princeton, NJ: Princeton University Press.

Sunstein, C. (2001b) 'The Future of Free Speech', *Little Magazine*, March–April: 'Looking Back'. Online. Available http://www.littlemag.com/mar-apr01/cass.html.

Tewksbury, D. and Althaus, S.L. (2000) 'Differences in Knowledge Acquisition among Readers of the Paper and Online Versions of a National Newspaper', *Journalism and Mass Communication Quarterly* 77 (3): 457–479.

Thornton, A. (2002) 'Does Internet Create Democracy?', *Ecquid Novi* 22 (2). Online. Available at http://www.zip.com.au/~athornto//thesis_2002_alinta_thornton.doc.

Wilhelm, A.G. (2000) *Democracy in the Digital Age: Challenges to Political Life in Cyberspace*, New York and London: Routledge.

Index